Jonathan Swift's prose has been discussed extensively as satire, but its major structural element, parody, has not received the attention it deserves. Focusing mainly on works before 1714, and especially on *A Tale of a Tub*, this study explores Swift's writing primarily as parody. Robert Phiddian follows the constructions and deconstructions of textual authority through the texts on cultural-historical, biographical, and literary-theoretical levels. The historical interest lies in the occasions of the parodies: in their relations with the texts and discourses which they quote and distort, and in the way this process reflects on the generation of cultural authority in late-Stuart England. The biographical interest lies in a new way of viewing Swift's early career as a potentially Whiggish intellectual. And the theoretical and interpretative interest lies in tracing the play of language and irony through parody.

CAMBRIDGE STUDIES IN EIGHTEENTH-CENTURY
ENGLISH LITERATURE AND THOUGHT 26

Swift's parody

Some recent titles

Plots and Counterplots:
Sexual Politics and the Body Politic in English Literature 1660–1730
by Richard Braverman

The Eighteenth-Century Hymn in England
by Donald Davie

Swift's Politics: a Study in Disaffection
by Ian Higgins

Writing and the Rise of Finance:
Capital Satires of the Early Eighteenth Century
by Colin Nicholson

Locke, Literary Criticism, and Philosophy
by William Walker

Poetry and Jacobite Politics in Eighteenth-Century Britain and Ireland
by Murray G. H. Pittock

The Story of the Voyage in Eighteenth-Century England
by Philip Edwards

Edmond Malone, Shakespearean Scholar
by Peter Martin

Swift's Parody
By Robert Phiddian

A complete list of books in this series is given at the end of the volume

Swift's parody

ROBERT PHIDDIAN

Flinders University
of
South Australia

Published by the Press Syndicate of the University of Cambridge
The Pitt Building, Trumpington Street, Cambridge CB2 1RP
40 West 20th Street, New York, NY 10011-4211, USA
10 Stamford Road, Oakleigh, Melbourne 3166, Australia

First published 1995

Printed in Great Britain at the University Press, Cambridge

A catalogue record for this book is
available from the British Library

Library of Congress cataloguing in publication data
Phiddian, Robert.
Swift's parody / by Robert Phiddian.
p.   cm. (Cambridge studies in eighteenth-century English literature and thought; 26)
Includes bibliographical references and index.
ISBN 0 521 47437 X (hardback)
1. Swift, Jonathan, 1667–1745 – Technique.   2. Parodies – History and criticism.
3. Rhetoric – 1500–1800.   4. Parody.   I. Title.
II. Series.
PR3728.P3P45   1995
828′.509–dc20   94-48353 CIP

ISBN 0 521 47437 X hardback

To Robyn,

the source of all my happiness and security.

Though sometimes distracting me from the mere execution of this work, she has made the life from which it comes worth living. The dedication of this book is poor recompense for the joy she gives me, but it is hers anyway.

Contents

Acknowledgments

As anyone who has read *A Tale of a Tub* can tell you, prefaces are dangerous supplements which can consume hundreds of pages and even entire books. Consequently, I will do my best to restrict myself to acknowledgments here. As it happens, the personal and intellectual debts I have incurred over the years are too numerous to itemise exhaustively, so even this will be a summary exercise.

My greatest intellectual debt is to Clive Probyn of Monash University, who has watched over this work through all its development with unfailing (or brilliantly simulated) sympathy and interest. He has contributed more than I dare to contemplate to my knowledge and ideas. I have also benefited from the attention and conversation of many other scholars, including Peter Steele, Ken Ruthven, and Bernard Muir of the University of Melbourne, Michael Meehan at Flinders University, Harold Love and Richard Overell at Monash University, and (scattered around the planet) Brean Hammond, Ian Donaldson, Hermann Real, David Nokes, Alan Downie, and David Woolley. To them and to all the others who have contributed to the ideas in this book, I give my thanks. I am also particularly indebted to three libraries: the Main Library, Monash University, particularly the Swift Collection; the Baillieu Library, University of Melbourne; and the British Library. I would like to thank the staff of all these institutions for their patient help, and also to thank the staff of the other libraries in Australia and the British Isles with which I have been more briefly acquainted in the course of my research. Sheila Wilson, Eileen Whittaker, and Jo De Corrado have also provided efficient and cheerful help in matters bureaucratic and bibliographical.

As for personal debts let me mention only the most obvious of them. I would like to single out my mother, Mary, and sisters, Carolyn and Jacquie, for the support and healthy scepticism which have always characterised conversation in the family. Thanks go to Carolyn in particular who, having heroically volunteered to proof-read an earlier version of this treatise, now knows more about Swift than your average electrical engineer. Thanks also to David Leslie, for his friendship and for serving as a model of how Swift's mind might have worked.

Abbreviations

A Tale *A Tale of a Tub, to which is added the Battle of the Books and the Mechanical Operation of the Spirit.* A. C. Guthkelch and D. Nichol Smith, eds. 2nd edn. Oxford: Clarendon Press, 1958; reprinted with corrections, 1973.

Corr. *The Correspondence of Jonathan Swift.* 5 vols. Harold Williams, ed. Oxford: Clarendon Press, 1963–65.

Journal *The Journal to Stella.* 2 vols. Harold Williams, ed. Oxford: Clarendon Press, 1948.

PW *The Prose Works of Jonathan Swift.* 14 vols. Herbert Davis, et al., eds. Oxford: Basil Blackwell, 1939–68.

Introduction

There is one Thing which the judicious Reader cannot but have observed, that some of those Passages in this Discourse, which appear most liable to Objection are what they call Parodies, where the Author personates the Style and Manner of other Writers, whom he has a mind to expose.[1]

The rhetorical flow of this sentence figures the process by which attention to parody has been overwhelmed by attention to satire in the study of Swift's prose. We are all, we eagerly assume, 'judicious Reader[s]', and, consequently, we can convert the parodies easily and accurately into attacks on the satirical objects whom the author 'has a mind to expose'. This assumption that parodic language is a transparent medium for the conveyance of satirical meanings has its problems, however. The history of the reception of Swiftian satire is one of disputed interpretations, and few of these disputes have been of the kind where a dialectical attrition of opinions has led gradually to a narrowing consensus. Fashions come and go, but we are no closer to agreement on whether the Houyhnhnms are paragons or monsters, whether *A Tale of A Tub* attacks or defends Anglican piety, or whether the *Argument against Abolishing Christianity* is for or against nominal Christianity. If, as *A Tale*'s apologist seems to suggest here, parody is merely the vessel carrying satiric meaning and satire is simply and obviously punitive, then it is hard to escape the conclusion that Swift is a failure as a satirist.

Yet such a patently perverse conclusion must be resisted, and the means of resistance lies latent in this statement. The apologist is seeking to make something complex and dangerous appear simple and inoffensive, but the matters of parody and personation which he glosses over are the points at which the authoritative transfer of satirical meaning becomes vexed. Critics have not, on the whole, attended much to these modes, assuming that Swift's powerful genius overpowers his demotic sources, but it is in parody rather than satire that the multiplication of dissonant possibilities begins. The use of parody decentres the voice of satirical authority (Juvenal's voice, for example) and replaces it with a parodied voice (Gulliver's, the *Tale*-teller's, any Modern discourse's) which exhibits error but must be converted

[1] *A Tale*, p. 7.

1

to produce truth. This conversion takes place across a silence, in a zone of uncertainty, where the judicious reader has to imagine authoritative meaning and where correctness of conversion is not signalled positively. The foolish intervention of injudicious readers in this process cannot be legislated against, and it remains possible that even a judicious reader (whoever that might be) can still get it wrong. Furthermore, because the satirist only leaves traces of his determinate convictions in the parody, it is not finally possible to prove that his whole self supports any particular judgement or pattern of judgements. The irreducible problem remains that the reader who wishes to turn parody into satire must convert ironies, and ironies (particularly the Swiftian variety) show a stubborn tendency to retain their openness.

I do not, therefore, propose to *solve* Swiftian satire in this book. I take that to be an impossible and misguided task. Instead, I intend to focus on parody, the mode Swift pre-eminently employs, with a view to understanding the terms of the play of signification and irony better. We can make a start by reading against the rhetoric of the passage quoted at the beginning of this section. While attempting to subordinate the problems inherent in parody in the interests of proclaiming the author's pious intentions, it also figures parody's basic themes and, consequently, the basic themes of this study. It betrays concern for the construction of authority and the author (personation), for the forensic role of the 'judicious Reader', for the textual function of parody in the realm of discourse ('Style and Manner'), and for the inescapability of a cultural-historical context, where actual 'Writers' need to be exposed. It is neither fanciful nor anachronistic to suggest that deconstruction occurs on all these levels, for parody is always an ironic and critical strategy which explores the cultural and textual terms of construction of discourses. Like deconstruction as a hermeneutic strategy, parody does not repudiate the texts on which it operates, but rather animates them in order to distort them, point out their limitations, and divide them against themselves. It is not simply destructive in the way 'pure' satire is destructive: Pope destroys Sporus/Lord Hervey in the *Epistle to Dr. Arbuthnot* with a single-mindedness similar to that of the ancient satirists who actually killed their victims with their curses,[2] whereas the corrupted minds and cultural/textual practices exposed in *A Tale* are deconstructed, which is to say that they are attacked from within their own terms of construction in an engagement no less hostile than Pope's but far more intimate.

This intimacy leads to the most unsettling aspect of Swiftian parody. While Pope and Juvenal (and the Swift of poems such as 'The Legion Club', for that matter) stand grandly apart from the vicious imbeciles they grandly expose, Swiftian parody weakens the barriers it transgresses. It both

[2] See Robert C. Elliott, *The Power of Satire: Magic, Ritual, Art* (Princeton: Princeton University Press, 1960).

employs and identifies textual and cultural subversiveness, and it can easily become subversive of itself. *A Tale* was received as a witty and destabilising attack on precisely those religious and philosophical propositions Swift claimed it had been written to support, and the persistent evasiveness of 'The Apology' suggests that the author himself was guiltily aware of the dangers of parodic reflexivity. Though it was an opinion current in the satiric theory of the age,[3] it is no more than a pious and enabling fiction to insist that truth is incontrovertible and therefore impervious to the attacks of ridicule, while error's deformities need only be repeated by the parodist to be exposed. There is a wildness and openness to subversive (or deconstructive) implications which, though formally denied, pervades Swiftian parody and involves it in the madness it seeks to expose.

For the purposes of this book, the madness Swift involves himself in is the burgeoning textuality of late seventeenth- and early eighteenth-century political and cultural dispute in England. To keep the project within a reasonable compass, it has been necessary to concentrate on the writings of Swift's 'English' period, before the death of Queen Anne, when Swift still imagined that his Irish birth was essentially an accidental misfortune to be redressed by a glittering career in the central, English culture. This allows us to distinguish between the very different characters of Swift's English writing and his later Irish concerns. The most remarkable recent book-length interpretations of Swift's works – Rawson, Steele, Fabricant, Wyrick, Eilon[4] – have tended to treat Swift's *œuvre* as of a piece, and consequently have been promiscuous in their attention to fragments of various texts from different periods. In the context of pursuing 'the character of Swift's satire',[5] this approach has been both valid and remarkably fruitful. It has, however, tended to suppress any sense of the differences between particular texts and periods. Consequently, the parodic intertextuality has been blurred into a vague compendiousness which can contain anything from the condition of books in an English library of the 1690's to the condition of Irish peasants

---

[3] See P.K. Elkin, *The Augustan Defence of Satire* (Oxford: Clarendon Press, 1973) for a survey of this opinion; a notable formulation of this theory, undervalued in Elkin's book and of particular relevance to my concerns, lies scattered through the Third Earl of Shaftesbury's *Characteristics* (1711).

[4] C.J. Rawson, *Gulliver and the Gentle Reader: Studies in Swift and our Time* (London and Boston: Routledge and Kegan Paul, 1973), Peter Steele, *Jonathan Swift: Preacher and Jester* (Oxford: Oxford University Press, 1978), Carole Fabricant, *Swift's Landscape* (Baltimore and London: Johns Hopkins University Press, 1982), Deborah Baker Wyrick, *Jonathan Swift and the Vested Word* (Chapel Hill and London: University of North Carolina Press, 1988), and Daniel Eilon, *Faction's Fictions: Ideological Closure in Swift's Satire* (Newark: University of Delaware Press, 1991). This is obviously a selective and subjective list, which focuses on interpretative works concerned primarily with Swift's published prose rather than his biography or poetry.

[5] Though indicative of the impetus of much modern criticism, the phrase is most notably Rawson's; see his essay 'The Character of Swift's Satire: Reflections on Swift, Johnson, and Human Restlessness,' in Rawson (ed.), *The Character of Swift's Satire: A Revised Focus* (Newark: University of Delaware Press, 1983).

in a famine of the 1720's. If it is a monolithic 'Swift' that we seek to interpret, then this act of comprehension is a necessary critical manœuvre, but if
we seek the parodic function of individual texts we need to situate them in
their culture and textuality. *The Battle of the Books* and the *Modest Proposal* disseminate in different ways in differently defined cultures; *A Tale* and *Gulliver's
Travels* do not share identical cultural loyalties. As I have argued elsewhere,
Swift's English writing is more playful, occasional, and textual than his more
committed and savage Irish work.[6] It plays parodically and *almost* freely in
the textual forms and cultural concerns of late seventeenth-century
England, lacking the satirical weight of political and moral conviction evi-
dent later, but attaining a brilliance of verbal wit and a complexity of irony
which have not been equalled.

Thus the English Swift is more of a parodist, the Irish Swift more of a
satirist. I do not wish to go any further with this distinction here, but it is
important for the reader to appreciate that, for the purposes of this study,
the 'normative' text of Swiftian parody is *A Tale* rather than *Gulliver's Travels*,
and that the normative context is late Stuart English cultural dispute rather
than early Georgian Irish cultural dispossession. *A Tale* exemplifies the
ironic scepticism and centrifugal textual playfulness to which the discoveries
of post-structuralist criticism apply most vividly, and what is true of *A Tale* is
not always or simply true of the more committed and less carnivalesque
texts. This book's trajectory, therefore, is towards *A Tale*, and its aim is to
learn how to equip ourselves theoretically and historically for the act of
reading its brilliant parody. The approach is not chronological, and, in fact,
we move backwards rather than forwards in time, from the stabler ironies of
1713 towards the elusive brilliance of the 1690s. This retrograde movement
is not only critically useful (a movement from the relatively simple towards
the complex); it has the added benefit of freeing us from expectations about
Swift's literary development so that we can see intimations not only of what
subsequently happened (the late masterpieces), but also of artistic and ideological potentialities within the early work which later achievements and
positions have tended to obscure.

We commence with theoretical orientations, using the language of deconstruction to help us see the way parody undermines (or erases) constructions
of textual authority. From there we move into cultural history, so that we
get an idea of the rhetorical and textual forms of the intertextuality in which
the early parodies operated. This entails some extensive redefinition of cultural terrain, the most notable aspect being a turning away from the
received reading of cultural history, based on metaphors of progress,
towards a revision of the age's intellectual enterprises in terms of restoration

---

[6] Robert Phiddian, 'The English Swift/The Irish Swift', Paul Hyland and Neil Sammells, eds, *Irish
Writing: Exile and Subversion* (London: Macmillian, 1992), pp. 32–44.

and the return to order. I do not seek to assert the historical truth (whatever that may mean) of this concentration on the reactionary elements of late Stuart culture, but rather to identify their importance in public language and forms of thought, and to see how cultural projections presented themselves as returns to fundamental and original truths rather than as novelties or improvements. In the third and subsequent chapters we move from these theoretical and historical generalities to focus more narrowly on the detail of textual skirmishing in Queen Anne's reign, looking at the function of parody in Swift's *Abstract* of Collins' *Discourse of Free-Thinking*, the *Argument against Abolishing Christianity*, and the Bickerstaff Controversy. The fifth chapter concludes with an investigation of the problem arising most insistently from these readings – the blank at the centre of the parodies where the Modern author has attempted to assume the voice of authority and failed. This erasure is the starting-point for the subsequent chapters on *A Tale*, which seek both to follow and to animate the process of parody in that brilliant and infuriating text. We look at the way it envelops a multitude of voices in its complex ironies while leaving us incapable of imagining Swift's authentic utterance. In the end, we do not discover a monolithic 'Swift', heroically disclosing truth or himself, but the disturbing possibility of various Swifts, whose self-shroudings and incompatible self-fashionings cannot be subdued any more satisfactorily than his parodic texts can be tied down to determinate meanings. I do not expect to prove Swiftian parody soluble, but intend rather to cast light on some of the ways in which it is brilliantly and disconcertingly readable.

1

Theoretical orientations

Three theories of quotation

If one were looking for a theory of quotation to describe the practice of Swiftian parody, it would be difficult to better this:

We now know that a text is not a line of words releasing a single 'theological' meaning (the 'message' of the Author-God) but a multi-dimensional space in which a variety of writings, none of them original, blend and clash. The text is a tissue of quotations drawn from innumerable centres of culture. Similar to Bouvard and Pécuchet, those eternal copyists, at once sublime and comic and whose profound ridiculousness indicates precisely the truth of writing, the writer can only imitate a gesture that is always anterior, never original. His only power is to mix writings, to counter the ones with the others, in such a way as never to rest on any one of them.[1]

Swift's parodic writing is restless, allusive, and eccentric, its status easily imagined as 'a multi-dimensional space in which a variety of writings, none of them original, blend and clash', and as 'a tissue of quotations drawn from innumerable centres of culture'. Swiftian narrators, 'those eternal copyists', are displaced from the authoritative centres of their texts, leaving a space that Swift fills only fugitively and problematically with his presence. They are sublime, comic, and profoundly ridiculous figures, who 'can only imitate a gesture that is always anterior, never original', and whose 'only power is to mix writings, to counter the ones with the others, in such a way as never to rest on any one of them'. Moreover, they are figures in both senses of the word, being tropes and verbal constructs as much as they are independent human characters.

Barthes continues his unconscious description of Swiftian parody by turning to the reader's role:

Once the Author is removed, the claim to decipher a text becomes quite futile. To give a text an Author is to impose a limit on that text, to furnish it with a final signified, to close the writing...In the multiplicity of writing, everything is to be *disentangled*, nothing *deciphered*; the structure can be followed, 'run' (like the thread of a

---

[1] Roland Barthes, 'The Death of the Author', *Image – Music – Text: Essays Selected and Translated by Stephen Heath* (London: Fontana Press, 1977), pp. 142–48 (p. 146); see Roland Barthes, *Essais Critiques IV: le Bruissement de la Langue* (Paris: Editions du Seuil, 1984), pp. 61–68 (p. 65).

stocking) at every point and at every level, but there is nothing beneath: the space of writing is to be ranged over, not pierced; writing ceaselessly posits meaning ceaselessly to evaporate it, carrying out a systematic exemption of meaning.[2]

It may be an exaggeration to suggest that what happens is as absolute as 'a systematic exemption of meaning', but in works such as *A Tale of A Tub*, the *Argument against Abolishing Christianity*, and *Gulliver's Travels*, there is no immanent 'Author' of certain authority to impose limits on the text and close the writing. There is a wandering sense of 'Swift', and moments (or traces) of concrete, determinate satire which indicate 'theological' meanings. Even in the wildest work, *A Tale of A Tub*, there is the description of Jack's later career, which, though it also has its cross-purposes, is essentially a clear and direct attack on Dissent. However, Barthes' distinction between deciphering (which most interpreters attempt) and disentangling (which is about as much as we can hope to achieve) is exactly right. To read Swiftian parody is to range over textual space without piercing it, to disentangle threads of quotation, allusion, and suggestion which, in turn, entangle us. These threads seldom lead to any simple solution, but are prodigiously productive of paradoxes and possible solutions. Barthes may not have compassed his revolutionary aim of describing all writing, but here he goes very close to Swift's bewildering practice:

Thus is revealed the total existence of writing: a text is made of multiple writings, drawn from many cultures and entering into mutual relations of dialogue, parody, contestation, but there is one place where this multiplicity is focused and that place is the reader, not, as was hitherto said, the author. The reader is the space on which all the quotations that make up a writing are inscribed without any of them being lost; a text's unity lies not in its origin but in its destination.[3]

It is not our concern here whether this constitutes an accurate – or even a useful – description of *all* writing. What interests us here is the precision with which it describes parody. The perception of parody – the recognition of quoted threads and the process of disentangling them – takes place in the reader. Furthermore, this perception is not a simple teleological process like allegory which, at least ideally, teaches us to see through the letter of the text to a determinate understanding.[4] Rather, it is a process of 'entering into mutual relations of dialogue, parody, contestation' with a miscellany of texts and their traces. There is no single and unified origin of sense or meaning, and no single role designated for the reader.

The only significant distortion engendered by the application of Barthes' theory to Swiftian parody is derived from its mood. Barthes liked to think of himself as a radical (if chic) intellectual, and, in the revolutionary locus of

---

[2] Barthes, *Image – Music – Text*, p. 147; *Bruissement*, pp. 65–66.
[3] Ibid., p. 148; p. 66.
[4] On allegory and its relationship to parody, see Maureen Quilligan, *The Language of Allegory: Defining the Genre* (Ithaca: Cornell University Press, 1979), particularly pp. 132–55.

Paris in 1968, he could make his joyous declaration of the rights of readers
against the oppression of author-ity with gay abandon. No such innocent
liberation characterises Swiftian parody, which engages in the multiplicity it
discovers as if it were a malign, as well as a comic, chaos. The hostility of
Swiftian parody towards its pre-textual materials, towards its readers, and
towards itself is palpable. The possibility of a judgemental sense of authority
is not realised in the parody, but, even in the most playful passages, it hovers, insisting that language should not be abused in this way. An immanent
hostility to uncontrolled engagement in textuality *is* realised in this other
theory of quotation, which, though it seems to describe a state of textual
integrity almost exactly opposite to the practice of Swiftian parody, enjoys
the status of being Swift's own (presumably) unironic opinion:

> I would say something concerning Quotations; wherein I think you cannot be too
> sparing, except from Scripture, and the primitive Writers of the Church. As to the
> former, when you offer a Text as a Proof or an Illustration, we your Hearers expect
> to be fairly used; and sometimes think we have Reason to complain, especially of
> you younger Divines; which makes us fear, that some of you conceive you have no
> more to do than to turn over a Concordance, and there having found the principal
> Word, introduce as much of the Verse as will serve your Turn, although in Reality it
> makes nothing for you. I do not altogether disapprove the Manner of interweaving
> Texts of Scripture through the Style of your Sermon; wherein, however, I have
> sometimes observed great Instances of Indiscretion and Impropriety; against which I
> therefore to give you a Caution.[5]

This avuncular warning against the incontinent use of quotation comes
from the *Letter to a Young Gentleman, Lately entered into Holy Orders* (1720), a text
published anonymously but definitely written by Swift.[6] It discusses sermons
in particular, but it is clearly interpretable as presenting an ideal for all
sober discourse. The main problem in reading it as a general advocacy of
the rhetoric of a small, clean, straightforward world is that the theory in it
does not fit the most memorable of Swift's own writings.

There is, of course, no logical reason for requiring Swift to agree with a
literary theorist 248 years his junior. Indeed, the shape of such an absurd
idea reminds one of the narrator's amusing solecism in *A Tale of A Tub* when
he criticises Homer for being unaware of Modern occult 'learning': 'his
Account of the *Opus magnum* is extreamly poor and deficient; he seems to
have read but very superficially, either *Sendivogius, Behmen*, or *Anthroposophia
Theomagica*'.[7] However, in his parodic practice Swift seems much closer to

---

[5] *PW*, IX, p. 75.

[6] Its original publication in Dublin, and its inclusion in both an expanded *Miscellanies* in 1721, and
in Faulkner's semi-authorised edition of Swift's *Works* in 1735, offer strong evidence for its authenticity. The clinching evidence, however, lies in the interventions Swift clearly made to improve the
text for the Faulkner edition. My thanks go to Mr David Woolley (whose letter this note clumsily
summarises) for relieving my concerns in this matter.

[7] *A Tale*, p. 127.

Barthes' precepts than to his own. His parodic writing is a comprehensive –
though, I assume, not a conscious – reversal of the *Letter*'s sober programme, even to the extent that he is profligate concerning quotations from
a multitude of sources, *except* the Bible and the Church Fathers.[8] From these
central sources of authority he claims very little language or imagery, while
he borrows prolifically from other, less prestigious forms of writing, often
using his audience and his pre-texts at least as unfairly as 'you younger
Divines' who 'having found the principal Word, introduce as much of the
Verse as will serve your Turn, although in Reality it makes nothing for you'.
The parodies are shot through with infidelities of the spirit in quotation, and
all kinds of misappropriation.

If we continue with Swift's strictures against incontinent (Barthesian) quotation, the reversal of his own practice is even more precisely articulated.
Strict terms are made for the admissibility and form of quotations even
from the Church Fathers, who 'I think...are best brought in, to confirm
some Opinion controverted by those who differ from us',[9] and whose opinions may otherwise be presented as the preacher's own, in his own words.
Modern authors are neither to be quoted nor named, and the use of Greek
and Latin is forbidden the pulpit. Then the question of commonplace books
is addressed:

> The Mention of Quotations puts me in mind of Common-place Books, which have
> been long in use by industrious young Divines, and, I hear, do still continue so; I
> know they are very beneficial to Lawyers and Physicians, because they are
> Collections of Facts or Cases, whereupon a great Part of their several Faculties
> depend: Of these I have seen several, but never yet any written by a Clergyman;
> only from what I am informed, they generally are Extracts of Theological and
> Moral Sentences, drawn from Ecclesiastical and other Authors, reduced under
> proper Heads; usually begun, and perhaps, finished, while the Collectors were
> young in the Church; as being intended for Materials, or Nurseries to stock future
> Sermons.[10]

Restricted by the patrician pretence that he has never actually seen one of
the beastly things, Swift is obliged to pretend to speculate on what a clergyman's commonplace book might contain. He suggests with deft accuracy:

> You will observe the wise Editors of ancient Authors, when they meet a Sentence
> worthy of being distinguished, take special Care to have the first Word printed in
> Capital Letters, that you may not overlook it: Such, for Example, as the *Inconstancy
> of Fortune*, the *Goodness of Peace*, the *Excellency of Wisdom*, the *Certainty of Death*; that

---

[8] See Charles Allen Beaumont's slender volume, *Swift's Use of the Bible: A Documentation and a Study in
Allusion* (Athens Ga.: University of Georgia Press, 1965), which manages to find and analyse just
about all there is in sixty-eight pages.

[9] *PW*, IX, p. 75.

[10] Ibid., pp. 75–76.

Prosperity makes Men insolent, and Adversity humble; and the like eternal Truths, which every Plowman knows well enough, although he never heard of Aristotle or Plato.[11]

From this sturdy pragmatism, he proceeds to judgement:

> If Theological Common-Place Books be no better filled, I think they had better be laid aside: And I could wish, that Men of tolerable Intellectuals would rather trust to their own natural Reason, improved by a general Conversation with Books, to enlarge on Points which they are supposed already to understand. If a rational Man reads an excellent Author with just Application, he shall find himself extremely improved, and perhaps insensibly led to imitate that Author's Perfections; although in a little Time he should not remember one Word in the Book, nor even the Subject it handled: For, Books give the same Turn to our Thoughts and Way of Reasoning, that good and ill Company do to our Behaviour and Conversation; without either loading our Memories, or making us even sensible of the Change. And particularly, I have observed in Preaching, that no Men succeed better than those, who trust entirely to the Stock or Fund of their own Reason; advanced, indeed, but not overlaid by Commerce with Books. Whoever only reads, in order to transcribe wise and shining Remarks, without entering into the Genius and Spirit of the Author; as it is probable he will make no very judicious Extract, so he will be apt to trust to that Collection in all his Compositions; and be misled out of the regular Way of Thinking, in order to introduce those Materials which he hath been at the Pains to gather: And the Product of all this, will be found a manifest incoherent Piece of Patchwork.[12]

Swiftian narrators are definitely not 'Men of tolerable Intellectuals' and they have little or no 'natural Reason' to trust to. They are plainly not 'improved by a general Conversation with Books', but rather degenerate by imitating other authors' imperfections. They quote indiscriminately and injudiciously, and are 'misled out of the regular Way of Thinking' by a determination to introduce all the materials they have gathered, regardless of sense. This is most comprehensively true of *A Tale*, which, at least if it is considered as the narrator's text, could not be better described than as 'a manifest incoherent Piece of Patchwork'. Its narrator even embraces this commonplace book theory of literary production and ingenuously admits its purpose:

> In my Disposure of Employments of the Brain, I have thought fit to make *Invention* the *Master*, and to give *Method* and *Reason*, the Office of its *Lacquays*. The Cause of this Distribution was, from observing it my particular Case, to be often under a Temptation of being Witty, upon Occasions, where I could be neither *Wise* nor *Sound*, nor any thing to the Matter in hand. And, I am too much a Servant of the *Modern* Way, to neglect any such Opportunities, whatever Pains or Improprieties I may be at, to introduce them. For, I have observed, that from a laborious Collection of Seven Hundred Thirty Eight *Flowers*, and *shining Hints* of the best *Modern* Authors, digested with great Reading, into my Book of *Common-places*; I have

---

[11] Ibid., p. 76.
[12] Ibid.

not been able after five Years to draw, hook, or force into common Conversation, any more than a Dozen. Of which Dozen, the one Moiety failed of Success, by being dropt among unsuitable company; and the other cost me so many Strains, and Traps, and *Ambages* to introduce, that I at length resolved to give it over. Now, this Disappointment, (to discover a Secret) I must own, gave me the first Hint of setting up for an *Author*; and, I have since found among some particular Friends, that it is become a very general Complaint, and has produced the same Effects upon many others. For, I have remarked many a *towardly Word*, to be wholly neglected or despised in *Discourse*, which hath passed very smoothly, with some Consideration and Esteem, after its Preferment and Sanction in *Print*.[13]

There is not even much difference in the form of words between a writer being 'misled out of the regular Way of Thinking, in order to introduce those Materials which he hath been at the Pains to gather', and being 'too much a Servant of the *Modern* Way, to neglect any…Opportunities, whatever Pains or Improprieties I may be at, to introduce' items from 'a laborious Collection of Seven Hundred Thirty Eight *Flowers*, and *shining Hints* of the best *Modern* Authors'. However, one writer is being criticised sincerely, while the other is praising himself.

The problem is that *A Tale*'s ironic expression of the Modern author's determination to use all his 'laborious Collection of Seven Hundred Thirty Eight *Flowers*, and *shining Hints*', which cannot be drawn, hooked, or forced into the more natural discourse of common conversation is a far more apposite description at least of the surface of Swiftian parody than the plain style advocated in the *Letter to a Young Gentleman*. Print is a culprit here, for, rather than enshrining ordered communication, it sanctions the incoherence of indiscriminately connected and larcenously collected fragments, and gives a false impression of integrity to the 'manifest incoherent Piece of Patchwork'. Print gives the illusion of being more permanent and separate from the act of writing than even the most formal of manuscripts which, when annotated, is supplemented in its own medium. As *A Tale* suggests, this is a purely mechanical way of giving words 'Preferment and Sanction', and it sets a false boundary marked by reverence between text and reader.

Therefore, though this passage from *A Tale* operates from under cover of irony, it figures what happens in the text as a whole far more accurately than the literary theory enshrined in the *Letter*. The idea of clear, simple, direct, and sincere preaching through which the priest can mediate God's meaning and be clearly understood finds no secure purchase in the flux of Swiftian parody. Moreover, if *A Tale*'s commonplace book theory of literary production is read without ironic transformation, it is very like an extravagant premonition of Barthes' proclamation of the necessary derivativeness of all texts. Swiftian parody is digressive and opaque, leaving no clear (or

---

[13] *A Tale*, pp. 209–10.

agreed) impression of authoritative intent. The prose can display a breath-taking economy, but that is used not to determine meaning so much as to cram in multiple meanings, by way of paradox, pun, and allusion. The *Letter* is very positive about how writing should be undertaken, insisting memo-rably that 'Proper Words in proper Places, makes the true Definition of a Stile'.[14] This may be what happens in Swift's sermons and relatively unironic writings, when he speaks for the ministry, for the whole people of Ireland, or for all citizens of sense. However, in the parodies the opposite occurs. Nor is the opposition a loose one, for we can invert Swift's own pre-cept exactly: 'Improper words in improper places, makes the true definition of a parodic style.' The parodies are formally and culturally transgressive, directly opposed in mode and resonance to the self-consciously orthodox writing, and not answerable to its canons of authority. They can be imag-ined as the praxis of a commonplace book theory of literary production, creating a place where textual fragments collide and multiply possible disso-nances of meaning.

The main problem with these exciting theories is that it is impossible to posit Swift's approval of them. Whether or not the preacherly Swift is some-how prior to, or more authentic than, the writer who generates such free-wheeling word-play, his hostility towards improper words is explicit, towards *A Tale*'s narrator everywhere implicit, and towards Barthes and other such trendy cultural relativists easy to imagine. As Ann Cline Kelly demonstrates, all of Swift's positive and unironic prescriptions for writing advocate a sim-ple, pure, unornamented diction.[15] The accurate transmission of meaning is presented as a necessary component of a healthy civil society. There is no room in these positive attitudes for the diffusion of meaning into quotation, allusion, parody, or sourceless indeterminacy. So how can we place the sta-tus of the parodies, when they show all the signs of the literary degeneracies which Swift explicitly rejected? We could follow Barthes out of this impasse by declaring the author dead (and therefore irrelevant as a source or deter-minant of meaning), but that is merely to deny complex and palpable dynamics in the play of signification, not to dissolve them. Rawson has put the case for an immanent and hostile Swift pungently:

But whether parody is present or not, the aggression I speak of is usually quite inescapable in Swift's satire. What is involved is not necessarily a 'rhetoric' or thought-out strategy, so much as an atmosphere or perhaps an instinctive tone. This is not to mistake Swift for his masks, but to say that behind the screen of indirec-tions, ironies, and putative authors a central Swiftian personality is always actively present, and makes itself felt.[16]

---

[14] *PW*, IX, p. 65.
[15] *Swift and the English Language* (Philadelphia: University of Pennsylvania Press, 1988).
[16] *Gulliver and the Gentle Reader*, p. 6.

Only the fool has said in his heart 'there is no Swift' – his presence broods in and around even in his most ironic texts although we cannot tell exactly where he stands. It may prove impossible to locate the proper noun 'Swift' determinately, but the adjective 'Swiftian' remains indispensable, and a sense of hostile urgency always disturbs anything like *jouissance*. A blankly doctrinaire post-structuralism (such as Barthes was never guilty of) might want to insist that the idea of 'a central Swiftian personality' is a mythic construct, empty of meaning and suggestive of a false and misleading priority of author over text. However, 'Swift' remains a necessary enabling concept in the negotiation of the parodies. Let us, therefore, have recourse to the Derridean notion of erasure as a metaphor for imagining both authorisation and method in Swiftian parody. There is no reason to believe that Swift would have had any more patience with Derrida than with Barthes or any other of us (post-) moderns, but the idea is useful, at least if we employ it warily.

The idea of parody under erasure

The Derridean notion of erasure mediates presence and absence; it covers the difference between something which has never been thought (or written) and that which has been cancelled. As such, it provides a potent metaphor for understanding the process of parody, particularly of parody as fugitive and indeterminate as Swift's.[17] In its simplest form, it is illustrated by a printed word with a line or a cross through it; for example, ~~Swift~~. Thus an idea is called up but its positive force is questioned, rendered dubious, and, ultimately, denied. It is not erased in the sense of being obliterated, for the page has not been returned to blankness. Rather, it appears under erasure, as a distinct trace, neither entirely present nor entirely absent.

The application of this metaphor to the perception of parody is obvious enough: all parody refunctions pre-existing text(s) and/or discourse(s), so it can be said that these verbal structures are called to the readers' minds and then placed under erasure. A necessary modification of the original idea is that we must allow the act of erasure to operate critically rather than as a merely neutral cancellation of its object. Parodic erasure disfigures its pretexts in various ways that seek to guide our re-evaluation or refiguration of

[17] This analysis has primarily a scavenger's interest in Derrida's complex philosophies of language. His rhetoric of absence (most notably ideas of textuality, erasure, and traces) provides a very useful shorthand for the discussion of issues, many (if not all) of which could be explained much more laboriously with traditional terms like irony and poetic licence. While this book uses deconstructive techniques and identifies such techniques in Swift's manipulations of texts, its preoccupations remain fundamentally logocentric in the most obvious sense – it hopes to provide ways of understanding the processes and meanings of Swiftian parody. *A Tale* shows little sympathy for those who try to supersede the texts they are supposed to be serving, and this is one Swiftian censure I hope to avoid.

them. It is dialogical and suggestive as well as negatively deconstructive, for it (at least potentially) can achieve controlled and meta-fictional commentary as well as purely arbitrary problematisation.[18] Keeping this important caveat in mind, the chief value of perceiving parody as a sort of erasure lies in the sense the idea captures of simultaneously recalling and displacing the pre-texts. In the specific instance of Swiftian parody, this process of erasure operates as a deconstruction of verbal, mental, ideological, and typographical patterns. As can be seen from the application of Barthes' theory of quotation to Swiftian parody in the previous section, what happens is very like deconstruction as it is understood by modern theorists.[19] However, as the previous section also indicates, Swift seems less than eager to embrace a full-blown relativism. Indeed, in places such as the *Letter to a Young Gentleman*, where he seems to be writing without irony, he expresses violent opposition to the newfangled process of piecing a text together from the fragments of other texts. What we have here is a paradox, a double erasure, whereby it is not only the pre-textual objects of parody that are deconstructed; the process of parody itself is erased, repudiated, and rendered problematic. As we will see often in the following pages, this second erasure can be seen both formally and psychologically, in the internal logic of the parodic texts and the literary-historical logic of Swift's career. The patterns of erasure are paradoxical, but some generalisations can be made as we set out.

Swiftian parody can be seen most obviously to operate under erasure in the way it opposes the expressed and, presumably, unironic opinions of the author and historical figure 'Swift' on the way language should operate in a properly functioning literary culture. These opinions were not espoused simply to be ignored, for there is a large body of prose where Swift seeks to write as an authoritative mouthpiece of various groups and institutions, using a stable and confident tone deeply antipathetic to the volatile eccentricities of the parodic works. Readers of Swiftian criticism will be aware of the division posited within Swift between the preacher and the jester, and there often do seem to be two bodies of work.[20] On the one hand (the right hand, if you like), there is the sober, serious writing in the name of church,

---

[18] For an extensive investigation of these aspects of parody, see Margaret A. Rose, *Parody // Metafiction: An Analysis of Parody as a Critical Mirror to the Writing and Reception of Fiction* (London: Croom Helm, 1979), particularly ch. 3; she has recently consolidated and expanded her ideas in *Parody: Ancient, Modern, and Post-modern* (Cambridge: Cambridge University Press, 1993).

[19] Clive T. Probyn, 'Swift and Typographic Man: Foul Papers, Modern Criticism, and Irish Dissenters', in *Reading Swift: Papers from the Second Münster Symposium on Jonathan Swift*, Richard H. Rodino and Hermann J. Real, eds. (Munich: Wilhelm Fink Verlag, 1993), pp. 25–43, faces this issue squarely and extensively, while it is an omnipresent consideration in Wyrick, *Swift and the Vested Word*. See also Carole Fabricant, 'The Battle of the Ancients and (Post)Moderns: Rethinking Swift through Contemporary Perspectives', *ECent*, 32 (1991), 256–73.

[20] The idea is most thoroughly and imaginatively investigated in Steele, *Jonathan Swift: Preacher and Jester*.

government, or established canons of taste, sense, or morality. We can see this most clearly in the sermons where, authorised by the established Church, Swift operates as a concise and chaste conduit of received teaching. The sermons are not, perhaps, undistinguished but they are *indistinguishable* from a long tradition of plain-speaking homiletics.[21] In their impersonal orthodoxy, they do not strike the reader as being written by anyone in particular, let alone by so wildly idiosyncratic a writer as the author of *A Tale*. They are simple and didactic, faithfully fulfilling the rhetorical programme advocated in the *Letter to a Young Gentleman*; they speak with the discursive propriety of properly constituted authority, all irony and verbal instability (as far as is possible) evacuated. Some of Swift's political writing seeks in varying degrees to attain this impersonal authoritativeness (*The History of the Last Four Years of the Queen*, *The Contests and Dissensions*, and *The Conduct of the Allies*, for example) and other pieces try to mix it with a reassuring draught of simple sincerity (*The Drapier's Letters* best illustrate this). On this right hand of Swift, whatever irony that appears is instrumental and, in Wayne C. Booth's sense, stable.[22] It is rhetoric of presence, conviction, and sincerity; the antithesis of the brilliant lies for which Swift is best remembered.

These brilliant lies thus lie under an external psychological erasure. They are works of Swift's left (*sinister/gauche*) hand, their right to exist denied both by explicit edict and by the authorised and approved workings of the (adroit) right hand. The formal correlative of this lies in the cultural status of the parodies and their pre-texts. I have remarked upon the self-conscious orthodoxy and legitimacy of Swift's 'right-handed' prose, but it is even more important to recognise the dubious marginality of the genres refunctioned in his parodies. If we consider the cultural status of each of Swift's parodies, we can see that none of them is of traditional or orthodox genre in its cultural context. *Gulliver's Travels* is a travel book, the *Modest Proposal* and the *Argument against Abolishing Christianity* are proposals by private citizens without authority to hold public opinions, the Bickerstaff Papers stem from an almanac and remain firmly in that ephemeral domain, *A Tale* is a riot of modern thoughts and forms. All these discourses are beyond the pale of authoritative discourse even before their unique absurdities become obvious. These kinds of writing lie under a formal cultural erasure. They are expressions of proliferating Modern[23] perversity which, from an authoritar-

---

[21] C. H. Sisson sees fit to reprint a couple of them in his edited anthology, *The English Sermon; Volume II: 1650–1750 – An Anthology* (Cheadle, Cheshire: Carcanet Press, 1976), and argues that it is for their own merits that they appear rather than because of the reputation of their author for other writings.

[22] Or at least aspires to and substantially attains stability. Even here Swift cannot always control his darker writerly urges. Booth explains the idea of stable irony in part I of *A Rhetoric of Irony* (Chicago: University of Chicago Press, 1974).

[23] Here and subsequently, I will use 'Modern' to indicate late seventeenth-century Modernity as a cultural movement, and 'modern' to indicate recent developments in the twentieth century.

ian perspective, should not exist in a healthy culture. The parody enacts the inevitable collapse of these feral and illegitimate discourses. In theory, therefore, the deconstructive process works as a kind of intellectual prophylaxis, but persistently the slipperiness inherent in the idea and practice of erasure asserts itself. If Swift in his preacherly aspect truly determined the implications of the work – if the right hand were securely prior to the left – the parody would work purely as destructive deconstruction of worthless discourses. However, paradoxical confusion penetrates this prophylactic minimalism in the form of a playful engagement with the debased verbal currencies. It is not that the illegitimate textuality is justified or dignified by coming into contact with Swift's 'high art', but it attains a mad brilliance and a sporadic lucidity which belie the flat-earth policies of sober orthodoxy.

At the centre of this confusion, the point at which the parodic depiction of illegitimate textuality slides guiltily from being simply an exposé into being also an engagement, there lies another formal erasure. It is like a death of the author, but it is not quite so total a disengagement with determinacy as that idea suggests. Essentially it is an erasure of authorial integrity and direction which can be seen under two aspects, both of which leave disjointed traces of authority. The first aspect is the erasure of Swift, the right-handed, institutionally authorised moralist, from the role of narrator in the parodies. The fully present, integral (that is, integrating and full of integrity) voices of the preacher, the ministerial spokesman, and the mouthpiece of the whole people of Ireland do not belong among these feral and illegitimate texts, whose terms of reference preclude authentic wisdom. If the parody were rigorously allegorical or instrumental, this displacement would be merely a sleight-of-hand, with Swift withdrawing from the position of narrator only to control the readers' reactions and judgements meta-textually by inscribing authoritative patterns for deciphering the apparent indirections. Certainly, in some works we can enjoy a level of confidence in looking past the narrator to Swift. An essay like the *Abstract* of Collins' *Discourse of Free-Thinking* functions as fairly stable suasive parody, as the reader finds it relatively easy to recognise error and to deduce Swift's idea of truth. However, *A Tale*, the *Argument against Abolishing Christianity*, and the fourth book of *Gulliver's Travels* generate endless critical industry, and will not be confined or reduced to any set of positive precepts indisputably informed by Swift. Meta-textual and allegorical interpretations abound, but none can drive out all competitors. A shadow falls between the readers and Swift which allows only teasing and inconsistent glimpses of an assertiveness which paradoxically also gives the impression of being vigorous and urgent. While it remains possible that this sense of urgency assumes a priority which is merely delusive (it is certainly deconstructible), we are never allowed to relax into a Shandean (or Barthesian) delight in indeterminacy and receding possibilities of communication. The will to truth and integrity is fugitive rather than simply absent, and the hermeneutic crisis revolves around the fact that we cannot determine which urgent truth we are being exhorted towards. We can generate a biographical picture from external information that allows us to allegorise plausible meanings from the marks on the page. We can privilege some statements or positions in the text as sincere, and discard or invert others as ironic. But the shadow has fallen: we cannot say certainly of this left-handed Swift's work that 'Swift tells us…'.

The shadow of this Swiftian dilemma marks the place where the second aspect of authorial erasure takes place. In right-handed, authentic discourse the narrator's, author's, and authority's voices seem to be identical, to be completely integrated. In the parody they separate and disintegrate. The narrators we are given are not simple, instrumental personae deployed by Swift to expose themselves and their ideologies to ridicule. They are not fully realised figures whose characters balance our impressions in the satiric message-structure. They are not the unmediated voice of Swift himself. They are erased sources of authority and authenticity, generally Modern, generally self-opinionated, generally inflated with their own wisdom and significance, and persistently inconsistent. They claim a central role in their texts, but the parody decentres them, breaching any reliable connections we might be tempted to make between them and Swift (either the historical figure or the Platonic authorial form). We cannot even rely on them to be wrong, and we cannot deny them some measure of partial domination over the wild works they claim to generate. Their authority is radically dubious and inconsistent, but not entirely vanquished; they operate unreliably, under erasure. So, with no focus of authority which is not decentred, the process of parodic quotation cannot channel the reader to certain conclusions. The illegitimate texts are called up and placed under a critical scrutiny which is deconstructive, but not entirely destructive. Erased but not obliterated, the parodied discourses retain traces of authority, but there is nothing to mark true perspectives in this realm of discursive conduct which, according to the precepts of the official (or right-handed) Swift, simply *should not exist*. We are led on a merry hermeneutic dance which is always energised by an urgent will to truth which always remains unfulfilled. From time to time certainties appear, but more often we are left with paradoxes.

And there is one more erasure which we must recognise and keep forever in mind, disconcerting though it may be. Not only is the race of critics a declared enemy in many of the works, the interpreter's role is also placed under erasure. We methodical commentators are not Swift's confederates, but his victims; our cure-all hermeneutic techniques are not only prefigured in the parodies, but also pre-emptively disfigured. The 'Apology' to *A Tale* assures us that 'Men of Wit and Tast'[24] will understand the author's mean-

24 *A Tale*, p. 20.

ing, but it is a brave fool who will count herself or himself in their number. Analysis itself is drawn under an erasure as we critics – whatever our ideological allegiances, from the textual scholarship of Bentley and Wotton to the most fashionably post-modern execution of the Derridean mysteries – tend to find the terms of our commentaries collapsed by reference to some inconvenient part of Swift's canon. The moment we try to dismember a paradox, the moment we start to make hermeneutic choices and attempt to reduce the texts to meanings, we fall under ironic erasure. Nor do the wise modern methods of deconstruction offer a safe defence from ridicule: to fall into witless *jouissance* is to admit kinship with the *Argument against Abolishing Christianity*'s 'young Men of Wit and Pleasure', who grasp the opportunity offered by scholarly dispute over the text of the Bible to 'by a sudden Deduction of a long *Sorites*, most logically conclude...; Why, if it be as you say, I may safely whore and drink on, and defy the Parson';[25] or to rejoice in the multiplicity of perpetually deferred plays of meaning is to endorse *A Tale*'s dubious approval of the sort of 'Scholiastick Midwifry' which delivers texts 'of Meanings, that the Authors themselves, perhaps, never conceived'.[26]

I make no claim to have escaped these curses and, for want of any real choice, embrace the ironic status of my enterprise. This defeatist method is not a renunciation of critical responsibility so much as a recognition that Swiftian parody is too paradoxical by nature to be solved, and that its issues and techniques are better kept in a living solution that allows us to engage in the risks of reading. Disentangling parodic threads rather than expecting to achieve final decipherment I often make epigraphs and starting points of clearly ironic statements within the parodies. This is illustrated above in my embrace of commonplace book theory – a theory which explains a great deal but whose truth-value is clearly erased by the irony both of its presentation and of its contradiction by Swift's positive precepts in the *Letter to a Young Gentleman*. Below I structure my entire reading of *A Tale* around slippery principles dubiously enunciated in the text.

But let us move on by illustrating the process in an emblem. This section is titled 'The idea of parody under erasure', and the gentle reader may have noticed a self-deflating irony in this. Swift's *Remarks* on Tindal's *Rights of the Christian Church Asserted* (written in 1708, but not published in Swift's lifetime) contains this remark: 'And since our modern Improvement of Human Understanding, instead of desiring a Philosopher to describe or define a Mousetrap, or tell me what it is; I must gravely ask, what is contained in the Idea of a Mousetrap?'[27] The idea of the mousetrap lies ready-sprung for all

[25] *PW*, II, pp. 30, 38.
[26] *A Tale*, p. 186.
[27] *PW*, II, p. 80.

our hermeneutic abstractions, and the idea of erasure will not save us from its destructive mechanism. Swift's parodies generate vexing circularities, for there is no positive meta-discourse that integrates all Swiftian paradoxes. Any proposition looks ridiculous from some angle. So what should we make of this fiendish frustration of hermeneutic mastery? One could, of course, refuse to read the stuff, but I prefer simply to accept the fact that no critical discourse lies beyond the reach of Swiftian irony and to proceed without worrying too much about my failure to achieve the impossible.

Illegitimate textuality: the pre-texts of Swiftian parody

Swift is invariably attacking what he impersonates. In other words, his technique is to become the thing he attacks, which is normally not a message or a political doctrine but a style or a manner of discourse.[28]

Parody is unavoidably occasional. Its first movement is never action, but reaction, and it cannot exist without having pre-existing verbal and/or intellectual formations to diverge from. Margaret Rose identifies this belatedness when she defines literary parody as 'the critical refunctioning of preformed literary material with comic effect'.[29] This is a splendidly succinct and useful definition, but it also points unwittingly to the reason for Swift's work being so seldom discussed in terms of parody. It suggests that parody and its pre-texts belong in the realm of the literary, and half suggests that the pre-texts being refunctioned will be in some degree canonical. Swiftian parody, on the other hand, does not rely on literary or dignified resources. Its pre-textuality affords us glimpses of an altogether more mechanical and miscellaneous discursive world, the political, cultural, and religious disputes of late Stuart England. Scholars interested in this archaeology of Swift's texts have tended to restrict themselves to source scholarship, identifying barbs and targets. There has seldom been much interest shown in how the final texts are informed by their sources, in the interpenetrating relationships a poststructuralist would call intertextual. In other words, Swift's texts have not generally been analysed as parody, because their pre-texts have not been considered literary or sufficiently significant of themselves.

The *Meditation upon a Broom-stick, According to the Style and Manner of the Honourable Robert Boyle's Meditations* (written c. 1703, published 1710) illustrates this hermeneutic slide well. It signals its parodic relationship to Boyle's *Occasional Reflections upon Several Subjects* (1665) quite explicitly in its title and all its parts, yet it is normally treated as a biographical detail, as a prank played on the Countess of Berkeley to expose her pomposity. No formalist interpre-

---

[28] Edward Said, 'Swift as Intellectual', *The World, the Text, and the Critic* (London: Faber and Faber, 1984), p. 87.
[29] *Parody // Meta-fiction*, p. 35.

tation goes any further than to remark that the piece is a parody and that it attacks the sentimental and self-satisfied moralism of Boyle's *Reflections*. So the intertextual relationship is not treated seriously because readers cannot bring themselves to take Boyle seriously (at least as a moralist). This is the basic form of the avoidance of parody in Swiftian scholarship: pre-texts and occasions are investigated chiefly as sources of targets and detail, so that Swift remains a satirist, criticising error from a distance. As a parodist, however, he has to be seen engaging in the textual madness as well as diagnosing it. Parody is a very intimate diagnosis of diseases in the plausible, not a grand and distant repudiation of error in the manner of Juvenal.

We will, therefore, start with the idea of non-literary parody, and look to see how Swift's works deform (and are deformed by) elements of the hurly-burly of late Stuart cultural, political, and religious dispute. As Edward Said reminds us, 'Swift is, I think, pre-eminently a reactive writer. Nearly every-thing he wrote was occasional, and we must quickly add that he responded to, but did not create, the occasions.'[30] We should take this sense of occasion seriously, and allow it to undermine our sense of Olympian satiric form, for the pre-texts are not merely neutral, plundered sources, but rather (as the term pre-text suggests) simultaneously the occasion, material, and supplement of the parody. Pre-textuality is provisional and accidental, but it is not unchanged by the parody nor is the parody unchanged by intertextual connections with it. The margins between parodic text and pre-text are not stable but are rather permeable and characterised by claims and transgressions which render interpretation fluid. Indeed, this hermeneutic fluidity is such that subsequent texts can be parodically refunctioned even though they cannot in an empirical sense have been directly imagined by the parodist. As occasional texts, parodies are useful from time-to-time, and it is an impoverished theory which refuses to allow that late twentieth-century economic rationalists are parodied in *A Modest Proposal* merely because Swift cannot have read their writings. However, the first occasion will inevitably have a particularly intimate relationship with its recombination in parody. As the two following illustrations from Swift's later 'Irish' career demonstrate, occasional specificity (both of reference and of intent) can be seen in even the most 'universal' moments of his most 'universal' texts.

A Modest Proposal can be usefully discussed as a great cry of anguish from the tortured human spirit, or as a brilliant illustration of ironic subversion, or as what you will. In short, it can be viewed *sub specie eternitatis* as a brilliant achievement of ideal literary form, but it also remains irreducibly a political document, speaking of a desperate situation in parodically marked language. We are shocked and exhilarated when we encounter such Baroque master-strokes of irony as:

---

[30] *The World, the Text, and the Critic*, p. 78.

Some Persons of a desponding Spirit are in great Concern about that vast Number of poor People, who are Aged, Diseased, or Maimed;...But I am not in the least Pain upon that Matter; because it is very well known, that they are every Day *dying*, and *rotting*, by *Cold*, and *Famine*, and *Filth*, and *Vermin*, as fast as can reasonably be expected.[31]

The language enacts a brilliantly horrifying marginalisation of human life, and we feel that we could imagine a crazed economist's or bureaucrat's mind that might indulge in such intellectual obscenity. But that is not the same as remembering an actual discourse. We are dragged away from general observations on man's inhumanity to man into the desperate political and social condition of Ireland (into the specific occasion) when we spot the parodic resemblance between this piece of satirical excess and the pioneering economic works of Sir William Petty. Petty was a senior public servant and certainly no lunatic, yet he could write in these terms of the constituents of Ireland's population during the Great Rebellion:

Whereas the present proportion of the British is as 3 to 11; But before the Wars the Proportion was less, viz. as 2 to 11. and then it follows that the number of British slain in 11 years was 112 thousand Souls; of which I guess two thirds to have perished by War, Plague and Famine. So as it follows that 37,000 were massacred in the first year of Tumults: So as those who think 154,000 were so destroyed, ought to review the grounds of their Opinion.

It follows also, that about 504 M. [i.e. 504,000] of the Irish perished, and were wasted by the Sword, Plague, Famine, Hardship and Banishment, between the 23 of October 1641. and the same day 1652.[32]

There is a casual brutality about this which Swift scarcely exaggerates, and we do well to recognise the intertextual link between the language of the 'obviously mad' Modest Proposer and that of the eminently respectable Sir William Petty. To the English eye – and to Swift's in many moods – the Popish Irish peasants were a threatening and alien majority, little better than animals.[33] As readers, we assume that Petty's description retains a discursive decorum which marks it as a legitimate discussion of these semi-humans, whereas the Proposer's project crosses a boundary into a zone of parodic invalidity. A reading attuned to the occasional context of the debate will notice the subtlety and unjustified arbitrariness of this distinction between the languages of wisdom and madness in a way that a general, rhetorical sense of satirical subversion can not. Parody, in other words, enters a deconstruc-

---

[31] *PW*, XII, p. 114.

[32] *The Political Anatomy of Ireland: with the Establishment for that Kingdom and Verbum Sapienti* (Shannon: Irish University Press, 1970; facsimile of first edn of 1691), p. 18. The text was probably written *c.* 1672.

[33] See David Nokes' two articles, 'Swift and the Beggars', *Essays in Criticism*, 26 (1976), 218–35, and 'The Radical Conservatism of Swift's Irish Pamphlets', *British Journal for Eighteenth Century Studies*, 7 (1984), 169–76.

tive dialogue with its pre-texts, and to miss this dialogue (or blur its particularity) is to lose contact with the precise dance of language.

An ear for intertextuality and the polemical moment is also of use in matters of hermeneutic detail, as can be seen here in that most universal of Swift's works, Book IV of *Gulliver's Travels*. Gulliver is explaining the causes of war to his Master Houyhnhnm, and 'Difference in Opinions' is one of them:

> Difference in Opinions hath cost many Millions of Lives: For Instance, whether *Flesh* be *Bread*, or *Bread* be *Flesh*: Whether the Juice of a certain *Berry* be *Blood* or *Wine*: Whether *Whistling* be a Vice or a Virtue: Whether it be better to *kiss* a *Post*, or to throw it into the Fire: What is the best Colour for a *Coat*, whether *Black*, *White*, *Red* or *Grey*; and whether it should be *long* or *short*, *narrow* or *wide*, *dirty* or *clean*; with many more. Neither are any Wars so furious and bloody, or of so long Continuance, as those occasioned by Difference in Opinion, especially if it be in things indifferent.[34]

Surely this is a high, Enlightenment dismissal of the violent and irrational conflicts of the Reformation? Every reader of this passage recognises the absurdity of going to war over points of theological speculation, and recognises Swift's sarcasm as a significant affirmation of sanity and common sense. It is a stern reminder that ideological purity is simply not worth the cost of a human life, but that is not all. On closer inspection of the polemical ramifications of this statement, it also becomes very partisan in a specific and particularly Anglican manner.

The intertextual thread from which this reading unravels is left hanging at the end: the phrase 'things indifferent' is far from indifferent in Anglican religious polemic, but rather an important notion introduced by Richard Hooker in his *Laws of Ecclesiastical Polity* (1594–7). It is the crucial idea sanctioning the Anglican middle way in matters doctrinal, as it allows for the possibility of a discretionary vagueness in disputed areas of doctrine and church discipline. In opposition to the fundamentalist Protestant reformers, who hoped to root out all vestiges of the ceremonial and mystical elements of received Christianity as well as the obvious administrative corruptions, moderate Anglicans advocated reform only of essential matters, leaving 'things indifferent' to be determined in practice and according to convenience. Dispute focused on the nature of the Eucharist, Catholics asserting that the real presence of Christ's body and blood (transubstantiation) occurs, Protestants insisting that the act is merely symbolic, with nothing physical actually happening to the bread and wine, and Anglicans trying to have a bit each way with a foggy doctrine called consubstantiation. In matters of ceremony, where the Protestants sought to cast out all ecclesiastical statues and furniture from the churches and to ban all music from services, the Anglicans hoped to retain some degree of ceremony while yet insisting that

[34] *PW*, XI, p. 246.

it could in no way make up for personal conviction. And on the vestments a minister should be permitted to wear, Protestants required extreme plainness, while Anglicans desired more ceremonial dress. In short, this satiric barb does not only advocate the common wisdom of pacifism, it also figures a number of partisan polemical points in exactly the fields of dispute it affects to despise. We witness simultaneously a general humanist point and a specific ideological reprise of Martin's case against Jack and Peter; and the doubleness has the irreducible openness of paradox.

The two levels of meaning are not logically compatible, but it is impossible to determine whether either of them is transcendently true. The necessary point for now, however, is that one of the levels is only available to a reading sensitive to intertextuality and a sense of polemical occasion. Whether we should call this dimension parodic in this instance can be questioned. It would certainly be fanciful to describe the passage as a parody of Hooker, but it might be seen as an approving reformulation of a more generally imagined Anglican apologetic. Anyway, such quotation inevitably opens the ironic space of parody, even if it does not seek to ridicule its object. What matters for the purposes of this book is not the decipherment of intended meaning, but the apprehension of quotation and distortion. This level of parodic interplay, feeding back into the discourses of cultural dispute, has been demonstrated here in two of the most general moments of Swift's two most approachable works. The entanglement in cultural occasion and warring discourses is only more essential to the earlier writings on which this study concentrates.

2

Restoration enterprises and their rhetorics

Perhaps no writer can easily be found that has borrowed so little, or that in all his excellencies and all his defects has so well maintained his claim to be considered as original.[1]

The burden of the past and a definition of restoration enterprise

That most self-conscious of public shapers, Joseph Addison, urbanely uncovers the central anxiety of his culture when he explains his purpose as an essayist in *The Spectator* no.262:

Among those Advantages, which the Publick may reap from this Paper, it is not the least, that it draws Mens Minds off from the Bitterness of Party, and furnishes them with Subjects of Discourse that may be treated without Warmth or Passion. This is said to have been the first Design of those Gentlemen who set on Foot the Royal Society; and had then a very good Effect, as it turned many of the greatest Genius's of that Age to the Disquisitions of natural Knowledge, who, if they had engaged in Politicks with the same Parts and Application, might have set their Country in a Flame. The Air-Pump, the Barometer, the Quadrant, and the like Inventions, were thrown out to those busy Spirits, as Tubs and Barrels are to a Whale, that he may let the Ship sail on without Disturbance, while he diverts himself with those innocent Amusements.[2]

In his measured way, Addison acknowledges the darkest fear of late Stuart England, the recent spectre of the 'Country in a Flame'. He commends the scientists for their efforts to create a better consensus in 'natural Knowledge' and to divert 'busy Spirits' from dangerous engagements in 'Politicks'. He modestly offers his own efforts to draw 'Mens Minds off from the Bitterness of Party, and furnish…them with Subjects of Discourse that may be treated without Warmth or Passion'. Terry Eagleton, following Habermas, has identified this endeavour as the constitution of a bourgeois 'public sphere'

---

[1] Samuel Johnson, 'Life of Swift', *Lives of the English Poets*, G. B. Hill, ed., 3 vols (Oxford: Clarendon Press, 1905), III, p. 66.

[2] 31 December 1711; *The Spectator*, Donald F. Bond, ed., 5 vols (Oxford: Oxford University Press, 1965), II, p. 519.

defined against the coercive certainties of absolutist cultures.[3] Dragged on by the relentless logic of Marxism, Eagleton sees *The Spectator* as a development, but Addison's project is also explicable as part of a socially conservative reaction against the chaos of the previous century. Addison is eager to avoid extremity, to construct a calmer, stabler culture in which the natural perversity of humanity can be accommodated benignly. He wants to swerve away from the recent past, to find sure grounds for cultural and rhetorical legitimacy.

The cultural history of the late Stuart period – the essential context for Swift's work – has tended to be written in terms of progress and innovation: the rise of the novel, the rise of the party system, the rise of Latitudinarianism, the rise of financial and administrative institutions, the rise of the periodical essay, the rise of science, the rise of reason, the rise of industry; all are ideas that illustrate this pervasive metaphor. Progress was not, however, the trope by which writers of the period figured their projects and experiences. They thought (or, at least, they wrote) in terms of reform, regularisation, restoration, and diversion of the vicious spirit of the age. If one attends to the public language of the late seventeenth century, the major epistemological break occurs at 1660, not 1689, for it was in 1660 that the sorts of political and religious debates, and the sorts of cultural forms which had sustained writers, changed. The crisis was sudden – as Karlis Racevskis puts it, summarising Foucault, 'when an epistemological break occurs it changes the basic configuration through which knowledge is legitimate'.[4] Dryden, with his exaggerated sensitivity to the change in climate, illustrates this point by writing the 'Heroic Stanzas' in praise of Cromwell in quatrains in 1658, then switching to heroic couplets and Charles II with 'Astræa Redux' in 1660. However, contrary to much Foucauldian theorising, a new episteme did not suddenly appear to fill the vacuum left by the old one. Rose Zimbardo has recently characterised the Restoration as a zero point:

The Restoration is a zero point in that, on the one hand, it responds to the abyss that is left when the idea of *essential* eternity embodied in medieval and Renaissance cultural forms is no longer tenable; on the other hand, however, it is also the point of maximum constructive power in that it was the time when the basic constructs of eighteenth-century 'modernity' were forged.[5]

[3] Terry Eagleton, *The Function of Criticism: From the Spectator to Post-Structuralism* (London: Verso, 1984), ch. 1; Jürgen Habermas, *The Structural Transformation of the Public Sphere: An Inquiry into a Category of Bourgeois Society*, trans. Thomas Burger (Cambridge, Mass.: MIT Press, 1989; 1st German edn, 1962).

[4] Karlis Racevskis, 'Genealogical Critique: Michel Foucault', *Contemporary Literary Theory*, G. D. Atkins and L. Morrow, eds. (Amherst: University of Massachusetts Press, 1988), pp. 229–45; quote, p. 231.

[5] Rose A. Zimbardo, 'At Zero Point: Discourse, Politics, and Satire in Restoration England', *ELH*, 59 (1992), 785–98; quote, 789.

With a vista of history running from medieval to modern, this draws a longer bow than is necessary for our present purposes, but the shape of the idea is important. In 1660, there were very few foundations of religion, thought, politics, literature, or rhetoric which had not been undermined in some way during the Civil War period.

New foundations were needed, but no one dared propose novelties. Authority had to be rediscovered and restored, for invention (in religion, with the Puritans, and in politics, with the Republicans) was the idea which had been most comprehensively discredited in the wars. Foucault's general proposition about 'Classical thought' is applicable at least to the rhetorical forms of Restoration writing:

> In Classical thought, the utopia functioned rather as a fantasy of origins: this was because the freshness of the world had to provide the ideal unfolding of a table in which everything would be present and in its proper place, with its adjacencies, its peculiar differences, and its immediate equivalences; in this primal light, representations could not yet have been separated from the living, sharp, perceptible presence of what they represent.[6]

'Restoration' took a long time – much longer than the period designated as the Restoration by historians. The 'Glorious Revolution' of 1688–9 did not bring the cultural process of restoration to an end. Rather, it was just another attempt to restore grounds for authority to a culture which had been lurching from one crisis to another for nearly a century. In the long view of the Whiggish narrative of British history, it was a successful compromise, but its ultimate success was not obvious in the public writing and public life of the nation for several decades. At least until the 1720s, and probably until the effective demise of the Jacobite alternative in the '45, English political culture (and the other elements of public culture) was marked more by an intense desire for order and arguments about what constituted that order, than by the fact of order itself.

Starting in 1660, and lasting nearly a century, the principle desideratum and site of conflict in public language was the nature, position, and possession of authority. Civil war, the execution of Charles I, Cromwell, the Republic, the disestablishment and re-establishment of the Church, the broadly accidental restoration of Charles II, the accession of a Catholic monarch, the 'Glorious' Revolution, the accession of a Dutch monarch, the Jacobite alternative, the Hanoverian succession; all these events fractured the impression of seamlessness on which immemorial authority relied.

---

[6] Michel Foucault, *The Order of Things: An Archaeology of the Human Sciences* (London: Tavistock, 1970), p. 262; see *Les Mots et les Choses: une Archélogie des Sciences Humaines* (Paris: Editions Gallimard, 1966), p. 274. By 'Classical' Foucault means (*sic*) seventeenth- and eighteenth-century French – the relevance of this imagery to British culture of the period should become clear in the course of this chapter.

Intellectuals of all types were often (almost habitually) engaged in attempts to recover order and unvexed authority. Even that most radical departure into a brave new world of Modernity, the new empirical science, presented itself as a return to purer sources of sense and reason than had been enjoyed amid the distracting sophistications of the Middle Ages. Whether this is what 'really' happened in the 'objective' course of history is not the point at issue. Again Foucault provides useful insight:

In the eighteenth century, to return to the origin was to place oneself once more as near as possible to mere duplication of representation...It was of little importance whether this origin was considered fictitious or real, whether it possessed the value of an explanatory hypothesis or a historical event.[7]

What I am looking for here are fledgling rhetorics of power, discourses which, by their terms of reference, try to erase the immediate past and to control the present. The name I will give to these projections of cultural and rhetorical power is restoration enterprise.

Restoration enterprises constructed themselves discursively as swerves away from the errors of the immediate past.[8] The swerves took three essential forms: (1) the idealistic (and often deeply rhetorical) loop back to an idea of original order and purity; (2) the pragmatic construction of a public sphere of controlled and limited contestation; and (3) the myopic veneration of established order and right. These movements were all evasions of the absolute and totalising claims which had characterised the middle of the seventeenth century, and had driven on the crisis of rebellion and revolution. Each was a refusal to claim an absolute authority, a refusal of what came to be called enthusiasm. Together, they led to public languages which claimed to place authority outside themselves, which eschewed inspiration and courted faithfulness to canons of truth, sense, and order. This is broadly the difference between seventeenth-century and eighteenth-century discourse, a difference which can be characterised (or caricatured) as the movement from Milton's 'Things unattempted yet in prose or rhyme' to Pope's 'What oft was thought, but ne'er so well expressed'.[9] My point is that the decades following 1660 form a fluid period of cultural making, a period of rhetorical flux which provides the textual context for Swift's early parodies.

---

[7] Ibid, p. 329; *Les Mots et les Choses*, p. 340.
[8] The theory of swerves is outlined in Harold Bloom, *The Anxiety of Influence: A Theory of Poetry* (New York and London: Oxford University Press, 1973). Obviously Bloom's ideas, constructed in response to psychoanalytical concerns about Romantic poets and poetry, have undergone a series of sea changes in their voyage to late Stuart cultural history. The career of Dryden, particularly as it is interpreted in Steven N. Zwicker, *Politics and Language in Dryden's Poetry: The Arts of Disguise* (Princeton: Princeton University Press, 1984), is the exemplary illustration of this anxiety of reconstruction.
[9] John Milton, *Paradise Lost*, I, l.16; Alexander Pope, *Essay on Criticism*, l.298.

In the course of this chapter, I will discuss several examples of the three kinds of swerve because Swiftian parody enters a disjunctive relationship with these cultural enterprises, invading their historical moments and deconstructing their rhetorics for parodic effect. Take, as an example, the way *A Tale of A Tub* engages with the passage from Addison with which we commenced this section. Here it is anachronistic but tempting to see *A Tale* as ridiculing Addison's calm proclamation of the tubbian nature of his enterprise:

The Wits of the present Age being so very numerous and penetrating, it seems, the Grandees of *Church* and *State* begin to fall under horrible Apprehensions, lest these Gentlemen, during the intervals of a long Peace, should find leisure to pick Holes in the weak sides of Religion and Government. To prevent which, there has been much Thought employ'd of late upon certain Projects for taking off the Force, and Edge of those formidable Enquirers, from canvasing and reasoning upon such delicate Points. They have at length fixed upon one, which will require some Time as well as Cost, to perfect. Mean while the Danger hourly increasing, by new Levies of Wits all appointed (as there is Reason to fear) with Pen, Ink, and Paper which may at an hours Warning be drawn into Pamphlets, and other Offensive Weapons, ready for immediate Execution: It was judged of absolute necessity, that some present Expedient be thought on, till the main Design can be brought to Maturity. To this End, at a Grand Committee, some Days ago, this important Discovery was made by a certain curious and refined Observer; That Sea-men have a Custom when they meet a *Whale*, to fling him out an empty *Tub*, by way of Amusement, to divert him from laying violent Hands upon the Ship. This Parable was immediately mythologiz'd: The *Whale* was interpreted to be *Hobs's Leviathan*, which tosses and plays with all other Schemes of Religion and Government, whereof a great many are hollow, and dry, and empty, and noisy, and wooden, and given to Rotation. This is the *Leviathan* from whence the Wits of our Age are said to borrow their Weapons. The *Ship* in danger, is easily understood to be its old Antitype the *Commonwealth*. But, how to analyze the *Tub*, was a Matter of difficulty; when after long Enquiry and Debate, the literal Meaning was preserved: And it was decreed, that in order to prevent these *Leviathans* from tossing and sporting with the *Commonwealth*, (which of it self is too apt to *fluctuate*) they should be diverted from that Game by a *Tale of a Tub*. And my Genius being conceived to lye not unhappily that way, I had the honor done me to be engaged in the Performance.

This is the sole Design in publishing the following Treatise, which I hope will serve for an *Interim* of some Months to employ those unquiet Spirits, till the perfecting of that great Work.[10]

The extraordinary thing about this passage is the exactness with which it parodies Addison's manifesto a decade before Addison wrote it. It is possible that Addison had this passage in mind when he wrote *The Spectator*, no.262, but it difficult to see how such a resonance might support his case. Rather, it is more interesting and informative to read *A Tale*'s tub as proleptically paro-

[10] *A Tale*, pp. 39–41.

dic of *The Spectator*'s. The passages share a mood of modest but practical public spirit, the images of the whale and the tub, the diversion of 'Mens Minds'
/ 'the Wits of the present Age' from 'Bitterness of Party' / 'pick[ing] Holes
in the weak sides of Religion and Government', and an admiration for corporate cultural effort (Addison explicitly expresses his enthusiasm for the
Royal Society, Swift's narrator mentions more vaguely a project settled upon,
for which his book is only an interim measure). Swift focuses unerringly on
the spirit of projection in the age, identifies the anxiety it attempts to cover,
and then pushes it until it looks ridiculous. The martial imagery colliding
with the imagery of print in the passage 'new Levies of Wits all appointed (as
there is Reason to fear) with Pen, Ink, and Paper which may at an hours
Warning be drawn into Pamphlets, and other Offensive Weapons', captures
exactly the way conflict was being quite consciously displaced by writers such
as Addison from the military realm into language. And, finally, the identification of Hobbes as the archetype of dangerous ideological error exposes the
way he was made to represent the ideological anti-matter of 'atheism' in this
age, the secular equivalent of Popery in religion.

In short, the expression of intent in *A Tale* goes right to the heart of
restoration enterprise, parodying it with dangerous and deconstructive irony.
The prophetic exposure of the Addisonian project is particularly vivid, but
this is only typical of the unsettling role Swiftian parody plays in an age of
projects, which were all attempting to constitute their own validity. Nicholas
Jose describes the parodic refunctioning of Dryden very aptly. He discusses
the moment in the *Battle of the Books* when Dryden enters a contest with Virgil
in extravagant armour, nine times too large for his puny physique:

Swift is ruthlessly sensitive here to the cultural and historical pretensions of the poet
of the Restoration. The modern anxiety to establish contact with a great ancient
tradition is seen by Swift as the merest vanity, when what should be most apparent
is the radical discrepancy between ancient values and modern capacities. Virgil's
armour is of gold, 'the others but of rusty Iron'. Swift considers it an evasion of self-
knowledge, and responsible self-scrutiny in the limited present, to go casting about
for large ideals, golden worlds, great traditions and remote utopias. To aspire to find
oneself in those terms is not to find oneself at all. And Swift's intuition is right. He
focuses on the gap between aspiring rhetoric and what can actually be
achieved...[T]hat gap is central to much of the writing of the Restoration years.
Swift, unlike Pope, makes little allowance for the historical pressures which forced
such a gap, and is impatient of the kinds of art, or of consciousness, which such historical pressures encouraged. Dryden, like Cowley, like Marvell, like Milton, was
troubled about the ways of providence, unsettled by history, and creatively driven
by the discrepancy between the two. And to say that is to discover that the major
poets of the 1660s were in touch with the central concerns of their time.[11]

[11] Nicholas Jose, *Ideas of the Restoration in English Literature, 1660–1671* (Cambridge, Mass.: Harvard
University Press, 1984), p. 173.

'He focuses on the gap between aspiring rhetoric and what can actually be achieved.' The parody attacks the self-aggrandising mood of these rhetorics of cultural regeneration; it is a dangerous supplement to these fledgling rhetorics of power, for it inevitably questions the authority of the discourses it invades. It hollows out the tropes at precisely the moments when appeals to order and original authority attempt to resound most convincingly. In the rest of this chapter, we will outline the logic of some of these tropes.

The restoration of true religion

In Christianity there can be no concerning truth which is not ancient; and whatsoever is truly new, is certainly false.[12]

The ideological and institutional restoration of the church, though relatively neglected by modern cultural scholars, was extremely important to the ideological self-image of the late Stuart period.[13] The Anglican Church had had a near-death experience during the Interregnum, from which it returned with a stronger doctrinal and institutional sense of itself than it had ever previously possessed.[14] This return was a major enterprise, marked throughout by a rhetorical desire to restore lost origins of order and authority. As we shall see further on, clerical rhetoric and activity provide examples of all three kinds of restoration enterprise that I have identified. However, the desire to proclaim restored authority is most clearly visible in the widespread opinion that the Church of England was almost perfectly reformed in imitation of the primitive church and had, therefore, regained the original Catholic and apostolic tradition which popish corruption had perverted. The confident expression of this controversial assumption is striking:

There are [some] who blame our Reformation as defective, as if the Church were not reformed, not purged enough from the errors it had before contracted; but if such would lay aside all prejudices and impartially consider the constitution of our church, as it is now reformed, they might clearly see that as there is nothing defective so neither is there anything superfluous in it, but that it exactly answers the pattern of the Primitive and Apostolical Church itself, as near as it is possible for a national church to do it.[15]

---

[12] John Pearson, *An Exposition of the Creed* (1659); quoted in John Gascoigne, *Cambridge in the Age of Enlightenment: Science, Religion and Politics from the Restoration to the French Revolution* (Cambridge: Cambridge University Press, 1989), p. 32. Pearson was subsequently Lady Margaret Professor of Theology at Cambridge (1661) and Bishop of Chester (1673).

[13] A large part of this gap has recently been filled by J. A. I. Champion, *The Pillars of Priestcraft Shaken: The Church of England and its Enemies, 1660–1730* (Cambridge: Cambridge University Press, 1992).

[14] See Robert S. Bosher, *The Making of the Restoration Settlement: The Influence of the Laudians, 1649–1662* (London: Dacre Press, 1951).

[15] William Beveridge, *Works*, 12 vols, Library of Anglo-Catholic Theology (Oxford, 1843–48), II, p. 444; quoted from Eamon Duffy, 'Primitive Christianity Revived: Religious Renewal in Augustan England', *Studies in Church History*, 14 (1977), 287–300; quote, p. 287.

This sense of providential destiny as the true body of Christ on earth was not confined to High Churchmen and erstwhile Laudians such as Beveridge. The idea had been argued at length by that very political Whig, Bishop Gilbert Burnet in his *History of the Reformation* (1679–1714), a work which provided a convenient bridge between the large project of the Reformation and the more partisan version ('our Reformation', as Beveridge has it) in the Anglican Church. The Latitudinarian bishop, Simon Patrick, shared the commitment to the local version of primitive christianity, proclaiming his convictions in these terms:

> Our Latitudinarians therefore are by all means for a Liturgy, and do prefer that of our own Church before all others, admiring the solemnity, gravity and primitive simplicity of it, its freedom from affected phrases, or mixture of vain and doubtful opinions; in a word they esteem it to be so good that they would be loth to adventure the mending of it for fear of marring it.[16]

The idea of 'primitive simplicity' being an unqualified virtue is telling, as is Patrick's later description of his party's doctrinal sources. Their doctrines are derived

> from the sacred writings of the apostles and evangelists, in interpreting whereof, they carefully attend to the sense of the ancient Church, by which they conceive the modern ought to be guided; and therefore they are very conversant in all the genuine monuments of the ancient Fathers, those especially of the first and purest ages.[17]

The validity of this return to the purity of original foundation became something of a shibboleth, even if, because primitive christianity could be made to mean different things for different purposes, a degree of creative misprision occurred. As Champion suggests, 'History was then a resource which intellectuals could employ to enshrine their particular ideals...The Restoration saw many rival claims to be the true religion.'[18] At a practical level, writers such as William Cave in his *Primitive Christianity: or, the Religion of the Ancient Christians in the first Ages of the Gospel* (1673) attempted to draw out its moral lessons, and there was a movement of societies for the propagation of these virtues.[19] However, the most extraordinary expression of devotion to the primitive can be seen in the efflorescence of patristic scholarship.[20] The Bible has little to say about the institution of a church and, as Anglicans were looking to restore the true church, the mediate evidence of the early years, recorded by the Councils and the Church Fathers, took on

---

[16] *A Brief Account of the New Sect of Latitude-Men, together with some Reflections upon the New Philosophy* (1662); quoted in Norman Sykes, *From Sheldon to Secker: Aspects of English Church History, 1660–1768* (Cambridge: Cambridge University Press, 1959), p. 147.

[17] Ibid., p. 147.

[18] Champion, *Pillars of Priestcraft*, p. 226.

[19] See Duffy, 'Primitive Christianity Revived' on these societies.

[20] See Sykes, *From Sheldon to Secker*, ch. 4.

an almost Scriptural significance. Dispute raged between Whigs, Tories, Catholics, and the heterodox (most notably and persistently William Whiston) as to the exact nature of this original ecclesiastical constitution and the terms of its apostolic filiation of authority. The more important point, however, is that no one doubted that it offered an ideal model which christians were commanded to imitate, and none of the Anglicans expressed any doubts about the essentially close congruence of their church to that model.

In their rhetorical attempts to restore legitimacy, however, the Tory High Churchmen tended to appeal less to primitive christianity and more to the rights of the church and the duties of the subject. These conservative clerics, who have been largely ignored by Whiggish history, formed a standing majority among priests and their texts dominated (at least numerically) politico-devotional debate. They saw rebellion as the great crime of the seventeenth century, and the execution of Charles I as the darkest moment in recent history. Their project was to restore order by developing a confessional state and inculcating proper obedience to civil and ecclesiastical authority. Had it not been for James II and the Revolution of 1689, Britain's constitutional and ideological development in the eighteenth century might have been much more like France's, because the Restoration and the Test Acts set up a political order which may well have proved durable. The events of 1688–9 split the legitimists between those who thought their duty of obedience irrevocable, even in the face of a Catholic monarch and exclusion from their livings, and those who took a more pragmatic line and cleft to Protestantism and the authority in place. The Nonjurors were never a significant political organisation, but (with writers such as Charles Leslie and George Hickes) they possessed a good deal of rhetorical power and operated as the chief ideological proponents of Jacobitism within Anglicanism. While arguments of obedience always had a Jacobite flavour after 1689, they did not lose their attraction for writers within the Church of England. In the reign of Queen Anne (who was conveniently English, Anglican, and relatively uninvolved in the events of the Revolution), Anglican divines as intemperate as Henry Sacheverell and as canny as Francis Atterbury busily asserted a legitimist constitution against what they saw to be the implicit rebelliousness of 'Revolution Principles'. This discourse of the confessional state remained dominant among Anglican clergy long after it became politically defunct under the Hanovers and, indeed, Bute made a notoriously unsuccessful attempt to revive it in the 1760s with the support of his pupil George III. It has a considerable importance for our understanding of Swift's work, because it governs his unironic writings on religious matters and is so conspicuously absent from his ironic writings.

This Tory concern with order, obedience, and proper authority slipped very easily from a veneration for *original* to *established* order. The restored

Church's other significant institutional preoccupation, the established rights, liberties, and structures of the Church of England, can be seen as like the pursuit of primitive christianity, but less confident in the belief that original purity can be reclaimed in a corrupt world. This preoccupation was digni-fied by the proposition that the Apostolic succession conveyed Christ's unbroken authority to his only truly Catholic, orthodox, and reformed church (the Church of England). Rights thus directly derived from God should therefore be inviolable and inalienable.[21] As with the development of the Common Law, this anxiety was expressed legalistically, in constant bick-ering among bishops, clergymen, and laymen over property rights and medieval precedents. As Dean of St Patrick's, Swift's troubles with his choir and Archbishop King derive from this mind-set, and its most important manifestation in public life was the conflict over the rights of the lower House of Convocation.[22]

The determination to uphold the rights of the church fits into the main-stream of Tory churchmanship; indeed, it practically defines it. High Churchmen vigorously asserted the proposition that the interests of church and state were intimately linked, holding that the church supported the state by teaching order and obedience, while the state should reciprocate by upholding the interests of the church. The origin of all authority for civil society was assumed to be God, and hence ideology and theology were practically identical, or, at least, existed in an close symbiotic relationship. This proclamation of the unity of church and state and the attendant deter-mination to discover and maintain (and dominate the terms of) a quiet and uncontentious orthodoxy was one of the clearest restoration enterprises. Doctrines of non-resistance and passive obedience were clearly employed to sublimate libertarian impulses and support the restored monarchy. We should not, however, assume that these doctrines were mere expedients designed to rationalise the encroachment of Stuart despotism during the reigns of Charles II and James II. They were seriously held political convic-tions sufficiently strong to drive a significant proportion of firmly Protestant clergy and laity into the Nonjuring schism and Jacobitism. Furthermore, they were ideas which retained considerable force in High Church rhetoric into the early Hanoverian period at least, and perhaps, as J.C.D. Clark has controversially maintained, throughout the eighteenth century.[23] We will

[21] Swift's intense hostility to Henry VIII, the expropriator of Church property, owes much to this tradition; see *PW*, V, pp. 247–51 and XIII, pp. 123, 126.

[22] See Sykes, *From Sheldon to Secker*, ch. 2. The most notable protagonists in this conflict were Francis Atterbury and White Kennett, both of whose biographies have been written by G. V. Bennett, *The Tory Crisis in Church and State, 1688–1730: The Career of Francis Atterbury, Bishop of Rochester* (Oxford: Clarendon Press, 1975), and *White Kennett, 1660–1728, Bishop of Peterborough: A Study of the Political and Ecclesiastical History of the Early Eighteenth Century* (London: SPCK, 1957).

[23] *English Society, 1688–1832: Ideology, Social Structure and Political Practice during the Ancien Régime* (Cambridge: Cambridge University Press, 1985).

look at this tradition of thought and rhetoric more carefully below, when we discuss the structure of political ideology and dispute.

More covert in its operation, but no less pervasive and more lasting in its consequences, was the way the stress on the church's establishment and orthodoxy functioned subtly as the final form of restoration enterprise: the displacement of open debate by a professionalisation of knowledge. In this period, the clergy asserted their control over the laity in theological dispute, professionalising the discourse so that only the qualified possessed either the right or the expertise necessary to controvert opinions. From a conservative point of view, the most volatile dynamic of the Civil War period had been the willingness of a relatively wide segment of society (including the Diggers, the Levellers, and the Agitators in the New Model Army) to dispute the question of Godly discipline. Now that the ecclesiastical structure was deemed by the terms of the Restoration and Revolution Settlements to be ideally and finally reformed (and, therefore, inviolable), the task of defining orthodox doctrine was ceded to the officers of the institution. The clergy formed a specialised corporate body with certain privileges, whose duty was to provide the laity with liturgy, doctrine, and morality. The majority of the population was therefore figured not as active believers, but as passive receptors of belief. Variety of opinions was limited in this sphere of religious debate, and controlled by the social and professional solidarity of the clergy. One manifestation of this solidarity was Atterbury's thwarted ambitions for Convocation (with two houses, as in Parliament, and with significant legislative power), which he wanted to establish as a permanent element of the constitution. However, we can see a more pervasive influence in the way priests dominated learned institutions and public discourse. Though literary history has tended to stress lay writers, clergymen played an almost pre-eminent role in the explosion of learned, devotional, and polemical print which characterises our age – Swift's career merely illustrates the extent to which clergy felt a natural entitlement to comment on all aspects of public life. Furthermore, the clergy had exclusive rights to the platform from which the majority of the populace received its only contact with structured language, the pulpit.

It was not only the voice of Divine Right loyalism which was heard from pulpits, however. The Whigs also had their clerical supporters, and these Low-Churchmen (often described as Latitudinarians, though that is to name them by the most extreme liberals among them) also had their restoration enterprises. The church they wished to restore was deeply opposed to Catholicism but inclusive of a wider range of Protestant beliefs than High Churchmen were willing to entertain. They stressed reason and morality above orthodoxy and obedience, seeing the best way to avoid a repetition of the conflagrations of the Civil War as building the Church of England on a broadly based coalition of Protestant opinion rather than a narrowly defined orthodoxy of doctrine and discipline. They saw themselves as basing their church on the fundamentals (which is to say, the necessary original principles) of Christian faith, while retaining unity at the price of a degree of flexibility in things indifferent. Consequently, even those two charitable and essentially Low-Church projects, the Society for the Propagation of the Gospel (established 1701) and the Society for the Propagation of Christian Knowledge (established 1696), attracted controversy and defence that was ideologically marked more by the rhetoric of restoration than of progress.[24] These and the other missionary and charitable institutions which burgeoned throughout the eighteenth century (charity schools, religious societies, public hospitals, lending and circulating libraries, etc.) mark a significant improvement in public philanthropy, but there was nothing socially progressive in their expressed aims. Rather they sought to inculcate virtue, obedience, and a firm sense of their social place in the masses. As late as 1745, Bishop Butler was still exhorting the bourgeois faithful to good works in these essentially negative terms:

But the principal Design of this Charity is to educate poor Children in such a Manner, as has a Tendency to make them good, and useful, and contented, whatever their particular Station be. The Care of this is greatly neglected by the Poor: nor truly is it more regarded by the Rich, considering what might be expected from them...

For if poor Children are not sent to School, several Years of their Childhood, of course, pass away in Idleness and Loitering. This has a Tendency to give them, perhaps a feeble Listlessness, perhaps an headstrong Profligateness of Mind; certainly an Indisposition to proper Application as they grow up, and an Aversion afterwards, not only to the Restraints of Religion, but to those which any particular Calling, and even the Nature of Society, require. Whereas Children kept to stated Orders, and who many Hours of the Day are in Employment, are by this Means habituated, both to submit to those who are placed over them, and to govern Themselves; and they are also by this means prepared for Industry, in any Way of Life in which they may be placed.[25]

The 'Restraints of Religion' and the social virtue of habituation 'both to submit to those who are placed over them, and to govern Themselves' bulk far larger here than the joys of salvation or the power of education to unlock the potential of 'mute inglorious Milton[s]' that Thomas Gray was writing of at the same time.[26] Again we have swerves rather than a progres-

[24] Gordon Rupp, *Religion in England, 1688–1791* (Oxford: Clarendon Press, 1986), pp. 289–321, demonstrates that these charitable efforts and institutions were not neatly attributable to particular parties within the Church of England or the Dissenters, but took their general colour from their Whiggish affiliations.

[25] Sermon preached in the Parish Church of Christ-Church, London, on the text Proverbs 22:6, delivered 9 May 1745; reprinted in Sisson, *The English Sermon*, pp. 346–58; quote, p. 354.

[26] In the *Elegy Written in a Country Church Yard* (1751), l.59; not that Gray, who goes on in the next line to muse about 'Some Cromwell guiltless of his country's blood' can be dragooned into the role of social progressive, either.

sion, shaped in language as a restoration and maintenance of order and motivated by reactionary anxiety concerning disorder.

Finally, we come to the other notably Whiggish religious project, the systematic investigation of the text of the Bible. We do well to remember here that the Bible was held by Protestants to be the fundamental text of christian society, literally true and prescriptive of social as well as ecclesiastical and moral order. The proposition that it might be textually defective and, therefore, potentially misleading in its received form, was radically deconstructive of all forms of ideological, intellectual, and institutional order. The French Jesuit, Père Simon, had his extensive biblical scholarship used as an argument for strong ecclesiastical control of doctrine against Protestant insistence on the need for individual believers to be immediately influenced by the Bible. Deists such as Toland, Collins, and Tindal used the new perspectives of biblical criticism to attack biblical authority and all things miraculous in religion.[27] While Jesuits and Deists were beyond the pale of legitimate discourse, and were roundly condemned, orthodox writers such as John Mill and Richard Bentley were also involved in narrow inspection of the text of Scripture.[28] They imagined themselves to be working towards reviving the true foundation of christianity, the exact and incorrupt form of God's revealed word. This is, of course, the basic Erasmian and moderate Protestant project of the Reformation, and history shows that even the most well-meaning efforts in this direction have tended to undermine precisely the faith in the literal and prescriptive authority of Scripture which they seek to affirm. However, it is significant that the revisionary tactic of textual scholarship (and it was obvious in the textual history of profane texts of the Ancients, as well as sacred texts) should have such a golden age in the decades after the Restoration of Charles II. The attempt to return to the certain source of an obscured seminal purity, symbolised here by the original God – or author – given text free from corruptions, was the central theme of the religious and intellectual endeavour in the age. It is no accident that the corruption and reformation of the original authoritative text is also the theme of the allegory in *Tale*.

The ordering of scientific language and method

Institutionalised religion is almost necessarily backward-looking, basing itself on original and revealed truths rather than promises of improvement in this world. Consequently, prophetic voices are always unsettling and usually

[27] For the story of the growth of systematic textual scholarship concerning the Bible and the attendant collapse of belief in its literal factuality, see Henning Graf Reventlow, *The Authority of the Bible and the Rise of the Modern World* (London: SCM Press, 1984) and Hans W. Frei, *The Eclipse of Biblical Narrative: A Study in Eighteenth and Nineteenth Century Hermeneutics* (New Haven: Yale University Press, 1974).

[28] See Adam Fox, *John Mill and Richard Bentley: A Study of the Textual Criticism of the New Testament, 1675–1729* (Oxford: Basil Blackwell, 1954).

intolerable within an established religious order. As intellectual history has usually been written, the true prophets of the modern world in late seventeenth century England were the scientists. However, in science we also find language and ideology marked more by the logic of restoration and the pursuit of order than by the proclamation of progress. It would be foolish and churlish to question the actual achievements of the age of Newton, Boyle, et al., but the rhetorics of scientific endeavours will bear further investigation. Let us consider the convergence of new science with language and propaganda in Thomas Sprat's *History of the Royal-Society* (1667). For our purposes, the crucial issue is the famous definition of an appropriate scientific prose:

[It] has been, a constant Resolution, to reject all the Amplifications, digressions, and swellings of style: to return back to the primitive purity, and shortness, when men deliver'd so many *Things*, almost in an equal number of *words*. They have exacted from all their members, a close, naked, natural way of speaking; positive expressions; clear senses; a native easiness: bringing all things as near the Mathematical plainness as they can: and preferring the language of Artizans, Countrymen, and Merchants, before that, of Wits, or Scholars.[29]

Sprat is too often taken at his own word as the mere amanuensis of a glorious scientific movement. The extraordinary rhetorical gesture of publishing a 'history' of the Royal Society only half-a-dozen years after its institution has seldom been questioned, perhaps because it has been justified after the fact by the long and successful career of the scientific programme it proclaims.[30] The language and enterprise are, however, performative rather than descriptive; the text is a manifesto rather than a history.

One of the text's most anxious moments comes just above our present passage where 'this trick of *Metaphors*' is forbidden in the meta-language of empirical science. It is not remarkable that metaphors appear, for, whatever Sprat might wish us to believe, metaphor (broadly conceived) cannot be eradicated (i.e. rooted out) from language. What is really remarkable in our present passage is that, though Sprat's *History* is sited in cultural history as a sort of Book of Genesis for the new empirical science and progress, the shape of the metaphors here figures the enterprise as reformation and restoration rather than as unmediated novelty. Joel Reed has identified the duplicity of Sprat's language well:

This passage is significant because of its interweaving of two important, complex themes. Sprat leads his readers back to Adamic language and forward to discourse

29 Thomas Sprat, *The History of the Royal-Society of London, for the Improving of Natural Knowledge*, Jackson I. Cope and Howard Whitmore Jones, eds. (St Louis: Washington University Press, 1959), p. 113.
30 On the fallacy of reading Sprat's book as guileless history, see Michael Hunter, *Science and Society in Restoration England* (Cambridge: Cambridge University Press, 1981), pp. 29–32, and P. B. Wood, 'Methodology and Apologetics: Thomas Sprat's History of the Royal Society', *BJHS*, 13 (1980), 1–26.

of science and rationality. The combination of these two themes exemplifies the heterogeneous structure of cultural formation that Raymond Williams posits in his discussion of dominant, residual, and emerging cultures...The double theme of Royal Society discourse – its reliance on the residual Judeo-Christian utopia of Eden and its evocation of the emerging discourse of scientific rationalism – plays important roles in legitimating the social order of the Restoration.[31]

Sprat's claims for language are shaped nostalgically. It should '*return back* to the *primitive* purity',[32] which is to say that purity is conceived of as anterior and original rather than a posterior and future goal. Hence the shape of linguistic reform is circular, a return to an Edenic correspondence between words and things which can only be achieved by looping backwards, around the corruptions inevitably attendant on the world's fallen state. The language of primitivism and pre-sophisticated simplicity continues with the exhortation to achieve 'a close, *naked, natural* way of speaking', 'a *native* easiness', 'the language of *Artizans, Countrymen,* and *Merchants*'. The ultimate goal of language is to come 'near the Mathematical plainness', but even that need not entail an attack on historical priority, for in a theocentric universe geometry (be it Euclidean, Cartesian, or, a few years on, Newtonian) asserted the ultimate priority of divine order, a determinate and stable system originating in the will of God for which mathematics was the purest descriptive language. Even in this most progressive of cultural enterprises, the *rhetorical* need for the authority conferred by priority – a priority whose significance was essentially mythic – is palpable and betrays a deep cultural anxiety, a desire to restore the certainties of an authentic and ordered world.

The age did not lack proposals of linguistic purification, whether in the promulgation of a scientific language or in the determination, led by Dryden, to tame the vigorous barbarity of English poetry and prose. The anxious desire to control passion and the dissemination of meaning can be seen in the proliferation of proposals for an English academy to be set up, along the lines of the French, to authoritatively control the nation's language and learning. Even Swift was touched by enthusiasm for such schemes, advocating 'a plan for a society or academy for correcting and settling our language',[33] in the *Proposal for Correcting, Improving and Ascertaining the English Tongue* (1712), though he also subverted the project by creating the Academy of Lagado. Sprat clearly had such regulatory ambitions for the Royal Society, but he went further by proposing a separate academy for the propagation of his linguistic programme. Again he lays bare his reactionary ideological motivations in suggesting that one of the new academy's principal functions would be to write an authorised history of the civil war period:

[31] 'Restoration and Repression: The Language Projects of the Royal Society', *SECC*, 19 (1989), 399–412; quote, 401.
[32] My emphasis in this and subsequent quotations.
[33] *PW*, IV, p. 5.

The effects of such a Work would be wonderfully advantageous, to the safety of our Country, and to His Majesties Interest: for there can be no better means to preserve his Subjects in obedience for the future, than to give them a full view of the miseries, that attended rebellion.[34]

You will search in vain to find an active member of the Royal Society who performed this noble function. The task finally fell to the great Tory, Clarendon, in his *History of the Great Rebellion* (1702–4), and that Sprat should have proposed something similar indicates the narrowness of the political spectrum. Here we have contemporaries, who have since come to signify the old world and the new, sharing an identical cultural ambition – the exposure of the evils of rebellion and the inculcation of social obedience.

Even in science, it was a culture looking to *renew* itself, but lacking the nerve or ideological resources even in its most confident moments to figure this as starting *anew*. As Steven Shapin and Simon Schaffer have shown in their important book, *Leviathan and the Air-Pump: Hobbes, Boyle, and the Experimental Life*,[35] the construction of experimental method and space was a significant restoration enterprise in its own right. In my terms, it was a revealing instance of the swerve away from the absolute claims of unitary systems of thought and cultural organisation into the limited plurality of a public sphere of polite contestation. As Shapin and Schaffer point out, 'The matter of fact was a social as well as an intellectual category'.[36] Sprat was quick to pounce upon and eulogise the social usefulness of experiment:

Experiments...will take away all pretence of idleness, by a constant cours of pleasant indeavors; they will employ men about profitable Works, as well as delightful; by the pleasure of their Discoveries they will wear off the roughness, and sweeten the humorous peevishness of the mind, whereby many are sowr'd into Rebellion.[37]

This concentrates on the decorums of discovering rather than on the truths discovered, and suggests that the process of experiment might act as a sort of social soporific. In this, Sprat was in perfect agreement with Addison in the passage from *The Spectator* which we have already studied: 'The Air-Pump, the Barometer, the Quadrant, and the like Inventions, were thrown out to those busy Spirits, as Tubs and Barrels are to a Whale, that he may let the Ship sail on without Disturbance, while he diverts himself with those innocent Amusements.'[38]

---

[34] Sprat, *History*, p. 42.
[35] *Leviathan and the Air-Pump: Hobbes, Boyle, and the Experimental Life*, (Princeton: Princeton University Press, 1985). Not only do the authors give a valuable description of the construction of the idea, space, and community of experiment, they also, particularly in ch. 7 ('Natural Philosophy and the Restoration'), suggest the shape of the larger cultural context upon which I am expanding here.
[36] Ibid., p. 69.
[37] Sprat, *History*, p. 428.
[38] 31 December 1711; *The Spectator*, Bond, ed., II, p. 519.

And the detail of the invention of experiment will support this analysis. The dispute between Boyle and Hobbes over the possibility of the existence of a vacuum in nature, chronicled by Shapin and Schaffer, clearly illustrates the clash between two orders of knowledge. Led by Robert Boyle's experiments on the vacuum, natural philosophers sought to swerve from the ideologically driven absolutisms of the previous age into a 'neutral' and consensually verifiable study of fact. Their dispute with Hobbes, who insisted, on theoretical grounds, that matter was continuous and that consequently a vacuum could not exist, was more than a simple intellectual disagreement. It was a dispute over what constituted a fact and the methods one might validly use to discover one. Hobbes, in science as in politics, demanded that authority should be central, systematic, absolute, and indivisible. He abhorred a vacuum, and the speculative, falsifiable method of experiment which was supposed to verify it, in the same way that he abhorred the idea that a commonwealth could be maintained by the balance of independent forces. Boyle and the experimentalists recoiled in turn from Hobbes' mechanical systematisation of certainty because they saw it as the same sort of intellectual 'enthusiasm' which had fractured the body politic. They sought to swerve away from the clash of irreconcilable certainties by constructing a negotiable and miscellaneous space for truth called fact, which could be ascertained by a common method called experiment. Hence truth ceased for them to be a matter of faith or obedience and became the supposedly neutral product of a supposedly neutral, and time-consuming, method.[39]

Restoration enterprises in other realms of culture

It is not necessary for our present purposes to survey thoroughly all aspects of late Stuart culture in terms of this idea of restoration enterprise. What is necessary is to grasp that the rhetorical inter-text in which Swiftian parody operates is not dominated by an ideal of progress, but by complex cultural and rhetorical reactions to perceived problems. The parody homes in on the swerves, the various projecting spirits of the age, and many of these do not fit in with the received Whiggish interpretation of cultural and political history. The rage for order, for original and/or settled institutions, and the displacement of intellectual extremism into a public sphere of limited debate, reveal anxious hindsight rather than prescient foresight in a number

---

[39] I stress 'supposedly' because, as Shapin and Schaffer demonstrate, access to experimental science was socially exclusive because of the massive expense involved in setting up and maintaining the apparatus needed. Moreover, the facts allegedly verified rested on a narrow experimental basis, because few air-pumps existed and it was some time before a successful replication of Boyle's famous experiments was made (see *Leviathan and the Air-Pump*, pp. 228–30). Hence, social and ideological solidarity among supporters played a larger part in the early success of experimental method than demonstrated facts.

of areas. Textual scholarship sought to restore the original form of biblical and classical texts after centuries of degeneration. The common law based itself on the massive originary fiction that the law was not made by judges and lawyers, only *declared*,[40] and concentrated on original rights, buttressed by such enabling fictions as the Norman Yoke and a libertarian interpretation of *Magna Carta*.[41] It was a regularising age, concerned with sound foundations, be they ideologies, institutions, academies, or philosophical systems. Geoffrey Holmes has identified our period as important in the development of professional bodies and professional status, as special skills came increasingly to rely on specialised, institutionally certified authority.[42] He has mapped the increased power, wealth, and status of doctors, lawyers, and the clergy as they improved the nature of their qualifications and cultivated the image of independent expertise. They worked on their corporate identities in an effort to prevent amateurs from intruding on their skills, and further professionalised their legal, medical, and theological discourses so that their language excluded laymen. Lawyers refined their professional rules, doctors stressed membership of the Royal College of Surgeons and university qualifications in order to distinguish themselves from midwives and apothecaries, and clergy claimed guardianship of doctrine, religious discussion, and salvation. The proliferation of such projects for suppressing unauthorised activity suggests a social anxiety, and the creeping credentialism lends itself to parody in Swift's works as narrator after narrator attempts to justify his utterance with flawed and poorly fabricated tropes of authority.

Few public rhetorics were unmarked by the desire to return to peace and order. In poetry the swerve away from the Miltonic ambition to pursue 'Things unattempted yet in prose or rhyme',[43] is very clear. The taming of the native wildness of English numbers, was prosecuted first by Dryden in the practice of his poetry and his critical theory, then followed to an inimitable pitch of controlled energy by Pope, and remained dominant as an ideal until the Romantics. It performed the dual cultural function of returning to original Classical ideals of form and style and of instituting a conservative literary culture, receptive to received ideas and wary of innovation. Literary culture became explicitly devoted to the emulative arts of translation, imitation, and

---

[40] On this myth of the pre-existent authority of the law in the eighteenth century, see Michael Meehan, 'Authorship and Imagination in Blackstone's *Commentaries on the Laws of England*', *Studies in the Eighteenth Century*, 16 (1992), 111–26.

[41] These legal propositions are discussed in J. G. A. Pocock, *The Ancient Constitution and the Feudal Law: English Historical Thought in the Seventeenth Century* (New York: Norton, 1967; 1st edn, 1957).

[42] *Augustan England: Professions, State and Society* (London: Allen and Unwin, 1982).

[43] *Paradise Lost*, I, l.16. Bloom, *The Anxiety of Influence*, and W. Jackson Bate, *The Burden of the Past and the English Poet* (London: Chatto & Windus, 1971), though they pursue different senses of tradition from that which I have followed, both bear fascinatingly on the matter of poetry's reaction to Milton. In my terms of reference, *Paradise Lost* is the literary equivalent of the regicide, a potent, dangerous, and obstructive overreaching of the assumed limits of human/artistic agency.

parody. Prose as well as verse was regularised by Dryden and his followers, to be turned into a sober public discourse, a vessel of ordered, communicable sense rather than a vehicle for virtuosity in speculation. Public language became more like the easy and sociable discourse of gentlemen and a medium for peaceful (which is to say non-military) conflict.

It is important not to mistake this aversion to innovation and intellectual experiment for a desertion of the public sphere by literature into a sort of artistic separatism – *Absalom and Achitophel*, *The Way of the World*, *The Spectator*, *The Dunciad*, and *Gulliver's Travels*, to mention only some major monuments, were all palpably public works. They were, however, reactive rather than 'primary' or speculative forms of writing, depending on pre-existing cultural and literary forms for their authority rather than on any claim to radical originality. *Absalom and Achitophel*, with its layered appropriations of biblical and political discourses and narratives, is typical of this flight from visionary claims. The public sphere which literature inhabited served social order: where it contained criticism, that criticism insisted that it remained constructive. When subversion did occur, it was contrary to the accepted theories of satire and ridicule expounded by commentators such as Dryden and Shaftesbury. These theories were based on the proposition that error is a weak growth while the truth is fundamental, ancient, and strong, so that ridicule will expose error and not damage truth.[44] One only needs to read *A Tale* or some of Pope's more scabrous attacks to realise that this wishful idealism is little more than an enabling fiction authorising extremes of wit or passion, but the rationalisation channels and contains the illegitimate utterance, transforming attack into the more acceptable guise of criticism. Within these limits, printed language offered an arena where differences could meet and coalesce into the relatively new (and potentially pluralist) idea of public opinion. While this can, of course, be characterised progressively as the freeing of the press and the triumph of the printed word[45] what interests us here is the reactionary motivation. The chief practical virtue of the opening up of a discursive space where rhetorics could do battle to define public perceptions and public policy, was that it distanced the prospect of military or authoritarian solutions. That there was nothing particularly deliberate or principled about this movement can be seen by the broadly accidental way that the centralised authenticating system of censorship lapsed in 1695 and by the sporadic acts of censorship by other means which followed from time to

[44] See Elkin, *The Augustan Defence of Satire*; John Redwood, *Reason, Ridicule and Religion: The Age of Enlightenment in England, 1660–1750* (London: Thames & Hudson, 1976); and Raymond A. Anselment, *'Betwixt Jest and Earnest': Marprelate, Milton, Marvell, Swift and the Decorum of Religious Ridicule* (Toronto: University of Toronto Press, 1979).
[45] For this, see John Feather, *A History of British Publishing* (London: Routledge, 1988); James Sutherland, *The Restoration Newspaper and its Development* (Cambridge: Cambridge University Press, 1986); and Alvin Kernan, *Printing Technology, Letters and Samuel Johnson* (Princeton: Princeton University Press, 1987).

time. But the very fact that censorship could be allowed simply to lapse indicates that variety of opinion was becoming less abhorrent than it had been. Textual authority no longer came from the centre, but from a text's own ability to validate itself in the eyes of the reader. This assumes a readership qualified to judge in matters of public importance (a right not willingly extended by any Tudor, early Stuart, or Cromwellian government and notably non-existent in Louis XIV's France or the other authoritarian regimes on the Continent), and affords an arena for a plurality of discourses bounded only by a consensual feeling for what was legitimate utterance and what illegitimate. Parody launches into this burgeoning textuality, but before we can judge its deformations of authenticity we need to find our bearings in the central field of restoration enterprise which determined images of authority and legitimacy: the structure and discourses of political ideology.

The structure of political ideology and discourse

The different programmes and principles of political (re-)construction, were most starkly opposed in political history and ideology. Here restoration enterprises were concerned urgently with problems of explaining recent history and restoring legitimacy to a fractured body politic. Practical projects and rhetorical projections abounded, before and after the watershed of 1688–89, and few writers recognised the inevitability subsequently ascribed to the course of events by the progressive, or Whig, reading of British history.[46] The historians have been well ahead of the literary scholars in revising our understanding of this period, re-emphasising the cross-currents and the arbitrariness of the events, and assessing the significance of contemporary conservative rationales for the course of events.[47] Even the patriarchalist notions of Sir Robert Filmer and others, so long held to have been demolished in Locke's *First Treatise*, had a sophisticated rationale, and were more widely accepted than contractarian ideology.[48]

Literary history has been slow to learn the lessons of revisionism, and there is much to be done in this area because some significant changes to

---

[46] J. P. Kenyon, *Revolution Principles: The Politics of Party, 1689–1720* (Cambridge: Cambridge University Press, 1977) surveys the various interpretations of the Revolution politically active in the decades following the event.

[47] For a survey of this conservative thought on political principle, see Mark Goldie's excellent (and mystifyingly unpublished) Ph.D dissertation, *Tory Political Thought, 1689–1714* (Cambridge University, 1978). For a trenchant but contentious argument that Tory thought remained central to political ideology throughout the eighteenth century until the Reform Acts of 1828–32, see Clark, *English Society, 1688–1832*. Linda Colley, *In Defiance of Oligarchy: The Tory Party, 1714–60* (Cambridge: Cambridge University Press, 1982) offers another explanation – based on ideas of opposition – for the persistence of Tory thinking and political organisation in the Hanoverian period.

[48] See Gordon J. Schochet, *The Authoritarian Family and Political Attitudes in Seventeenth Century England: Patriarchalism in Political Thought* (New Brunswick: Transaction Books, 1975).

our understanding of the rhetorical logic of texts have become necessary. The Whig reading has been determined to foreclose on the Restoration, yet no one was aware of a sudden accession of political and ideological stability when William and Mary ascended the throne. Charles II had been restored only a generation earlier, and there was little reason to believe that James would not expect as much support as Charles received from other Catholic monarchs and from British loyalists, so there was the constant and real threat of a Jacobite restoration. Moreover, the Revolution Settlement itself meant radically different things to people of differing ideological bents. Locke's suggestion in his *Two Treatises of Government* (1690) that it affirmed private liberty, vanquished tyranny, and demonstrated (via the idea of the social contract) the right of the people to dissolve their government if displeased, should be seen as the partisan (and extreme) statement that it was in context. Mark Goldie has described it as 'the unacceptable face of Whiggism'[49] and, certainly, it was not received at the time as the obvious explanation of political principle and events Whig historians have since taken it to be.[50] Events fell out more messily, and historians have supplied a variety of dates for the appearance of stability (variously defined) which might be taken to suggest the boundaries of the period I would like to define as one of restoration following the crisis of the middle of the seventeenth century. They date the arrival of real stability from the accession of George I (1714),[51] the collapse of the Tory party after 1714,[52] from the institution of Walpole's 'Venetian Oligarchy' in the 1720s,[53] and finally from the demise of the Jacobite alternative (1745).[54] It has even been suggested that 'Political stability was not achieved until the reign of George III [1760] when *de facto* and *de jure* merged. He was the King of all his subjects and the opposition was now, at last, His Majesty's Opposition.'[55]

---

[49] 'The Revolution of 1689 and the Structure of Political Argument: An Essay and an Annotated Bibliography of Pamphlets on the Allegiance Controversy', *Bulletin of Research in the Humanities*, 83 (1980), 473–564; quote, 518.

[50] Gerald M. Straka, *Anglican Reaction to the Revolution of 1688* (Madison: The State Historical Society of Wisconsin, 1962), H. T. Dickinson, *Liberty and Property: Political Ideology in Eighteenth-Century Britain* (London: Weidenfield and Nicolson, 1977), ch. 2, and Goldie, *Tory Political Thought* provide plentiful material to suggest that Locke's contribution to debate over the nature of civil society and the Revolution Settlement was swamped by comparison with the great flood of more traditional legitimist tracts. Even moderate Whigs claimed that royal authority was being in no way diminished, just being returned to its original, authentic terms after the encroachments made on liberty by a Catholic tyrant.

[51] Christopher Hill, *The Century of Revolution, 1603–1714* (London: Thomas Nelson and Sons, 1961).

[52] Bennett, *The Tory Crisis in Church and State*.

[53] J. H. Plumb, *The Growth of Political Stability in England, 1675–1725* (London: Macmillan, 1967).

[54] Eveline Cruickshanks, *Political Untouchables: The Tories and the '45* (London: Duckworth, 1979).

[55] Cruickshanks, 'Religion and the Royal Succession: the Rage of Party', Clyve Jones, ed., *Britain in the First Age of Party, 1680–1750: Essays Presented to Geoffrey Holmes* (London: Hambledon Press, 1987), p. 41. A recent survey of the debate over political stability is Jeremy Black, 'Introduction: an Age of Political Stability?', Jeremy Black, ed., *Britain in the Age of Walpole* (London: Macmillan, 1984), pp. 1–22.

It is not my intention to stop the music in this game of historiographical musical chairs. The important thing is to recognise the period – which coincides even at the most conservative estimate with Swift's first half-century of life – as a time not of reliable progress, but as a time of reaction, a time of various ideological projects attempting to fill the vacuum in the principles of authority created first by the execution of Charles I in 1649 and reformulated by the effective deposition of James II in 1689.[56] It was a time of absolutism on the continent and a time of nostalgia in England for a pure, primitive institution of politics, religion, the other elements of culture.[57] Even Locke imagined civil government as radiating from an original social contract, when people agreed to submit to laws and governance for mutual benefit. Though the evidence suggests that he conceived this as an enabling metaphor to explain current social and political structure, his nearest intellectual allies (contractarians such as Sidney, Tyrell, and Hoadly) were more orthodox in attempting to stress the historicity (and hence the logical priority) of the original contract.[58] They were all engaged in restoration enterprises, seeking to identify the pure source of social and political authority so that the world might be remodelled along its original lines, thus skipping back beyond the recent errors to primal and seminal (and, presumably, God-given) form. It was not considered blockish literal-mindedness to criticise Locke's theories by asking when the social contract had actually, historically been promulgated, and his inability to point to a primal moment was only partly covered by the construction of a more passive theory of ongoing consent.[59] For contractarians, the difficulty of discovering a unified, seminal moment of transfer from a state of nature to civil government was as devastating as the problem faced by Filmerians in identifying the legitimate hereditary descent of divine authority from Adam to Charles II or Queen

---

[56] Most, including Parliament, clung to the fiction that James had deserted and/or abdicated the crown, despite James' and his successors' inconvenient insistence that no such abdication had occurred. Only committed Whigs (a minority) accepted the proposition that resistance to the crown had actually occurred, and only a few extremists among them were willing to suggest that the resistance which had occurred at the Revolution could legitimately be repeated. See Kenyon, *Revolution Principles*, pp. 5–60, and Goldie, '1689 and the Structure of Political Argument'.

[57] It should be assumed throughout that my statements refer only to that small section of the community that might be described as the political nation. In describing the electorate, W. A. Speck, *Tory and Whig: The Struggle in the Constituencies, 1701–1715* (London: Macmillan, 1970), gives a sense of the size and composition of this group. Speck estimates (pp. 16–17) that by 1715 approximately 250,000 men had the franchise, i.e. 4.3 per cent of a population of approximately 5,826,000. The cultural discourse of the landed, the monied, and the literate is all we have that is available to the sort of analysis on which I am engaged. What the powerless and sub-literate thought of these debates of principle and policy generated no public, recorded language, and cannot be recovered except in tiny, mediated fragments. By focusing on printed discourses, this study restricts its focus inevitably to the small, dominant group in English society, and its internecine anxieties.

[58] See Dickinson, *Liberty and Property*, p. 65.

[59] See Schochet, *The Authoritarian Family*, pp. 254–64, particularly p. 262.

Anne. My point is that it was typically an atavistic sort of legitimacy being disputed, not a forward-looking or even particularly pragmatic one.

I do not mean to suggest that any of the restoration enterprises did, or should be expected to, appropriate the ideal past in anything like a historically accurate manner. The past has always been a bountiful field for creative misprision and political wish-fulfilment. When Swift wrote glowingly of the marvellous 'Gothic Institution' of annual Parliaments,[60] his admiration was not based on careful research into Anglo-Saxon politics and culture, but rather on a rhetorical need to demonstrate the illegitimacy of Walpole's introduction of septennial parliaments. The important thing is that the ideal is not conceived of as abstract, appealing merely to reason, but original, that is given or revealed and, consequently, open to corruption. Only the primitive origin was certain, and until that state of purity could be reformed, individual human reason could only approximate to truth inaccurately. Thus lawyers did not concern themselves with abstract notions such as justice or equity, but regarded only precedent and the letter of statute. As Pocock has demonstrated, they were intellectually equipped to discover only those constitutional structures shrouded in the authority of priority. For them and the rest of the political nation, the only valid constitution was the Ancient Constitution. It was Cromwell, the regicide usurper, who had attempted to impose such destructive novelties as a parliament of saints (the 'Barebones Parliament') and succeeded by virtue of the 'New Model Army' – no one in the sphere of orthodox utterance used such language after 1660.

The sphere of orthodox utterance

The great project of restoring authority to a fractured polity generated three realms of principle and discourse, each seeking to constitute its own exclusive legitimacy. These ideological realms can be broadly described as Tory, Whig, and heretical. There were many subtler distinctions and semi-distinctions between individual rhetorics, and these grand allegiances suggest sharp boundaries and unified purposes that were often blurred in practice. Goldie, for example, makes a tripartite division of principles in the allegiance controversy (Whig, Tory, and Nonjuror), then sub-divides these into eight sub-groups.[61] Dickinson describes only orthodox politics when he discusses Tories' loyalty to an ideology of order and Whigs' to government by consent, and he identifies a further variable in court-country allegiances.[62] Burtt cuts across accepted categories in pursuit of a politics of virtue.[63] However,

[60] *PW*, IX, p. 32.

[61] '1689 and the Structure of Political Argument', p. 508.

[62] *Liberty and Property*, part 1.

[63] Shelley Burtt, *Virtue Transformed: Political Argument in England, 1688–1740* (Cambridge: Cambridge University Press, 1992).

for the purposes of literary and historical mapping, it is important to see some model structuring the political rhetorics, because politics happened within this discursive field. The two recognised groupings of ideology, Tory and Whig, were the ones which commanded real political support and could expect to have opportunities to put their ideas into action. They shared an underlying allegiance to England's mixed constitution which could not be assumed among the heretical or unorthodox writers (such as Hobbes and his followers, Jacobites, Republicans, Papists, Dissenters, deists, and other assorted 'atheists'), though they idealised this allegiance in very different ways. The bedrock of consensus in orthodox politics entailed a conviction that legitimate power was divided constitutionally between the crown and Parliament, that the common law protected common rights which could not be denied by executive government, that local government was essentially the business of local gentry and magnates, and that the Church of England as by law established was the national church with inalienable rights superior to any sect's. This sums up the essential ingredients of the supposedly timeless constitution restored against Republican chaos in 1660, and again against Stuart Popish absolutism in 1689.

These very different occasions of 'restoration' also mark the points at which the Whig and Tory legitimating enterprises most clearly diverge. Though the ancient constitution was deemed to have been restored in both 1660 and 1689, the ideological complexion of each event contrasted dramatically with the other. Tory pamphleteers were most at home discussing the transcendent loyalism of the Restoration, whereas the Whigs were happier discussing Revolution principles and the preservation of liberty from tyranny. Tories commemorated the anniversary of Charles I's 'martyrdom' with sermons reminding the faithful of national apostasy and humiliation. They figured their discourses around ideas of loyalty to the crown and the Church of England, and for them the idea of passive obedience to proper authority held vivid attractions. Their ideal was a political culture dominated by a privileged hierarchy, in which authority on an absolutist model would be followed naturally, or obedience compelled validly. Whigs shaped their thinking around principles of liberty and freedom, with their major anniversary being a celebration of William of Orange's coming over on the 'Protestant wind'. They were not in any sense democrats – for them, liberty was imagined as a form of property rather than as an inalienable right. This is to overdraw distinctions which are much harder to demonstrate definitively in detail, particularly when attitudes to landed versus financial or trading wealth and affiliations of court and country are taken into consideration, but it presents two poles which attract and repel actual political rhetorics in orthodox debate, as we will see often in following pages.

These poles created an axis of legitimacy in political debate which formed the common ground for a party political structure. The consensus

was narrow and bitterly contested, particularly at first, but it created *de facto*
a negotiable centre to political debate. This effective concession of a public
sphere where public policy could be hammered out without recourse to
physical force and (increasingly) without the instinctive equation between
opposition and treason being made, was one of the most lasting restoration
swerves. It relied on recognition of the fact that a stable polity could be
maintained by the opposition of more-or-less permanent interests and that
the public interest was not a simple unity. This was very seldom recognised
in the rhetoric of disputants, but it is recognisable in their actions. We can
see this at an institutional level in the rise of party politics in Parliament,
where the warring interests of Whig and Tory, court and country, were represented and public policy was decided by vote. Parliament represented the
political nation (wealthy, landed, Anglican, conservative) and its concerns,
so parliamentary opinion was substantially self-censoring. The range of
legitimate utterance which could be expressed in this sphere was restricted
to arguments within the consensus about loyalty to the crown and the established order. Explicit Jacobite or pro-Catholic statements were impossible,
and support for Dissenters needed to be extremely qualified; loyalty to the
crown imposed restrictions on the extent of criticism which could be aimed
at the king's or queen's government; the interests of the lower classes were
entirely subordinate to social order and the ruling class. Parliamentary
utterance was governed by a consensual system of decorums, and transgressions such as the occasional (heavily coded) suggestion of Jacobite sympa-
thies, of the kind William Shippen was famous for throughout the early
decades of the eighteenth century, were immediately recognised.

The margins were slightly wider and less distinct in the public sphere
being created in a politically sensitive and manipulative press.[64] Entrance to
Parliament was more socially exclusive than entrance to this sphere, and the
range of legitimate utterance in print was broader. It was, however, only a
difference of degree. Only a restricted range of opinions were legitimate,
and beyond this axis of ideas bounded by Whig and Tory were the various
regions of heterodoxy, of treason, and of illegitimate textuality: in short, of
otherness. These other political and ideological enterprises were not entertained as part of a vague latitudinarian plurality, but rather were viewed
with great consternation by orthodox thinkers within the pale of legitimacy.
The heterodox were by definition affiliated to alternative images of social,
political, and religious order and, hence, were hostile to the present
(re-) established pattern of authority. Their ideas and discourses became
various kinds of ideological anti-matter; destructive of unity and order,

[64] See J. A. Downie, *Robert Harley and the Press: Propaganda and Public Opinion in the Age of Swift and Defoe*
(Cambridge: Cambridge University Press, 1979); and James O. Richards, *Party Propaganda Under
Queen Anne: The General Elections of 1702–1713* (Athens, Ga.: University of Georgia Press, 1972).

repelling and/or polluting legitimate patterns of thought and language. Conceived under labels such as Popery, Dissent, Hobbism, Atheism, Deism, Jacobitism, Nonjuring, and Republicanism, these ideologies inhabited a transgressive and demonised territory, stigmatised by and distinguished from established order and its allegiances.

At the beginning of the period we can see this new sense of transgression being enacted when Puritanism shifts its status to become Dissent. Before 1660, most Puritans had imagined themselves as within the national church, seeking to reform it along godly lines, and to negotiate the terms of its doctrinal, liturgical, and institutional establishment. The Presbyterians, in particular, never sought to become a sect but rather worked for more than a century following the Reformation to establish 'Godly Discipline' (that is to say, a national church like the Scottish Kirk, without bishops and other vestiges of Popery) in the Church of England. Presbyterianism collapsed in the 1660s because it failed to have the restored Church reformed along Presbyterian lines, and it could not accommodate itself to the congregationalist model forced on Dissenters in the Test Acts. Puritans achieved only a bare toleration, defined as dissent from the (re-)established political and religious order. Their allegiances were held to fall outside the restored constitution, and hence they were allowed only restricted freedoms (or liberties) under it. They bore a lasting reproach as the party which had driven on the Rebellion, and their discourses became formally illegitimate. The cultural act of naming was a matter of fundamental importance. In a conflict of dogmas commanding allegiance, dispute was not essentially rational: to succeed in naming an opponent as 'other' was enough. What happened in the period of restoration was a hardening of the divisions between legitimate and illegitimate thought and utterance. The transformation of Puritanism into Dissent illustrates this hardening clearly, but the shape of this transformation was repeated in many other aspects of political and cultural life. A polity conscious of its fragility generates many demons, for any ideological dissonance is perceived as a threat. Furthermore, the consensus was narrowly and polemically defined. Dissent was a threat to it, but so were Popery, Republicanism, and absolutism. Indeed, any germ of disloyalty to the mixed constitution was a danger, an affiliation to a destructive otherness.

The secular archetype of this otherness in the demonology of the day was Thomas Hobbes and his 'atheistical'[65] political theories, most notoriously propounded in *Leviathan* (1651). Though it predated the historical Restoration by several years, Hobbes' treatise responded in its own idiosyn-

[65] 'Atheism' in the seventeenth and eighteenth centuries did not mean anything resembling the systematic rejection of divinity expected of modern atheists. Even quite esoteric doctrinal errors (such as mistaking the exact nature of the Trinity) could earn one the label 'Atheist'. See Redwood, *Reason, Ridicule and Religion*, particularly Ch. 3, 'Atheism as a Political Cause'; and Hunter, *Science and Society*, ch. 7, 'Atheism and Orthodoxy'.

cratic way to the same historical issues and problems of collapse of authority which generated the plethora of restoration enterprises. It was no less than an investigation of the origins and the play of authority and subordination in civil society. He sought to define 'that great LEVIATHAN called a COMMON-WEALTH, or STATE',[66] and to turn to those pure principles which would ensure order and peace in the face of the collapse of civil order during the Civil War. The reception of these ideas was almost universally hostile because, for more orthodox thinkers, they courted the wrong sorts of order and scorned many traditional pieties.[67] Hobbes' attention to scientific, metaphysical purity of thought, and his systematic materialism in searching for causes and effects cast him beyond the pale of legitimate ideology. He did not mystify his analysis by claiming to be searching for a (pseudo-) historical origin of authority and he made it clear that he saw civil order as man-made, not God-given. Consequently, his was considered a feral discourse, an attempt to subvert the constitution; it was heresy in religion/ideology[68] and treachery in politics. To be a Hobbist was to be an enemy both of morality and the state, and so the *Leviathan* resonated through at least the rest of the seventeenth century as the primal site of Modern apostasy. The volatile potential of such subversive allegiances in the intertextual combat of parody will be a constant theme in the analyses which follow, but before we go on it is worth noting that Swift's *A Tale* figures itself as a distraction to save the ship of the Commonwealth from the whale of '*Hobs*'s *Leviathan*, which tosses and plays with all other Schemes of Religion and Government'.[69]

At this point it must be confessed that I have not presented an extensive documentary proof of the hypothesis concerning restoration enterprises and the structure of their ideological conflicts at a cultural historical level. To do so would require at least another book. Rather, I have here mapped out a rhetorical and polemical space the contours of which we need to understand before we can appreciate the peculiarities of Swift's early prose parodies fully. To read the intertextual transformations intelligently, it is necessary to have in mind a sense of the absolute (yet disconcertingly negotiable) distinc-

---

[66] *Leviathan*, C. B. Macpherson, ed., (Penguin: Harmondsworth, 1968), p. 81.

[67] For the contemporary reaction to Hobbes, see John Bowle, *Hobbes and his Critics: A Study in Seventeenth Century Constitutionalism* (London: Frank Cass, 1969; 1st edn, 1951); Samuel I. Mintz, *The Hunting of Leviathan: Seventeenth-Century Reactions to the Materialism and Moral Philosophy of Thomas Hobbes* (Cambridge: Cambridge University Press, 1962); and, for a corrective to the tendency of these two books to exaggerate the universality of the opposition, Quentin Skinner, 'The Context of Hobbes's Theory of Political Obligation', Maurice Cranston and Richard S. Peters, eds., *Hobbes and Rousseau: A Collection of Critical Essays* (New York: Doubleday, 1972), pp. 109–42.

[68] On the proposition that ideology in this period is more closely related to 'Religion' than 'Politicks', see my 'The Reaction to Collins's *A Discourse of Free-Thinking* "Not Politicks"?' *Swift Studies*, 4 (1989), 63–76.

[69] *A Tale*, p. 40.

tion between loyal and subversive affiliations, between legitimacy and illegitimacy of discourse. However, our attention will fall mainly on the margins, for parody occurs in the negotiations and transgressions of the boundaries between legitimacy and other. Let us turn to the way this worked in polemical practice, where texts and discourses were warring in public over the voice and image of authority.

3

Parody and the play of stigma in pamphlet warfare

The Case the Book pointed at, was to speak in the first Person of the Party, and then, thereby, not only to speak their Language, but make them acknowledge it to be theirs, which they did so openly, that confounded all their Attempts to deny it, and to call it a Scandal thrown upon them by another.[1]

Pamphlet warfare and appeal to public opinion became necessary in the new political world of late Stuart England, but they remained radically dubious in the eyes of many, not least because of their origin in the anarchic days of the Civil War. The languages generated in this novel forum sought to define the sort of constitution which was being 'restored', and so rhetorical skirmishes tested the margins of orthodox utterance, with combatants attempting to appropriate authority for their own discourse and to stigmatise as potentially treasonous the language of their opponents. Steven Zwicker has characterised this culture as inhabited by various rhetorics of disguise,[2] and there is much truth in this analysis, for truth, conviction, and motivation were generally covert elements of texts. In this nascent public sphere writers attempted to define and dominate the terms of the developing consensus on what constituted ideological validity. The process was often, almost typically, oppositional, as various ideologues sought to draw out the infidelity implicit in their opponents' principles, to expose the Commonwealthman behind the Whig and the Jacobite behind the Tory. Though the Whigs won in the long run, the contest between the major parties was reasonably even. It was by no means certain that the Tory political and rhetorical programme was doomed to failure. For example, when the Anglican incendiary, Henry Sacheverell, was tried in 1709–10 for provocatively preaching on passive obedience before the Lord Mayor and Aldermen of London on the day of the Whigs' great anniversary, 5 November (the day William landed in England in 1688), Revolution Principles and the High-Church arguments against them were put on trial.[3]

---

[1] Daniel Defoe, *The Present State of the Parties* (London, 1712), p. 24.
[2] *Politics and Language in Dryden's Poetry*, particularly ch. 1.
[3] For a compelling account of the trial, see Geoffrey Holmes, *The Trial of Doctor Sacheverell* (London: Eyre Methuen, 1973).

In law (or at least in the irrefutable logic of Whig majorities in both houses of Parliament bringing the impeachment), the Whig case was so unassailable that Sacheverell's lawyers made shifts only to deny that the sermon's words meant what they palpably said. However, the political repercussions diverged drastically from this, and there was a massive mobilisation of public opinion for Sacheverell, starting principally among the lesser clergy and reaching the pitch of riots and looting of Dissenting meeting-houses in London. The trial in the House of Lords became the single most popular show in the country. And, most importantly, it triggered a Tory renaissance which led to parliamentary victory at the next election, Tory government for the last years of Anne's reign, and a temporary ascendency for Tory political rhetorics. Were it not for the political events and allegiances surrounding the Hanoverian succession (or had Bolingbroke and Atterbury managed to engineer a Jacobite restoration), these might well have remained the accepted terms of the settlement.

The circumstances of publication of Clarendon's *History of the Rebellion* illustrate both the persistence of dispute over the nature of the restored polity and the sort of charge seemingly innocent texts could take on in the environment of the paper wars. The *History* always was a major political statement, of course, expressing conservative horror at the excesses of the Civil War and providing an apologia for Clarendon's career. However, it had a fresh political pertinence for his sons, the second Earl of Clarendon and the Earl of Rochester (to whom the discretion of when to publish had been left), and their High Tory supporters when it was ushered into print in annual instalments between 1702 and 1704. They had held off publication until the reign of William and Mary, with its dubious origin, toleration for Dissenters, and Whig-dominated politics, was over. The new queen, Anne, was English, a Stuart, and a staunch adherent of the Church of England. Though the problem of the Pretender remained to confuse pure pedigrees of loyalty, James himself was dead, and here was an English queen well disposed towards Tory ideals and a proper object for Tory obedience. It looked like the dawn of a new age for legitimist ideology, based on principles of loyalty rather than principles of liberty and limitation of royal prerogatives. The uneasy period following the Revolution Settlement of 1689 looked set to have a Tory rather than a Whig conclusion, and, in this context, Clarendon's *History* became a living political discourse, a central part of a project to redefine the Revolution Settlement in Tory terms. Consequently, Rochester's preface to the first volume was statesmanlike in its charity to opponents but firm in its Tory principles of passive obedience and Stuart loyalism.[4] As the second and third volumes came out in the fol-

---

[4] See Edward Hyde, Earl of Clarendon, *The History of the Rebellion and Civil Wars in England, begun in the Year 1641*, 6 vols, W. Dunn Macray, ed., (Oxford: Clarendon Press, 1888); quote, I, pp. xix–xx.

lowing years, and it became clearer that Anne and her ministers wished to avoid domination by intemperate Tories such as her uncles, Rochester's mood moved from sternly monitory (volume two, 1703) to become 'an unashamed party manifesto'[5] (volume three, 1704). The history of the Civil War period and the seminal Restoration grappling with its implications were not matters of antiquarian interest at the turn of the eighteenth century, but were rather significant sources of rhetoric and symbolism for a new order which only narrowly failed to assert itself. Clarendon's massive exercise in hindsight became part of a later restoration enterprise prosecuted in politics by Rochester and Nottingham (and, subsequently, Harley and Bolingbroke) and in print by propagandists such as Henry Sacheverell,[6] Charles Leslie, Francis Atterbury, and others, aimed at giving England's mixed constitution a Tory rather than a Whig explanation. This is how political dispute operated in the reigns of William and Anne.

Intertextual insults: political debate and the sin of faction

At the end of the previous chapter we posited a polar model for the structure of ideological dispute in the decades following 1660, with an axis of legitimate debate between the positions of Whig and Tory, and a much broader band of heterodox conviction on either side of these limits. The shape of this thinking suggests a narrow consensus concerning the fact of a mixed and restored constitution, surrounded by a less narrow area of intense and acrimonious (but still legitimate) debate over the constitution's nature. For any thinking which cast beyond this pale of legitimate debate, however, there was deep intolerance. Dissent of any kind from this relatively restricted body of ideas and discourses was construed as more than mere difference of opinion – it was treachery (intellectual and practical) against the settled and original constitution of the land. The rationales of loyal opposition and passive dissent were not extensively developed, and those who held the power simply did not trust people who could not share their oaths of loyalty and ideas of legitimacy. The restricted and restrictive terms of the Toleration Act illustrate this distrust far more forcefully than they illustrate any essential growth in the spirit of freedom, and even Locke, in his radically pluralist *Letter Concerning Toleration* (1689) withheld the vote from Catholics. Faction meant division rather than balance – we need to grasp this idea before it can be possible to understand the religious intolerance of the age as anything more

---

[5] Kenyon, *Revolution Principles*, p. 82. My analysis of the publication and political resonance of the *History of the Rebellion* follows Kenyon's closely.

[6] The resurgence of Tory rhetoric at this time (and its peculiarly Anglican emphasis) is most intemperately illustrated by Sacheverell's sermon, published as *The Political Union: A Discourse Shewing the Dependence of Government on Religion in General: And of the English Monarchy on the Church of England in Particular* (Oxford, 1702). Oxford was very much the home of this matrix of ideas.

than mindless bigotry. In a society without centralised administrative and police power, peace was maintained by voluntary self-control and co-operation, particularly from the country's 'natural' governors, the local JPs. The only glue with which to maintain order was the idea of allegiance, and dissent (whether in religion or politics) implied, at best, an impurity in the body politic or, at worst and by logical extension, a determination to destroy the *status quo*. Protestant Dissenters, Catholic recusants, republicans, Jacobites, Nonjurors, and atheists were all lumped together conceptually as fifth columnists, owing allegiance to some alternative polity, some alternative settlement. But their ideas and discourses were more than alternative, they were heretical, which is to say practically and positively dangerous.

Ideological illegitimacy was a threat, and it follows that the languages generated by its various manifestations bore a stigma of treason and sedition. Sacheverell was, after all, prosecuted for seditious language which was held to have undermined the settled constitution, and the Whigs used the political and legal processes to stigmatise his utterances formally. However, the more common (and less extreme) method was to engage in an intertextual process of stigmatisation, of consigning the acts and discourses of the opposition to the margins of illegitimacy and showing how they overtly or covertly transgressed the boundaries of ideological orthodoxy. The way to grasp the direction of this process in the battles of Whig versus Tory is to review what the two great moments of restoration repudiated, for each crisis was held to be not only a great victory for one body of principles, it was also a rejection of the excesses of the other. The Restoration asserted Tory loyalism and repudiated republicanism; the Revolution asserted English liberties and repudiated tyranny. The first term of each of these equations is orthodox and associated with the legitimate body of one of the parties, whereas the second term is unorthodox and associated with the illegitimate extreme of the other party. In practice the extent to which Whiggism could be equated with sectarian Protestant, regicide republicanism, or Toryism with Catholic, Jacobite tyranny, went a long way towards determining the outcome of political disputes and realignments of power.

Sacheverell was convicted of sedition for advocating opinions too close to those which Whigs believed the Revolution had repudiated. On the other side of politics, rumours persisted throughout the period of the existence of a republican 'Calves' Head Club' which was supposed to gather on 30 January every year to celebrate the execution of Charles I. Whether or not such gatherings ever occurred – no positive evidence exists and it seems unlikely that they did – they entered the political demonology of the time as examples of appalling disloyalty, and when Swift was searching in 1712 for a symbolic way of chastising the Duke of Nottingham for joining with the Junto Whigs against Harley's ministry, he hit upon the idea of 'Toland's Invitation to Dismal to Dine with the Calves' Head Club'. Nottingham's conduct, essentially an accommodation in the horse-trading of power politics and shifting alliances, is cast in the poem as terrible apostasy. The age's most notorious deist extremist, John Toland, is depicted as inviting Nottingham (until now the incarnation of Anglican loyalism) to come and celebrate as tyrannicide the event that Nottingham himself had always commemorated as a martyrdom. Again, martyrdom was considered an appropriate (i.e. orthodox) naming of the royal execution, whereas tyrannicide was heretical. Swift's poem achieves its polemical effect by associating the orthodox political figure with the heretical companion and the heretical symbol – Nottingham is damned by association with illegitimate images.

The shape of this strategy is parodic: it refunctions Nottingham's public image by translating it into another field of associations, convicting him of hypocrisy in his 'published' image of himself as a paragon of Tory and Anglican respectability. The real bite lies in the way that a cynical piece of political manœuvring is identified as treason, as a betrayal of the royal authority around which Nottingham claimed to have figured his political career. This is not just a cheap coincidence remarked upon to connect my meditations on restoration ideologies to the literary themes of this study, for there is an important sense in which polemical dispute in this period – Swift's essential discursive environment – operates on parodic lines. Whig writers were forever trying to rewrite the Tory agenda as Jacobite absolutism; Tory writers sought to represent Whigs as sectarian anarchists. On each issue, polemical language sought to constitute the transcendent orthodoxy of the ideology it supported and/or push the principles of its opponents into the illegitimate margin of cultural life. As Paula Backscheider has commented: 'Just as the Whigs hoped to expose the Jacobite face behind the Tory mask, so did Leslie and the Tories hope to reveal a commonwealthman behind the Whig façade.'[7] We will now investigate two such projects of hostile naming, which themselves used sophisticated techniques of literary parody. Defoe's *Shortest Way with the Dissenters* (1702) and Swift's *Abstract* of Collins' *Discourse of Free-Thinking* (1713) were both concerned with matters which the twentieth century might wish to marginalise as narrowly religious, but I hope to demonstrate that their political and ideological resonances apply vividly to larger disputes. Both were relatively small parts of corporate restoration enterprises seeking to name opponents hostilely and to parody them into the illegimate margin of cultural life.

Defoe's *Shortest Way with Dissenters*: encoded triggers to parodic reading

The *Shortest Way* shares the same historical and polemical moment as the first publication of Clarendon's *History of the Rebellion*, only it enters the pub-

---

[7] *Daniel Defoe: His Life* (Baltimore and London: Johns Hopkins University Press, 1989), p. 167.

lic stage from the other side.[8] Written in reaction to the great outpouring of Tory and High-Church rhetoric which greeted the accession of Queen Anne, it is an attempt to stem that flood by deconstructing its terms into absurdity and (more importantly) illegitimacy. It works over more extreme and occasional writers than Clarendon, who were busily seizing the moment in order to assert the Tory image of political, religious, and ideological order, particularly against what they saw as the dangerous inroads of the Dissenters under William III. Writers such as Henry Sacheverell:

> They [i.e. Dissenters] are not therefore to be Look'd upon as a *Religious Sect* whose Design only is a *Particular* way of Worship, but as a *Political Faction* in Our State, as a *Combination Against Our Settlement*, not only Uneasy under Its Laws, and Unwilling to Pay Obedience to 'em, but Affronting Its Authority, Denying Its *Legal* Power, endeavouring to Supplant Its Jurisdiction, and to Wrest the Reins of Dominion out of Our Rulers Hands.
>
> ...
>
> And 'tis as Unaccountable and Amazing a Contradiction to Our Reason, as the Greatest Reproach and Scandal upon Our Church, (however Others may be Seduc'd, or Mis-led) that Any Pretending to that Sacred and Inviolable Character, of being *Her True Sons, Pillars,* and *Defenders,* should Turn Such *Apostates* and *Renegadoes* to Their *Oaths* and *Professions;* such False *Traytors* to Their *Trusts,* and *Offices,* as to *Strike Sail* with a Party, that is such an Open and Avow'd Enemy to Our *Communion;* and Against Whom, every Man, that Wishes Its Welfare, ought to Hang out the *Bloody Flag,* and *Banner* of Defiance.
>
> ...
>
> In short, if Their Number and Quality are so great that the *Government* must *Endure* Them, how Highly does it Concern It to carry a very Watchful Eye, and Strict Guard upon these *Domestick Enemies,* in whom It can never repose the least Confidence, or Dependance, but at Its Injury and Peril! For No *Principles,* but those of the *True Church of England,* can ever make the *English Crown* to Set Easy on the Head of Majesty; and it will be found an Infallible Truth, that Phanaticism is as

---

[8] J. A. Downie, 'Defoe's *Shortest Way with the Dissenters*: Irony, Intention and Reader-Response', *Prose Studies,* 9 (1986), 120–139, would have us further specify the occasion as the debate in Parliament during the winter session of 1702–3 over a bill condemning occasional conformity. Downie suggests that the essay was intended to arouse moderate opinion in favour of the Dissenters so that the bill would not pass through the Lords. It is not necessary for my purposes to be so exact, and Downie's conclusions are not beyond dispute. He is more convinced than I (or many of Defoe's contemporary readers) that pointers to irony appear early and unequivocally in the text so that moderate readers could not have misconstrued it. Ironic potential is everywhere, but I lean towards Paul Alkon's opinion (in 'Defoe's Argument in *The Shortest Way with the Dissenters*', *MP,* 73 (1976), 512–23) that the pamphlet is most remarkable for the way it avoids becoming explicit, recoiling from literal language into disembodied metaphors whenever extreme expressions of genocide are called for. The other problem with Downie's proposed occasion is that it would make the *Shortest Way* Defoe's only published defence of occasional conformity, a practice against which he wrote many pamphlets. The single passage from *The Consolidator* which Downie (p. 127) offers as Defoe's explanation for his momentary change of heart expresses only a general abhorrence of the extreme High Churchmen, and it seems wiser to see the pamphlet as opposed to a general mood rather than to a specific legislative goal.

utterly Irreconcilable and Inconsistent, as *Popery* itself, with Our Establish'd Constitution and Monarchy.[9]

The phrase 'the *Bloody Flag*, and *Banner* of Defiance' became a notorious commonplace of Anglican excess, but Sacheverell's bombastic ragings offer more than mere rhetorical excess to the *Shortest Way*'s pre-textuality. The first passage illustrates the way Tory thinkers equated sectarianism in religion with sectarianism (or 'faction') in politics, as they could not conceive of civil obedience which was not based on comprehensive assent. The paranoid assumption is that a sect cannot rest until it has overcome the majority, that its members can owe no true obedience to the settled constitution in politics and religion and must be forever 'Uneasy' and plotting, in '*Combination Against Our Settlement*'. Defoe makes much of this sort of conspiracy theory, but it is important to realise that the feeling that Dissenters (especially Quakers) could not be trusted or held to oaths was widespread, and only Sacheverell's *expression* of the idea was extreme. Similarly, though the language be incontinent, the call to the Church of England's '*True Sons, Pillars*, and *Defenders*' to come to the aid of their holy institution against such '*Apostates*', '*Renegadoes*', and 'False *Traytors*' as would undermine it, really defines the purpose of the 'Church' party, for its members seriously felt that their church was in danger.

However, it is the third passage which most clearly suggests Defoe's strategy. It states the central High-Church conviction that 'No *Principles*, but those of the *True Church of England*, can ever make the *English Crown* to Set Easy on the Head of Majesty.' The political imagery of this idea resonates in two important ways. It reminds us of the primal act of national sin when the Dissenters led the nation in removing the crown from Charles I's head and his head from his shoulders.[10] A more subtle resonance comes from the word '*Principles*', for it enshrines a rebuke for the Whig explanation of recent history, and its insistence on the efficacy of 'Revolution Principles' in bringing the constitution to 'Settlement' in 1689. The only true principles which support the crown, Sacheverell asserts, are Anglican principles of obedience; 'Revolution Principles' of liberty are, it is hinted, false and dangerous. But it is the wistful tone of this passage's rejection of a 'Final Solution' for Dissenters which is closest to Defoe's pamphlet. The rejection comes across as an unwilling recognition of political expediency, rather than as an acceptance of humanitarian principle. Moreover, it is expressed in the conditional mood – 'if Their Number and Quality are so great that the *Government* must *Endure* Them' – and is used as the pretext for mounting a strict guard over and persecution of these cuckoos in the nest of the body politic. This is no

---

[9] *The Political Union* (1702), pp. 55–56, 59, 60–61.

[10] Such thinkers made no distinction to match the modern historian's differentiation between Puritans (pre-1660) and Dissenters (post-1660). Fanatic sectarians were all one to them.

very long step at all from Defoe's parodic proposal of eradication, and it is tempting to see a direct link between the two texts. As Defoe himself later admitted, such a link exists:

Some People have blam'd the Author of the aforesaid Pamphlet, called *The Shortest Way*, &c. for that he did not quote either in the Margin, or otherwise the Sermon of *Sacheverell*, aforesaid, or such other Authors from whom his Notions were drawn, which would have justified him in what he had suggested; but these Men do not see the Design of the Book at all, or the Effect it had, at the same Time, taken off the Edge of the Book, and that which now cuts the Throat of the whole Party, would not have then given the least Wound. The Case the Book pointed at, was to speak in the first Person of the Party, and then, thereby, not only to speak their Language, but make them acknowledge it to be theirs, which they did so openly, that confounded all their Attempts to deny it, and to call it a Scandal thrown upon them by another.[11]

This expression of intent, though clarified by a decade of hindsight, rings true. The pamphlet's aim went beyond individual targets such as Sacheverell to expose the absurdity and viciousness of the High Churchmen by speaking 'in the first Person of the Party', to imitate their tyrannous and illegitimate language and 'make them acknowledge it to be theirs'. This is at once a process of parody and a process of political stigmatisation; it calls up a body of discourse and seeks dialogically to define it as other. Let us see how it works.

Consider this lengthy passage from the *Shortest Way*, and its triggers to critical (that is, stigmatising) parodic reading:

Now let us examine the Reasons they pretend to give why we shou'd be favourable to them, why we should continue and tollerate them among us.

First. THEY are very Numerous, they say, they are a great Part of the Nation, and we cannot suppress them.

To this may be answer'd, 1. THEY are not so Numerous as the Protestants in *France*, and yet the *French* King effectually clear'd the Nation of them at once, and we don't find he misses them at home.

---

[11] *The Present State of the Parties*, p. 24. In *A Brief Explanation of a Late Pamphlet, entituled, 'The Shortest Way with the Dissenters'* (London, 1702–3), Defoe enumerates his sources as 'The Sermon preach'd at *Oxford*, the *New Association*, the *Poetical Observator*, with numberless others' (p. 2). The sermon was Sacheverell's, the *New Association* was a pamphlet written by Charles Leslie, and the *Poetical Observator* was an ephemeral newspaper which we can assume was virulently Tory in tenor, though it has left almost no trace. Miriam Leranbaum, '"An Irony Not Unusual": Defoe's *Shortest Way with the Dissenters*', *HLQ*, 37 (1973–74), 230, suggests that, to her knowledge, only one copy of one issue exists. I have not been able to track down even this. Backscheider, *Daniel Defoe*, pp. 95–96, argues persuasively that the particular model for the *Shortest Way* was an anonymous text entitled *The Establishment of the Church, The Preservation of the State: Shewing the Reasonableness of a Bill against Occasional Conformity* (London, 1702). Though the connections are reasonably extensive, however, it does not follow that this (quite obscure) pamphlet should be the only or even the primary target of Defoe's parody. It is in the nature of parodic textuality that more than one particular pre-textual target may be hit if more than one pre-text can be recognised in its negative (parodic) exemplar. In this instance, it seems possible that Defoe modelled his text on *The Establishment*, but it is clear (as his comment above suggests) that the irony was intended to expose a body of pre-textuality of which Sacheverell's text was a notorious member.

But I am not of the Opinion they are so Numerous as is pretended; their Party is more Numerous than their Persons, and those mistaken People of the Church, who are misled and deluded by their wheedling Artifices, to join with them, make their Party the greater: but those will open their Eyes, when the Government shall set heartily about the work, and come off from them, as some Animals, which they say, always desert a House when 'tis likely to fall.

2dly. The more Numerous, the more Dangerous, and therefore the more need to suppress them; and God has suffer'd us to bear them as Goads in our sides, for not utterly extinguishing them long ago.

3dly. If we are to allow them, only because we cannot suppress them, then it ought to be tryed whether we can or no; and I am of Opinion 'tis easy to be done, and cou'd prescribe Ways and Means, if it were proper, but I doubt not but the Government will find effectual methods for the rooting the Contagion from the Face of this Land.

ANOTHER Argument they use, which is this, That 'tis a time of War, and we have need to unite against the common Enemy.

We answer, this common Enemy had been no Enemy, if they had not made him so; he was quiet, in peace, and no way disturb'd, or encroach'd upon us, and we know no reason we had to quarrell with them.

But further, We make no question but we are able to deal with this common Enemy, without their help; but why must we unite with them because of the Enemy, will they go over to the Enemy, if we do not prevent it by a union with them – We are very well contented they shou'd; and make no question, we shall be ready to deal with them and the common Enemy too, and better without them than with them.

Besides, if we have a common Enemy, there is the more need to be secure against our private Enemies; if there is one common Enemy, we have less need to have an Enemy in our Bowels.

'Twas a great Argument some People used against suppressing the Old-Money, that 'twas a time of War, and was too great a Risque for the Nation to run, if we shou'd not master it, we shou'd be undone; and yet the Sequel prov'd the Hazard was not so great, but it might be master'd; and the Success was answerable. The suppressing the Dissenters is not a harder Work, nor a Work of less necessity to the Publick; we can never enjoy a settled uninterrupted Union and Tranquility in this Nation, till the Spirit of Whiggism, Faction, and Schism is melted down like the Old-Money.

...

We are not to be frightned with it; this Age is wiser than that, by all our own Experience, *and theirs too*; King *Charles* the First, had early supprest this Party, if he had took more deliberate Measures. In short, 'tis not worth arguing, to talk of their Arms, their *Monmouths*, and *Shaftesburys*, and *Argiles* are gone, their *Dutch-Sanctuary* is at an end, Heaven has made way for their Destruction, and if we do not close with the Divine occasion, we are to blame our selves, and may [hereafter] remember that we had once an opportunity to serve the Church of *England*, by extirpating her implacable Enemies, and having let slip the Minute that Heaven presented, may experimentally Complain, *Post est Occasio Calvo.*[12]

[12] *The Shortest Way with the Dissenters and Other Pamphlets* (Oxford: Basil Blackwell, 1927), pp. 121–24.

Where does this transgress the boundary of legitimacy and wander into the region of cultural, political, ideological, or logical heresy? Or, to put it another way, at what point(s) can we see this violate the decorum of imitation and become parody? To see this clearly, we must pretend that we are readers contemporary to the text's initial production (to keep our modern preoccupations out of the discovery of hints) and that we do not know that Defoe is its author. Anonymity is deeply inscribed both in Swiftian parody and the entire culture of late Stuart polemical pamphleteering; it is crucial to Defoe's effect here. Many of the pamphlet's original readers failed to discover cues to parodic reading before they discovered the author's identity,[13] and we need to pretend innocence before we can decide whether the process of parodic stigmatisation is unequivocal, independent of knowledge of the author's intention.

The clearest piece of 'objective' discursive illegitimacy is the attitude towards France. It is simply unimaginable in post-1689 Protestant England that an orthodox political writer might so openly approve of Louis XIV's religious policies: 'the *French* King effectually clear'd the Nation of them [the French Protestants] at once, and we don't find he misses them at home'. This is the point at which we can most clearly see Defoe pushing his Tory persona over the line from orthodox Tory allegiances into Jacobitism. The tyranny of the revocation of the Edict of Nantes (1685) was already a Whig cliché, that Tories dared not question, and the flood of Huguenot refugees in the years since the revocation was a constant reminder of the human effects of the religious principle. By using this example of absolutist Popish tyranny as evidence for his proposal, the narrator marks himself as at best a blinkered divine right of kings theorist ('Louis is king and can therefore do as he pleases, and note how effectually he has managed to work his will'), or at worst a Jacobite (Louis was James II's great protector and so to be praised in all things) and a Papist (how, after all, could anyone approve of such treatment of fellow Protestants?). There is an unbecoming and (in historical context) misguided brutality about the sentiments that was and is likely to shock readers out of sympathy with the narrator and awaken critical faculties.

The francophilia reappears when we are asked to believe that the common enemy, with whom England had been at war for more than a decade over (among other things) the future of Protestantism in Europe, is a lover of peace stirred to rage by England's irresponsible aggression. We are assured that it is only our Dissenters that have made him an enemy: 'this common Enemy had been no Enemy, if they had not made him so'. Furthermore, we are asked to believe that before English intervention, Louis 'was quiet, in peace, and no way disturb'd, or encroach'd upon us'. This

---

[13] See L. S. Horsley, 'Contemporary Reactions to Defoe's *Shortest Way with the Dissenters*', *SEL*, 16 (1976), 407–20.

bizarre reading of seventeenth-century history has one tenuous claim to validity in that France had not actually declared war on England, but she had gone to war with England's allies regularly and harboured a pretender to the English throne, giving him sporadic material support for his invasion plans. To offer this scenario to us as peaceful coexistence seems to go beyond the bounds of stupidity, and begins to look either like an attempt to deceive the audience or an invitation to parodic reading. We can maintain an image of a Tory squire or parson unironically expressing his sincere opinions only by redefining him as a Jacobite. Furthermore, if we insist on this the text becomes self-parodying, first because of the clumsy veiling of treasonous intent, and second because support for France and the Pretender was inadmissable within the terms of public discourse. To voice such opinions, even subtly and/or seductively coded, was a radical lapse of decorum. It introduced a deconstructive agent into the text whose final term was inevitably treason.

A further trigger in the passage comes in the paragraph commencing "Twas a great Argument some People used against suppressing the Old-Money...'. Here the reflective reader might well pause to wonder at the propriety of equating people with coins. In one way, the argument that difficult things may yet be achieved in difficult times is analogically triumphant; in another, it is inhuman. It may well be true that 'The suppressing the Dissenters is not a harder Work, nor a Work of less necessity to the Publick', but there is a moral difference between killing people and reworking metal. Our moral sensibilities are offended by the casual brutality of the equation, and we are likely to be disturbed by the final metaphor which gleefully informs us that 'we can never enjoy a settled uninterrupted Union and Tranquility in this Nation, till the Spirit of Whiggism, Faction, and Schism is melted down like the Old-Money'. Moreover, the nearest thing to melting coin, when applied to humans, is burning them – conduct Protestants of the age of the Counter-Reformation would be very unwilling to approve of. Thus critical attention to the metaphor transforms what is ostensibly a benign prophylactic measure into a disturbingly literal image of cruelty and agony; we recoil from the narrator and are apt to suspect that the text itself authorises our revulsion.

It is a matter of historical record that casual and committed readers managed to pass over such hints and continued to read the text approvingly or disapprovingly as a simple and positive enunciation of religio-political opinions.[14] However, once a trigger has been identified, the perception of parody proceeds to ramify almost uncontrollably. A reader whose suspicions have been alerted by the moral and political blemishes is likely to see a textual trigger in the excessive rhetoric of 'effectual Methods for the *rooting the*

[14] See particularly ibid.

Contagion from the Face of this Land.[15] She or he is also likely to become disenchanted with the (self-serving) providential rhetoric about God having made 'an opportunity to serve the Church of England, by extirpating her implacable Enemies', and is liable to discover further intellectual triggers – points at which the narrator loses touch with 'logic'. At an empirical level, such lapses could be merely signs of ineptitude, but they can also play a part in an accumulating awareness of parody. A clear example of this in the passage under discussion comes when the narrator twists away from describing the peacefulness of Louis XIV's intentions to tell us that 'we' can deal with the common enemy on our own, then questions whether the Dissenters mean to go over to the enemy if we do not unify with them, and concludes triumphantly that we can quite happily defeat them and the common enemy as well, if needs be. The way this tumbles out and the odd juxtapositions it makes with the adjacent arguments suggest that logic has become handmaiden to opinion and that the narrator has lost control of his rhetoric. This makes us willing to imagine that the essay's apparent author does not comprehend the authoritative meaning of his text, and that he is running counter to the tenets of authority and legitimacy, into moral, ideological, and intellectual treason. The parody is practical in nature, imitating and interrogating (which is to say, deconstructing) a body of discourse to which the actual author is opposed, and laying upon it the stigma of illegitimacy.

When the enterprise backfired, at least at a personal level, and Defoe was prosecuted, it was in exactly such terms of ideological legitimacy that he sought to justify himself:

The Author professes he thought, when he wrote the Book, he shou'd never need to come to an Explication, and wonders to find there should be any reason for it.

If any man take the pains seriously to reflect upon the Contents, the Nature of the Thing and the Manner of the Stile, it seems Impossible to imagine it should pass for any thing but an Irony.

That it is free from any Seditious design, either of stirring up the Dissenters to any evil practice by way of prevention; much less of animating others to their destruction, will be plain, I think, to any man that understands the present Constitution of *England*, and the nature of our Government.[16]

'[F]ree from any Seditious design', its innocence plain 'to any man that understands the present Constitution of *England*, and the nature of our Government', Defoe's 'irony' is defended from the vices it has tried to fix on others. The dangerous doubleness of parody is demonstrated in the way the stigma has come to rest on the mirror rather than on the discourses it parodically reflects, but the aim of the project is clear. 'By an *Irony not Unusual*',[17]

---

[15] My emphasis.

[16] *A Brief Explanation*, p. 1.

[17] Ibid., p. 2.

Defoe was trying to place his political and religious opponents outside 'the present Constitution of *England*', to prohibit their language and ideology by identifying them as the verbal and intellectual forms of sedition. The '*Irony not unusual*' expresses the shape of much interplay between restoration enterprises, because the distinctions and deconstructions of irony were fraught with political meaning. Let us turn now to one of Swift's simpler efforts in the genre.

Swift and Collins: the play of parodic stigma

As I have demonstrated elsewhere,[18] critics have been too willing to take Swift at his word in the *Journal to Stella* when he describes the pamphlet, soon to be published as *Mr. C----ns's Discourse of Free-Thinking, Put into plain English, by way of Abstract, for the Use of the Poor*, as 'a little Whim wch just came into my Head' and 'a little Pamphlet I have written; but not Politicks'.[19] Only by the narrowest definition of the word 'Politicks' can Swift's pamphlet and the controversy it enters be excluded from the political sphere, for both are deeply embroiled in discriminations of ideological legitimacy. It is a relatively simple parody by Swift's standards, because its argument remains pretty clear. Its ironies do not remain completely stable, but in its context it retains an essentially suasive function that makes a useful counter-point to the more anarchic implications of the *Argument against Abolishing Christianity* and *A Tale*. 1712–13 was a bad time for the Whigs; they were very much in retreat before the rampant Tories, led by Harley and Bolingbroke in politics and by Swift in print. A JP and provincial magnate of moderate importance, Collins was identified with the Whigs politically, and his ideas had their natural home on the radical fringe of Whiggish libertarian thinking.[20] The particular problem posed by his *Discourse* was the licence it took with notions of liberty and freedom. These were the fundamental principles of the Whig-defined Revolution Settlement, yet here they were being made to support heterodox religion and uncontrolled intellectual speculation. That a real risk of having these central principles stigmatised existed can be inferred from careful attention to the shape and nature of the orthodox Whiggish response, which sought assiduously to distinguish between legitimate and illegitimate notions of liberty.[21] However, my primary interest here is to investigate the way that Swift sought to enact this

---

[18] 'The Reaction to Collins'. This section reproduces much of the article's material, though with different emphases and to different ends.

[19] 16 and 21 January 1712–13; *Journal to Stella*, II, pp. 603, 605.

[20] On Collins' life, works, and connections with more influential liberal thinkers such as Locke and Shaftesbury, see James O'Higgins, S. J., *Anthony Collins: The Man and his Works* (The Hague: Martinus Nijhoff, 1970).

[21] This is a rough summary of the argument of my article; refer to it for the detail which supports these interpretations.

stigmatisation parodically, to rework Whiggism as speculative atheism in politics and ideology as well as in religion.

The slide from innocence to anxiety is crucial in the process of suasive parody. Once the propriety of the model text (or discourse) has been breached, it is important for the readers to see the unravelling of its plausibility and to recognise for themselves the dangerous ramifications it attempts to decentre or obscure. A discourse is pushed into the margin of illegitimacy, and the readers are taught to condemn it. A problem often arises in that once the innocence of simple reading is lost it is very difficult (and often rather arbitrary) to stop the deconstructive process and the slippage into the receding possibilities of anarchic parody is always available.[22] However, reading parody in the suasive mode – figured as a process of revision and reassessment – is a real possibility. It begins in the editorial passages, which frame the summary of Collins' text and place readers who are alert to polemical resonance firmly into a context of ideological judgement. Swift's title page offers a compact and pungent suggestion that the enterprise is dubious, marginal, and subversive, if only we have eyes to see and ears to hear. The expression of purpose, 'Put into plain *English*, by way of Abstract, for the Use of the Poor', works in several ways. First there is the simple meaning, innocent of parody, which offers the pamphlet as a dissemination of valuable information to a public ill-equipped to appreciate the original in all its complexity and subtlety of thought. Given the notoriety of Collins' *Discourse*, however, it is unlikely that anyone ever read only this sense of the words. They ask to be interpreted ironically, and a contemporary reader would probably have started with the phrase 'For the Use of the Poor'. In an age deeply anxious about popular uprisings and nervously aware of the religiously inspired chaos of the Civil War period, even the most conservative attempt to influence the opinions of the poor was extremely suspect. To appeal to them for any purpose other than the pious improvement of their morality was to invite anarchy and subversion of the settled order, to risk a return to the chaos of the Interregnum and the destructive rule of the mob.

When we have been alerted to the suspicious resonances of attention to the poor, so plain a phrase as 'Put into plain *English*' begins to generate malign possibilities. The pre-parodic meaning figures the enterprise as a faithful and valuable translation of complex ideas into readily understandable terms, but this meaning does not remain stable for long. By becoming

---

[22] For a fuller negotiation of the very provisional distinction between suasive and anarchic parody, see the discussion of the *Argument against Abolishing Christianity*, in ch. 4. For essays that deal with these issues in the context of the *Abstract*, see Clive T. Probyn, '"Haranguing upon Texts": Swift and the Idea of the Book', *Proceedings of the First Münster Symposium on Jonathan Swift*, Hermann J. Real and Heinz J. Vienken, eds. (Munich: Wilhelm Fink Verlag, 1985), pp. 187–97; and Judith C. Mueller, 'The Ethics of Reading in Swift's *Abstract* on Freethinking', *SEL*, 31 (1991), 483–96.

the vehicle for disseminating ideological heresy among the mob, 'plain
English' loses its habitual sturdy connotations. Moreover, the idea that its
polite guise of intellectuality is being removed and its truly subversive implications are being exposed in 'plain *English*' makes a sharp comment on
Collins' *Discourse*. The subversiveness which Collins attempts to disguise with
the sophistications of scholarship is seen in all its deformity in a simpler,
purer discourse. Consequently, the text parodied and its notional process of
popularisation are stigmatised, while the wisdom of 'plain *English*' is
reasserted.

We turn the page to find the objects of stigma being given current political names, to see the great Whig restoration enterprise being implicated in
Collins' private heresies. The introduction begins:

> Our Party having failed, by all their Political Arguments, to re-establish their Power;
> the wise Leaders have determined, that the last and principal Remedy should be
> made use of, for opening the Eyes of this blinded Nation; and that a short, but per-
> fect, System of their *Divinity*, should be publish'd, to which we are all of us ready to
> subscribe, and which we lay down as a Model, bearing a close analogy to our
> Schemes in Religion.[23]

The Whigs are named and implicated in the first words as 'Our Party' – in
1713 there was no ambiguity or evasiveness in saying the party out of
power, for it was merely a circumlocution designating the Whigs. They are
presented as an organised faction acting under the direction of their 'wise
Leaders', who have determined, 'for opening the Eyes of this blinded
Nation', to publish (and presumably work to establish) their 'System of their
Divinity'. The intimate relationship between religion and public ideology is
seldom made more obvious in the period, even by Sacheverell and Leslie,
for the text says that if the right religion can be established political power
will follow. As parodic readers, we are, of course, expected to notice this
blithe determination to change the ancient constitution. And if we miss this
nuance in the first sentence, the point is hammered home in the next lines:

> Crafty designing Men, that they might keep the World in Awe, have, in their several
> Forms of Government, placed a *Supream Power* on *Earth*, to keep human Kind in fear
> of being *Hanged*; and a *Supream Power* in *Heaven*, for fear of being *Damned*. In order to
> cure Mens Apprehensions of the former, several of our learned Members have writ
> many profound Treatises in *Anarchy*; but a brief compleat Body of *Atheology* seemed
> to be wanting, till this irrefragable Discourse appeared.[24]

The nexus between religion and social order could hardly be more starkly
exposed, and our conservative instincts are supposed to recoil at the terrible
prospect of a new ideological axis balanced on one side by anarchy and on

[23] *PW*, IV, p. 27.
[24] Ibid., p. 27.

the other by atheology. The morphological parallelism is particularly effective, though it strikes something different from the triumphant chord desired
by the apparent author. The great public anxieties of the restoration era,
anarchy and atheism, are here linked under the banner of Whiggery. The
declension of ideas suggested is something like 'Liberty, Apostasy, and No
Peace without Spain', and to insist further on the practical implications of
errant (and innovating) ideology, the last paragraph of the preface commences: 'For I am sensible that nothing would more contribute to the *contin-
uance of the War*, and the Restoration of the late Ministry, than to have the
Doctrines delivered in this Treatise well infused into the People.'[25] The
volatile play of stigma pushes the Whigs into the margin of illegitimacy,
depicting them as trying to subvert the ancient constitution in favour of
anarchy and atheism. The identification may not be wholly successful, but it
leaves a stain which the body of the *Abstract* seeks to darken. Parody is here,
as it was for Defoe, a weapon in ideological conflict, as it attempts to show
orthodox Whigs – their ideas, political programmes, and their discourses –
keeping company with heterodox subversives.

The text of the *Abstract* contains some unmistakable political pointers,
ranging from the blunt to the subtle. At one extreme, there is the raw anti-
clericalism and blatant political expediency in this suggestion of an
exchange of priests between England and Siam:

> I heartily wish a Detachment of such Divines as Dr. *Atterbury*, Dr. *Smalridge*, Dr.
> *Swift*, Dr. *Sacheverell*, and some others, were sent every Year to the furthest part of
> the Heathen World, and that we had a Cargo of their Priests in return, who would
> spread *Free-thinking* among us; then the War would go on, the late Ministry be
> restored, and Faction cease, which our Priests enflame among us by haranguing
> upon Texts, and falsly call preaching the Gospel.[26]

This nominates the best known and most political of the High Churchmen
for exile, criticises them for their misleading preaching, and suggests that
Whig political goals would be immediately achieved if these Tory voices
were silenced. This may seem like a clumsy interpolation of politics into religion, but Swift is only being (nearly) faithful to his model. The passage to
which this corresponds in the *Discourse* commences with a heavily ironic suggestion that, as missionaries rely on the freethinking of heathens, so English
christians should be willing to return the favour by thinking freely about the
opinions of heathen clergy. This leads to the suggestion that the Tory
divines should be sent to encourage the heathens to think freely and thus to
convert to Christianity on its rational merits:

[25] Ibid., p. 28.
[26] Ibid., p. 31.

And Oh! that the proper Persons were but employ'd for the Execution of so glorious
a Work! That such zealous Divines as our S-----ls, our At-----ys, our Sm----ges, our
St--bs's, our Higgins's, our M---rns, and our Sw-fts, were drawn out annually, as our
military Missionarys are, to be sent to foreign Parts to *propagate the Gospel* (a Service in
which such conscientious Men must rejoice, since preaching the Gospel to infidel
Nations is no doubt contain'd in *Christ's Commission,* whatever *haranguing upon a Text*
among Christians, by some call'd *preaching the Gospel,* may be) we might then hope to
see blessed Days, the *Doctrine* and *Discipline of the Church of England* triumph throughout the World, and Faction cease at home; as by the means of the others of our
Arms triumph abroad, and we securely take our rest at night, and travel by day
unmolested.[27]

So, all of Swift's material comes from his model, and is close to being a
faithful summary, except that it is more blunt and it deliberately miscon-
strues the shape of Collins' snide irony to expose (make plain) his real political desires. It is parodic distortion rather than a clumsy attempt to widen
the scope of the ridicule.

After all, it is the threads of discursive affiliations that parody works
among. So interpretation is very much a function of the reader's stance:
once we have been placed to read the parody broadly, as the title page and
preface insist we should, the general application of parodic detail need not
be continually insisted on. Indeed, Swift ties his text so very closely to
Collins' that to make too many extraneous political connections would
breach the *Abstract's* internal logic. Furthermore, it would be unnecessary.
Once we have been alerted to the nature of the guilty parties, the deconstruction of Collins' obviously heterodox text can proceed with the affiliations in the readers' minds. We have been taught to recognise a fabric of
associations that share a common thread of error and, while we may only
be inspecting a small part of the fabric in detail, we are positioned to know
that the whole piece is fatally flawed.

Swift treats Collins roughly, reducing the text to absurdity and interpolating the occasional barb, in a virtuoso deconstruction of the *Discourse's*
integrity. His first paragraph collapses thirteen pages of Collins' careful reasoning into a paragraph of self-exposing cant:

I send you this Apology for *Free Thinking,* without the least hopes of doing good, but
purely to comply with your Request; for those Truths which no Body can deny, will
do no good to those who deny them.[28]

This sounds trite and self-satisfied, but the beauty of the ploy is that this is
copied directly from two passages of the model text's introduction, and
unhappily mixed. First, the empty commonplace of epistolary convention is

---

[27] Anthony Collins, *A Discourse of Free-Thinking, Occasion'd by the Rise and Growth of a Sect call'd Free-
Thinkers* (London, 1713), p. 43.
[28] *PW,* IV, p. 29.

echoed; Collins wrote 'It is therefore without the least hopes of doing any good, but purely to comply with your Request, that I send you this *Apology for Free-Thinking*',[29] which sounds artificial enough among men of letters but becomes positively inane when placed in an explicitly popular treatise. Then the parodist moves from Collins' exact words to paraphrase his mildly pompous opening sentence, 'Apologies for *self-evident Truths* can never have any effect on those who have so little Sense as to deny *them*',[30] into something only slightly different but significantly sillier, 'for those Truths which no Body can deny, will do no good to those who deny them'. This illustrates with economy and clarity Swift's main strategy, to condemn Collins so far as possible in his own words.

The paragraph continues:

The Clergy, who are so impudent to teach the People the Doctrines of Faith, are all either cunning Knaves or mad Fools; for none but artificial designing Men, and crackt-brained Enthusiasts, presume to be Guides to others in matters of Speculation, which all the Doctrines of Christianity are; and whoever has a mind to learn the Christian Religion, naturally chuses such Knaves and Fools to teach them.[31]

This does more than merely deconstruct the text towards absurdity; it also glosses its terms into more orthodox (and accusing) language, and makes Collins' coy suggestions of infidelity very plain indeed. The first part of this sentence is based on ideas in the *Discourse* (though the words are changed significantly), while later parts repeat the model almost exactly:

But Men who deny what is self-evident, are not only destitute of the *Principles of Knowledge*, but must in virtue of such their Denial have *Principles* inconsistent with the *Principles of Knowledge*, and consistent with the *greatest Absurditys*. And under that dis-temper'd State of Mind, it remains only for them to take up with some disorder'd Fancys of their own; or, which is much more common, with the Dictates of artificial designing Men or Crack-brain'd Enthusiasts: for as none else presume to be *Guides* to others in Matters of *Speculation*, so none who think they ought to be *guided* in those Matters make choice of any but such for their *Guides*.[32]

The *Abstract* draws out Collins' latent anti-clericalism and infidelity by nam-ing the 'Men who deny what is self-evident' as 'The Clergy' and 'the *greatest Absurditys*' (which are 'inconsistent with the *Principles of Knowledge*') as 'the Doctrines of Faith'; to 'Matters of *Speculation*' it appends 'which all the Doctrines of Christianity are'; it keeps whole Collins' most canting and excessive phrases, 'artificial designing Men, and crackt-brained Enthusiasts', drawing further attention to their unbalanced (or incontinent) diction; it sup-

---

[29] Collins, *Discourse*, p. 4.
[30] Ibid., p. 3.
[31] *PW*, IV, p. 29.
[32] Collins, *Discourse*, pp. 3–4.

presses the quiet admission that individuals can have 'disorder'd Fancys of their own'; and it identifies priests as misguiding 'Knaves and Fools' vigorously where Collins only insinuates his hostility. This makes plain the implications hidden in Collins' more neutral terms, and provides us with language that triggers another set of allegiances. These allegiances are towards a common faith, obedience, intellectual and moral order – the central precepts of Tory loyalism – and they keep recurring in the *Abstract* writer's mistranslation of his model. This presence of a positive understanding, pointed to through the errors of the model, is the clearest sign of suasive parody, of parody which seeks to punish and enlighten. It is, as we shall see in discussing more complex parodies (notably *A Tale*), a rather arbitrary requirement which stems the deconstructive flow of signification artificially, but it is an important strategy of polemical combat, often used in the period.

At this point, Swift leaves out five pages of carefully argued definition and defence of freethinking, leaving us with only the bald and distorted assertions of a few lines. This hiatus leaves a substantial hole in Collins' reasoning, and to bring the point home, the précis leaps straight to the sorest point, Collins' desire to think freely about (or, as we might say, deconstruct) the Bible and its authoritative interpretations:

Now the *Bible*, which contains the Precepts of the Priests Religion, is the most difficult Book in the World to be understood; It requires a thorow Knowledge in Natural, Civil, Ecclesiastical History, Law, Husbandry, Sailing Physick, Pharmacy, Mathematicks, Metaphysicks, Ethicks, and every thing else that can be named: And every Body who believes it, ought to understand it, and must do so by force of his own *Free Thinking*, without any Guide or Instructor.[33]

This corresponds to more than two pages in the *Discourse*,[34] and strips bare both the absurdity and dangerousness of Collins' position from a Tory point of view. Clive Probyn has discussed the anxiety of textual and conceptual uncertainty concerning western culture's centrally authoritative text which runs under this passage,[35] but it is the more thinly disguised and broadly political implications that concern us here. This declaration of independence from priestly oversight is made to sound hollow, foolish, and self-serving. It is reduced to the absurd paradox that *because* the Bible is such a complex and important book, we should approach it ignorantly and without guidance. This is not exactly what Collins wrote, but parody can make it look as if he did.

One could continue to compare Swift's parodic deconstruction with Collins' text almost interminably, but that would be to little purpose. The

---

[33] *PW*, IV, p. 29.
[34] Collins, *Discourse*, p. 10–12. It is worth noting that, despite this compression nearly half of the sentence uses Collins' exact words and a significant part of the rest is accurate paraphrase.
[35] "'Haranguing upon Texts'".

methods become repetitive, and the opening paragraph is such a triumph of malicious concentration that the rest of the pamphlet is almost a let-down. The important thing to recognise is the significantly different perspective on Collins' text and the issues it raised displayed by Swift when compared to other of Collins' answerers whose churchmanship was of a Whiggish hue.[36] While Swift gleefully stuffed Collins' words back down his throat and sought to implicate his political opponents in the ideological heresy, Whiggish writers were obliged to defend several of their most sacred principles from Collins' misapplications of them. They had to disassociate their views and the shape of their thinking from the heterodox extensions of similar notions in the *Discourse*. Swift depicted Collins' whole enterprise as illegitimate – in Error – even managing to entangle it in the works of the Devil. Consider the suspiciously illogical cant of:

If you are apt to be afraid of the Devil, *think freely* of him, and you destroy him and his Kingdom. *Free-thinking* has done him more Mischief than all the Clergy in the World ever could do; they *believe in the Devil*, they have an *Interest* in him, and therefore are the great Supports of his Kingdom. The Devil was in the *States General* before they began to be *Free-thinkers*. For *England* and *Holland* were formerly the *Christian* Territories of the Devil; I told you how he left *Holland*; and *Free-thinking* and the *Revolution* banish'd him from *England*; I defy all the Clergy to shew me when they ever had such success against him. My Meaning is, that to think freely of the Devil, is to think there is no Devil at all; and he that thinks so, the Devil's in him if he be afraid of the Devil.[37]

Swift has hit upon one of the *Discourse*'s most obvious weaknesses here, for it is not at all clear whether Collins (pp. 27–32) disbelieved in the works of the devil (as a progressive freethinker of the period would have had the intellectual resources to do) or whether he actually and superstitiously considered freethinking a useful talisman against the devil, more efficacious than a crucifix. However, the interesting thing is the way the parody manages to suggest the possibility of a diabolist plot in which the author and other freethinkers are involved, either as fools or knaves.

Whiggish divines, on the other hand, had to erect a more subtle barrier between themselves and Collins so that they could distinguish between their laudable ideals of liberty and his flawed practice. For them, Collins is not so much in Error as guilty of errors of detail and interpretation. A lapidary illustration of this point can be seen in the contrary directions of criticism exercised by Swift and Bentley over this point in the *Discourse*:

St *Paul* likewise went frequently into the Synagogues of the *Jews*, and *reason'd* with them; which was not only putting the *Jews* upon *Free-Thinking* on matters of Religion, but taking (according to the present Notions of *Christians*) a very extraordi-

---

[36] For the detail of this argument, refer to my 'Reaction to Collins'.
[37] *PW*, IV, p. 30.

nary step to put them upon *Free-Thinking*. For should *William Penn* the *Quaker*, or other religious Person differing from the *Establish'd Church*, come to *St. Paul's* during the time of *Divine Service* to *reason* with the *Court of Aldermen, Preacher*, and *Singing-Men*, or *Mr. Whiston* into the *Lower House of Convocation*, to *reason* with them; it is certain, that pursuant to the false Notions which now universally prevail, the *one* would be treated as a *Madman* and *Fanatick*, and the other as a *Disturber of the Proceedings of the Holy Synod*, which assumes a right to determine without *Reasoning* with the Person whose Opinions they condemn.[38]

Swift turns this into a canting incitement to chaos in public assemblies:

I have another Project in my Head which ought to be put in execution, in order to make us *Free-thinkers*: It is a great Hardship and Injustice, that our Priests must not be disturbed while they are prating in their Pulpit. For Example: Why should not *William Penn* the Quaker, or any *Anabaptist, Papist, Muggletonian, Jew* or *Sweet Singer*, have liberty to come into St. *Paul's* Church, in the midst of Divine Service, and endeavour to convert first the Aldermen, then the Preacher, and Singing-Men? or pray, why might not poor Mr. *Whiston*, who denies the Divinity of Christ, be allow'd to come into the Lower House of Convocation, and convert the Clergy? But alas we are over-run with such false Notions, that if *Penn* or *Whiston* should do their Duty, they would be reckoned Fanaticks, and Disturbers of the Holy Synod, although they have as good a Title to it, as St. *Paul* had to go into the Synagogues of the *Jews*; and their Authority is full as Divine as his.[39]

This commences with an exposure of narratorial stance reminiscent of *A Tale* ('I have another Project in my Head') and proceeds to stress the social absurdity of the situations projected by Collins. St Paul is relegated to the end of the passage so that his authority for 'reasoning' with priests is not activated until lines after the outrageous statement first strikes us: 'It is a great Hardship and Injustice, that our Priests must not be disturbed while they are prating in their Pulpit.' Swift then undermines the stature of the likely interrupters by interpolating a list of increasingly extreme figures to accompany the relatively respectable Quaker leader, Penn. 'Any *Anabaptist, Papist, Muggletonian, Jew* or *Sweet Singer*' encompasses images of heresy, fanaticism, and general baseness: these social and ideological incendiaries are not attempting to reason with the clergy and congregation, as Collins would have it, but are rather attempting to convert their audience to their own heresies. Similarly, the introduction to Convocation of the noted Arian, William Whiston,[40] is coloured not as reasoned debate but as an attempt to convert the clergy to disbelief in 'the Divinity of Christ'. Such freedom of thought appears in Swift's text as entailing, at best, disruption of the peace and, at worst, the dissemination of dangerous errors. St Paul is brought in at

---

[38] Collins, *Discourse*, pp. 44–45.

[39] *PW*, IV, p. 31.

[40] Who, as it happens, also wrote a reply to Collins' *Discourse* called *Reflexions on an Anonymous Pamphlet, Entituled, A Discourse of Free Thinking* (London, 1713).

the end – the reverse of his position in Collins' structure of ideas – to confirm the reverse of Collins' argument that freethinking is commanded by God. When we read that 'they have as good a Title to it, as St *Paul* had to go into the Synagogues of the *Jews*; and their Authority is full as Divine as his', we are forced by the parody to differentiate between St Paul's authentic, divinely inspired teaching and the indirections of heterodoxy. He had authority to teach and oppose the Jewish priests, but that authority came not from freethinking. It came directly from God, and was conveyed by way of the apostolic succession to the established Church, not to modern heretics. Divine authority filiates from a divine origin in the Tory intellectual patterns we are being taught – it does not inhere in the individual soul or intellect.

There is a substantial cultural gap between Swift's roundly destructive ridicule of Collins' premises and Bentley's narrower criticism on this point, and it is a gap that reflects more than just the temperamental distance between two very disparate clergymen. Bentley writes:

> St. *Paul*, says he, *when he went into the Synagogues of the Jews, and reason'd with them, took a very extraordinary Step*, as now it would be look'd on: and so he compares it to *Penn* the *Quaker* going into St. *Paul's*, or Mr. *Whiston* into the *House of Convocation*, to reason there against the *Establish'd Church*...But how ignorant and stupid is this Writer with his foolish Comparison? The Fact, he speaks of and quotes *Acts* XVII, 2,3. was done at *Thessalonica* a Pagan City in *Macedonia*: and was the *Jewish* Synagogue the *Establish'd Church* there? or rather allow'd on *Toleration*? But to pardon him this, and suppose the thing done in *Judea* it self, where our Saviour often did the same: was it any thing like to *interrupting Divine Service*, or *disturbing the Proceedings of a Synod*? Our Author knows not one tittle of the manner and custom of a Synagogue. After reading a few Sections out of the Law and the Prophets; the ablest men of the Assembly us'd to stand up and expound the Passages read: and if any Stranger or person of Note chanc'd to be there; he was ask'd by them, if he had any Discourse to impart to the Congregation. This is expressly affirmed by *Philo* the *Jew*, and others; and appears clearly from *Acts* XIII, 15. where at *Antioch* in *Pisidia* the Rulers of the Synagogue, seeing *Paul* and *Barnabas* Strangers there, *sent unto them, saying, Ye men and brethren, if you have any word of exhortation for the people, say on.* So that if even *Penn* and *Whiston* should do no more, but speak when desir'd by Authority, it would be no *extraordinary step* at all. The only *step* here that appears very *extraordinary*, is our Author's bold Leaping into the Dark; and blundering about matters, where he's quite blind and ignorant.[41]

The tactics and terms of discrediting are different from Swift's. Bentley courts scholarly objectivity, masquerading throughout his *Remarks* as Philaleutherus Lipsiensis, a theologian from Leipzig, who is moved to write by the many errors he sees in the *Discourse*. Unlike Swift, he goes to great

---

[41] *Remarks Upon a late Discourse of Free-Thinking: In a Letter to FHDD by Philaleutherus Lipsiensis* (London, 1713), pp. 48–49.

lengths to keep anything resembling a political dimension silent. This is a crucial displacement of all that is contingent and volatile in the controversy, in that it immediately distracts our attention from implications for public order, ideology, and morality, and focuses instead on matters of intellectual accuracy. Bentley's *Remarks* neutralises Collins' *Discourse*, showing that the claim that heterodox thinkers should dispute freely with clergy in churches and Convocation is irrelevant because it is based on a misunderstanding of Jewish customs.

This is the opposite direction from the trajectory of Swift's criticism, which engages hostilely and intertextually with its object, to emphasise the *Discourse*'s dangers and absurdities. Both critics use quotation, but in diametrically opposed ways. Swift entangles his victim text in its malign possibilities, changing the frames of reference and expanding, contracting, and interpolating at will, but always staying so close to Collins' words that the validity of the criticisms can scarcely be denied. As readers, we are taken inside Collins' discursive world and shown it without the window-dressing and concealments that hide its 'true' implications from public view. We are taken beneath its veneer of plausiblity, to see its errors enacted while simultaneously we learn to reject them. Bentley, on the other hand, uses quotation to keep his target at arm's length, to displace it from the centre of our attention so that we can look at it critically, judge it, and find it wanting on grounds of intellectual rigour and historical accuracy. While Swift exaggerates the text's intellectual life, Bentley restricts it, redirecting our attention from central issues to matters of competence in detail. Swift concentrates the text by parody so that we can see and reject its true nature, whereas Bentley atomises it by impersonal criticism, breaking the text up so that it can be taken away in little pieces. Bentley exposes textual illegitimacy, whereas Swift catches it parodically in the act of self-exposure.

The political implications of these two trajectories were not accidental. Whereas Swift was attempting to spread the stigma of freethinking deism over the whole spectrum of Whiggish politics and Latitudinarian churchmanship, the Whigs and Latitudinarians, led by Bentley, needed to isolate the implications and, in particular, to separate some important parts of their ideology from Collins' illegitimate misapplications of them. Parody was the last method of criticism that they would have employed, because it exaggerates the characteristics of its model and sends implications running deconstructively. They needed to restrict Collins to a cultural margin, carefully distinguished from their own legitimate principles. Swift draws out the 'true' (which is to say conservative or Tory) implications of Collins' language and opinions compellingly, as the vulnerability and fallibility of the individual mind exercising unguided liberty becomes apparent when compared to the greater and more unified certainty of corporate, established authority. This distrust of individual cognitive freedom expresses a widespread (and broadly ascendent) cultural distrust of unguided speculation, so the stigma of Collins' heterodox thought can be spread widely. In deconstructing Collins' faith in individual free reason in such a hostile manner, Swift is attacking the whole shape of libertarian thought, showing the way it fragments common order and common sense.

At the beginning of the controversy, the Whiggish newspaper *The Britain* had admitted the general reference of Collins' extreme formulations of freedom candidly:

Wou'd this Sect of Men have thought how they might abuse the *Whigs*, they cou'd not any way more effectually have done so, than by Printing this Jargon of Inconsistency, the Labour of many Hands, and to use their own fine Expression, only *Consistent with the Greatest Absurditys*.[42]

By depicting liberty and its languages in the act of collapsing under their own contradictions, Swift sought to enact this abuse even more incriminatingly as self-abuse. But the anonymous author of this admission also figured the Whiggish reaction to the threat to this central plank of their ideology. The Whigs needed to marginalise Collins' heterodox extension of their thinking, to restrict its reference as tightly as possible to Collins alone. Whereas Swift sought to name the *Discourse* as a Whig manifesto, fully expressing the treason and perversity of that faction's spirit ('a brief compleat Body of *Atheology*' to support their 'many profound Treatises in *Anarchy*'), the Whigs themselves sought to name it as 'this Jargon of Inconsistency,...only *Consistent with the Greatest Absurditys*'. In the long term, individual liberty rather than passive obedience came to be seen as at the root of the English constitution, so the Whigs must be said to have won the war, but the volatility of this intertextual skirmish should not be underestimated.

---

[42] *The Britain*, no. 3 (12 January 1712–13); a brief characterisation of this otherwise unremarked newspaper appears in my 'Reaction to Collins', pp. 71–72.

4

The problem of anarchic parody: *An Argument against Abolishing Christianity*

It is commonly assumed that parody is a sub-genre of satire, a kind of partisan diagnosis of diseases in the plausible. This view projects it as a form of rhetorical interrogation which is implicitly oppositional – it seeks to expose the absurdity of errant texts and discourses and to apportion blame. As we have seen, Defoe's *Shortest Way with the Dissenters* and Swift's *Abstract* of Collins' *Discourse of Free-Thinking* are functional texts in this way, aimed at identifying error and its religio-political affiliations. While a thoroughgoing investigation of the ironies can turn up more subversive implications in these texts, they operate primarily as suasive parodies: they deconstruct their victim-texts in order to persuade readers of the truth of a solution which is retrievable from the parodic text. The satirically 'true' meta-texts (the wisdom of toleration in the *Shortest Way*, and the need for intellectual and religious authority in the *Abstract*) can be identified by accurate interpretation of hints embedded in the errant languages being parodied. Certainly it is possible to argue that slippages into discourses altogether more subversive occur at the edges of these texts. Some readers have felt that Defoe mimics his victim so closely that he obscures the positive counter-message and becomes an imitator rather than a parodist. Similiarly, in the *Abstract* Swift can be accused of destabilising more than he manages to establish. However, these slippages occur only in the margins of the way these texts function in their polemical culture, for once fundamental orientations are made, the respective places of the *Shortest Way* and the *Abstract* in the pamphlet wars are not significantly equivocal. The same cannot be said of the *Argument against Abolishing Christianity* (written 1708, first published in the *Miscellanies* of 1711).

Certainly a bit of contextual ground-clearing will dissolve some of the more obvious misconceptions to which the *Argument* has given rise. The debate over whether the essay attacks Whig and Dissenting desires to abolish the Test Acts or deist efforts to undermine orthodox Christianity becomes a non-issue (a distinction without a difference) when we recognise that the majority of conservative readers would have seen only an unimportant difference of degree between the two programmes – both would have been viewed as fundamental attacks on true religion, which was to say primitive Christianity, which was to say the Church of England as by law established.[1] However, this does not resolve all hermeneutic problems, and neither would a solution to the question of whether the text advocates real or nominal Christianity.[2] The process of parodic erasure loses a confident sense of direction in this text, making all meta-textual solutions unverifiable. This is not to say that meta-texts cannot be projected – the text both awakens and thwarts readers' desires for a solution – but rather that we can construct many interpretations which are not compatible with each other. The text is opened to possibilities that, in a literary and political culture committed to restoring authoritative meaning, become distinctly anarchic.

The *Argument* positions itself in the context of late Stuart culture in a disturbingly anomalous way. The narrator begins by apologetically proclaiming his purpose, and projects a grotesquely distorted version of the recent past:

[I]n the present Posture of our Affairs at home or abroad, I do not yet see the absolute Necessity of extirpating the Christian Religion from among us.

This perhaps may appear too great a Paradox, even for our wise and paradoxical Age to endure: Therefore I shall handle it with all Tenderness, and with the utmost Deference to that great and profound Majority, which is of another Sentiment.

And yet the Curious may please to observe, how much the Genius of a Nation is liable to alter in half an Age: I have heard it affirmed for certain by some very old People, that the contrary Opinion was even in their Memories as much in Vogue as the other is now; and, that a Project for the Abolishing of Christianity would then have appeared as singular, and been thought as absurd, as it would be at this Time to write or discourse in its Defence.[3]

Swift's (as distinct from the Arguer's) irony is initially very easy to interpret here. Clearly the 'wise and paradoxical Age' which has allowed religious indifference so to triumph is being dispraised ironically. Readers with High-Church inclinations would have been particularly alert to the disregard for orthodoxy and the established Church displayed. However, simple reversal

---

[1] This perspective suggests that the dispute over whether the exact occasion of the *Argument* was Dissent and the Test Acts (Irvin Ehrenpreis, *Swift: the Man, his Works, and the Age*, 3 vols (London: Methuen, 1962–83), II, pp. 280–88, 294–97; and Frank H. Ellis, 'The *Argument against Abolishing Christianity* as an Argument against Abolishing the Test Act', *Reading Swift: Papers from the Second Münster Symposium on Jonathan Swift*, Richard H. Rodino and Hermann J. Real, eds. (Munich: Wilhhem Fink Verlag, 1993), pp. 127–40); or deism (Robert M. Philmus, 'Swift's "Lost" Answer to Tindal', *TSLL*, 22 (1980), 367–93; Davis, *PW*, II, pp. xvii-xix; and Philip Harth, 'Ehrenpreis's Swift: The Biographer as Critic', *MP*, 67 (1970), 273–78) builds a false opposition. Both programmes were under a severe stigma from the High-Church point of view and, being members of the same malicious plot, could be held to stand synechdochally for each other.
[2] Issues most convincingly canvassed by Mary F. Robertson, 'Swift's *Argument*: The Fact and Fiction of Fighting with Beasts', *MP*, 74 (1976), 124–41.
[3] *PW*, II, p. 27.

will not suffice to unravel the meaning, for the previous age, though prepared to stand up for its convictions and its conflicting images of true religion, was also the age of the civil conflicts of the middle of the seventeenth
century. As I have suggested in previous chapters, abhorrence of this excess
of enthusiasm did much to shape the political and religious culture of the
subsequent century. Defence of religion could be perceived as both
admirable and dangerous, and there is no clear marker here or throughout
the text as to which of these attitudes is finally privileged. This parodic text is
conscious of its cultural context but fits uneasily into it. There is a duplicity (a
space for uncertainty) implicit in parody because the reader is required to
interpret very actively, to translate the apparent meaning of the words on the
page into a deeper understanding significantly opposed to that apparent
meaning. In suasive parody, the reader is guided closely through this process
of deconstruction towards determinate conclusions. In more open modes of
parody, however, the irony embedded in the process of saying one thing and
'meaning' another – of saying 'the thing which is not' – can become reflexive
and plural in its implications. And that is precisely what happens here: the
reader is left stretched between interpretations that valorise either flaccid
indifference or dangerous enthusiasm, with no middle way readily apparent.
In a process I will describe (perhaps a little melodramatically) as anarchic
parody, determinate meaning gives way to an openness of implication.

Parody as homily: the pious solution

The assertion needs to be tested, and the most rigorous way of doing this is
to attempt to read the *Argument* extensively as suasive parody. Let us see if
we can discover a language and an ideology which the text is teaching us to
cleave to in the face of the errant discourses and loyalties attacked in the
parody. The likeliest place to find this authentic wisdom is the institution
and discourse of Swift's deepest loyalties, High-Church Anglicanism. The
essay was, after all, first published in 1711 between two demonstrably
Anglican documents, *The Sentiments of a Church-of-England Man with Respect to
Religion and Government* and *A Project for the Advancement of Religion and the
Reformation of Manners*, in a volume designed to show that the author's seeming apostasy from Whigs to Tories was not a piece of opportunism but the
expression of sustained loyalties.[4] This argument is corroborated by events
of the moment of its composition, particularly the ascendent condition of
the Whigs, described well by Geoffrey Holmes:

---

[4] See *PW*, II, pp. xxxii-lx; and Ehrenpreis, *Swift*, II, pp. 422–24 for accounts of the *Miscellanies'* publication and its biographical logic. For an excellent analysis of the genre and implications of the volume, see Anne Cline Kelly, 'The Semiotics of Swift's 1711 *Miscellanies*', *Swift Studies*, 6 (1991), 59–68.

After their success at the 1708 Election there were many prophecies that they [i.e. the Whigs] would try to repeal the Test Act in the 1708–9 session; indeed, Lord Weymouth was so certain of it that he dispatched an urgent message to Bishop Hooper, bidding that worthy prelate brave the snow between Wells and London in order to save his Church and country. But by the middle of January 1709 it had become clear that whatever plans the Whigs had formed for this purpose, if any, had been shelved, and even Wharton's much-publicised intention of abolishing the test in Ireland during his two viceregal visits in 1709–10 came to nothing. It seems by no means unlikely, however, that had the Whigs enjoyed power longer in the middle of the reign they would have attempted to remove the civil disabilities of the Protestant nonconformists.[5]

The *Argument* fits this historical moment very precisely. The Church of England felt itself to be threatened with a loss of privileges that was widely (if hyperbolically) described as a threat to its very being. The established nature of Swift's own Church of Ireland (of which he was the official representative on the matter of the First Fruits) was being openly attacked under the administration of Wharton as Lord Lieutenant. The Arguer's opinions concerning the unfashionableness of speaking in support of religion (quoted above) exclude and ignore the existence of an important body of rhetoric which was constituted under the banner of 'the Church in Danger'. If we treat this as a deliberate and audible omission, it can provide us with a meta-textual key to the essay's enigmas. Where the Arguer alleges that the times are so transformed from the recent past 'that a Project for the Abolishing of Christianity would then have appeared as singular, and been thought as absurd, as it would be at this Time to write or discourse in its Defence', he makes what in the context of early eighteenth-century pamphleteering is an audible omission. The silence only becomes louder further down the page when the Arguer distinguishes himself from a group of lunatics whom he claims are very marginal:

I hope, no Reader imagines me so weak to stand up in the Defense of *real* Christianity; such as used in primitive Times (if we may believe the Authors of those Ages) to have an Influence upon Mens Belief and Actions. To offer at the Restoration of that, would be a wild Project; it would be to dig up Foundations; to destroy at one Blow *all* the Wit, and *half* the Learning of the Kingdom; to break the entire Frame and Constitution of Things; to ruin trade, extinguish Arts and Sciences with the Professors of them; in short, to turn our Courts, Exchanges and Shops into Desarts.[6]

This passage fairly bristles with submerged metaphors of the rhetoric of High-Church Anglicanism: '*real* Christianity', 'as used in primitive times', 'Restoration', 'wild Project', 'Foundations', 'Frame and Constitution'. This

---

[5] *British Politics in the Age of Anne* (London: Macmillan, 1967), p. 105.
[6] *PW*, II, p. 27.

ideologically significant language has been only half-erased in the parody, leaving traces of a discourse that might be taken to be authoritative. The writers whose discourse is being ironically excluded here – those who were willing 'to stand up in the Defense of *real* Christianity' – equated the reformed and restored Church of England with the Apostolic Church. They were happy to lose the dubious benefits of modern wit and civilisation adumbrated here if they frustrated the higher goal of establishing and protecting primitive/orthodox/established/Anglican Christianity. Wit, learning, fashion, trade, arts, sciences, experts, courts, and retailing were scarcely positive virtues in the small, clean, pious, and obedient world they desired; and the obliteration of these innovations would be a small price to pay for the achievement of pure morality and religion.

The ideas and discourses of High-Church paranoia provided a dominant code in religious controversy in the first decade of the eighteenth century, and we can be sure that, to the common reader of 1708 (or 1711) they were audibly absent from Swift's *Argument*. It is a language further implicated by the grim irony of this passage:

Nor do I think it wholly groundless, or my Fears altogether imaginary; that the Abolishing of Christianity may perhaps bring the Church in Danger; or at least put the Senate to the Trouble of another Securing Vote. I desire, I may not be mistaken; I am far from presuming to affirm or think, that the Church is in Danger at present, or as Things now stand; but we know not how soon it may be so, when the Christian Religion is repealed. As plausible as this Project seems, there may be a dangerous Design lurk under it. Nothing can be more notorious, than that the *Atheists, Deists, Socinians, Anti-Trinitarians*, and other Subdivisions of Free-Thinkers, are Persons of little Zeal for the present Ecclesiastical Establishment: Their declared Opinion is for repealing the Sacramental Test; they are very indifferent with regard to Ceremonies; nor do they hold the *Jus Divinum* of Episcopacy. Therefore this may be intended as one politick Step towards altering the Constitution of the Church Established, and setting up *Presbytery* in the stead; which I leave to be further considered by those at the Helm.[7]

Circling anxiously around the resonant phrase itself, this activates the rhetoric of 'the Church in Danger' and skilfully suggests the institution's importance and beleaguered status. The circumlocutions which seem intent on avoiding the outright admission that the abolition of Christianity would undermine 'the present Ecclesiastical Establishment' may seem merely comic, but the game has specific political resonance as well. In 1705 a particularly intemperate High-Church pamphleteer, James Drake, had published *The Memorial for the Church of England*, which argued that the Church was in grave danger from the machinations of Dissenters and the Whiggish ministry. The Queen was offended that her government should be accused of endangering her Church, and the pamphlet was burnt as seditious. To capitalise on this, the Whigs

7 Ibid., pp. 36–37.

forced a debate on the issue in the House of Lords, which concluded with a resounding resolution proclaiming Parliament's trust in its good Anglican Queen, her loyal ministry, and her wise episcopal bench. In the first securing vote alluded to by the Arguer, Parliament assured the world at large that the Church could not be in safer hands or a more flourishing state, and that (and here is the twist) anyone who claimed that she was in danger must be a treacherous, treasonous, and incendiary liar with evil designs on both church and state; a secret or open Jacobite.[8] Parliament had declared, therefore, that it was sedition to allege that the Church was in danger, and Henry Sacheverell was (in part) prosecuted on these grounds in 1708–9. The Arguer is clearly mindful of this legal constraint, and goes to great lengths to assure us that 'I am far from assuming to affirm or think, that the Church is in Danger at present'. He then proceeds to dance around the obvious in a hilarious and ponderous parody of circumspection and politic avoidance of offence. He will not willingly be a martyr for his opinions, but he cannot help but imagine that the Church would be in some danger in the imminent event of Christianity's abolition. Having to go through the charade of sophistry illustrates the threatening stranglehold which the destructive forces of Whiggery, Dissent, and Republicanism have on the situation: while they attack the Church, one is not even allowed to rise in its defence.

Similarly, the enthusiastic pro-clericalism of the High-Churchmen is directly implicated in the ironic comparison made between those two symbols of city and country virtue, the country parson and the courtly wit:

It is likewise urged, that there are, by Computation, in this Kingdom, above ten Thousand Parsons; whose Revenues added to those of my Lords the Bishops, would suffice to maintain, at least, two Hundred young Gentlemen of Wit and Pleasure, and Free-thinking; Enemies to Priestcraft, narrow Principles, Pedantry, and Prejudices; who might be an Ornament to the Court and Town: And then again, so great a Number of able (bodied) Divines might be a Recruit to our Fleet and Armies.[9]

As with all the Arguer's prudential assessments, the equation is drawn up as a comparative cost-benefit analysis. We are asked to choose between funding a regiment of clerics deployed throughout the country and a handful of rakes centred in London. Reduced to these terms, the Arguer decides in favour of the clerics.

However, the grounds he presents for his preference are brilliantly perverse in their rigorous expedience. Furthermore, a just analysis is figured forth against the Arguer's grain, both by the basic and hackneyed iconography and by direct intervention in the detail. Thus the Arguer demonstrates the expedient case against the proposition by suggesting that it would be convenient 'that in certain Tracts of Country, like what we call Parishes,

---

[8] This account of the course of events follows Kenyon, *Revolution Principles*, pp. 98–101.
[9] *PW*, II, p. 30.

there should be *one* Man at least, of Abilities to read and write', and that such a sum of money as would support ten thousand pastors and the bishops as well could scarcely be expected to make so many as one hundred young gentlemen 'after the modern Form of Speech, ...*easy*', 'to the present refined Way of Living', let alone the two hundred proposed. But it is an older, colder voice, one with undertones of passion and authority, that calls us to consider the future 'of the Race of Men in the next Age, if we had nothing to trust to, besides the scrophulous consumptive Productions furnished by our Men of Wit and Pleasure'. It is the voice of long-suffering clerical frustration, harbouring a long resentment of the pillage of Church property by Henry VIII and his confederates, which speaks in a tone of bleak irony commending the idea of 'ten Thousand Persons reduced by the wise Regulations of *Henry* the Eighth, to the Necessity of a low Diet, and moderate Exercise, who are the great Restorers of our Breed'. Finally, it is the apocalyptic voice of the prophet that gives us the vision that without this good moral stock, 'the Nation would, in an Age or two, become but one great Hospital'. The proclamation makes us see the priesthood as the salt of the earth upon whom the health of society depends. And the ideal of free-thinking discourse, the man of wit, leisure, and liberal views, becomes a cancerous growth in the body politic who consumes wealth 'and entail[s] Rottenness and Politeness on...Posterity'.[10]

Overdetermined silences: problems with the pious solution

There is a major problem, however, in the way this hermeneutic pattern of escape into pious certainty tends also, disconcertingly, to become an escape from the words on the page into another text. Such a text might have been written by Sacheverell, Atterbury, Smallridge, Leslie, or any one of a number of Anglican apologists – even by the unironic Swift of the sermons and the *Project for the Advancement of Religion*. However, it bears no very close resemblance to the text we read as *An Argument against Abolishing Christianity*. Furthermore, this is not simply a procedural problem. Suasive parody can operate fairly unproblematically as a self-consuming artefact, where error is animated and systematically evacuated, while a positive course of action or understanding is clearly indicated. The *Argument*, however, will not stop signifying so conveniently. It is not just that there are insufficient pointers towards the meta-text for the decipherment of the victim-text to be 'safe'. Where there should be codes which can be rigidly decoded, there are, instead, important nodes of indeterminacy, which can point towards quite disparate interpretations.

Take the issue of scriptural authority raised in the image of the brutish libertine who justifies his conduct thus:

[10] Ibid., pp. 30, 31, 32, 35, 38.

This was happily expressed by him, who had heard of a Text brought for Proof of the Trinity, which in an antient Manuscript was differently read; he thereupon immediately took the Hint, and by a sudden Deduction of a long *Sorites*, most logically concluded: Why, if it be as you say, I may safely whore and drink on, and defy the Parson.[11]

The homiletic point is easy enough to see here: if society lets the standards of orthodoxy slip it will end inevitably in widespread godlessness, for the sinful laity are always willing to take the least shadow of doubt as a general licence for vice. In a more precisely political vein, the Whig-Latitudinarian project of biblical textual criticism is being identified as an invitation to apostasy in the face of conservative High-Church insistence that the laity were better kept in ignorant obedience than in ill-informed disobedience. All this seems orthodox enough. However, if we re-examine the idea of deducing 'a long *Sorites*' a problem arises. Is not this pietising reading of the essay precisely a long series of tightly targeted deductions? We have started with a hypothesis and proceeded to twist everything towards the goal of its validation. We have translated the language of parody blankly and teleologically, without reference to the ironic doubleness (or, to use Derridean terminology, the dangerous supplement) it carries with it. It is all very well to condemn wilful libertine deductions, but can that criticism be quarantined so that it casts no shadow of doubt on a meta-textual enterprise so heavily dependent on long partisan deductions, merely because they are on the 'right' side of religio-political dispute? The process of parody is structurally dependent on dialogical doubleness, and this sits uneasily with a monological solution to the issues at hand in a particular text, particularly one as pervasively ironic as the *Argument*. Parodic interplay works by erasure rather than obliteration of errant discourses, and sometimes the erasures, being intrinsically partial, leave traces that fight back to undermine the supposed goal. The places where this sort of dangerous supplementation is particularly notable are nominalism, the cynical critique of religion as socially and politically useful, the analysis of 'the Spirit of Opposition', and the duplicity of the 'positive' arguments for nominal Christianity. We will first discuss the way these nodes of multiple meanings resonate, then we will look at how the *Argument*'s entire mode runs counter to a message of simple and pious obedience.

One of the *Argument*'s most striking passages is the playful but not altogether frivolous discussion of the casual connection between human signified and verbal sign:

THERE is one Advantage, greater than any of the foregoing, proposed by the abolishing of Christianity; that it will utterly extinguish Parties among us, by removing those factious Distinctions of High and Low Church, of *Whig* and *Tory*, *Presbyterian* and *Church-of-England*; which are now so many grievous Clogs upon publick Proceedings, and dispose Men to prefer the gratifying themselves, or depressing their Adversaries, before the most important Interest of the State.

[11] Ibid., p. 38.

I CONFESS, if it were certain that so great an Advantage would redound to the Nation by this Expedient, I would submit to be silent: But will any Man say, that if the Words *Whoring, Drinking, Cheating, Lying, Stealing*, were, by Act of Parliament, ejected out of the *English* Tongue and Dictionaries; we should all awake next Morning chaste and temperate, honest and just, and Lovers of Truth. Is this a fair Consequence? Or if the Physicians would forbid us to pronounce the Words *Pox, Gout, Rheumatism*, and *Stone*; would that Expedient serve like so many *Talismans* to destroy the Diseases themselves? Are Party and Faction rooted in Mens Hearts no deeper than Phrases borrowed from Religion; or founded upon no firmer Principles? And is our Language so poor, that we cannot find other Terms to express them? Are Envy, Pride, Avarice and Ambition, such ill Nomenclators, that they cannot furnish Appellations for their Owners? Will not *Heydukes* and *Mamalukes, Mandarins* and *Potshaws*, or any other Words formed at Pleasure, serve to distinguish those who are in the *Ministry* from Others, who *would be in* it *if they could.*[12]

If one were determined to turn this into the Tory jeremiad I have proposed as the meta-textual message, one would point in a general way to its focus on sin and perversity as fundamental to human existence. There is also a barb aimed at Latitudinarian projects for ecumenical unity among Protestants which, it is implied, neglect to allow for the deeply ingrained perversity of the sectarians. Such explanations might be just enough to cover the first paragraph, but something altogether more dangerously speculative happens in the second. The cynical critique of public life and personal morality here sounds more like Rochester's 'Satyr against Reason and Mankind' than an inverted but recoverable homily. Only supreme confidence in the saving rhetoric of Anglicanism could decipher the implications of this systematic nominalism positively, and keep them from running into a sort of Hobbesian materialism of human motivation. This is amorality, treating '*Whoring, Drinking, Cheating, Lying, Stealing*' as elements of the human condition no less inalienable than illness, for which the empty sounds of moralising nomenclature act as disguises or pretexts. Matters of political principle merely provide the occasion (the neutral structure) for the expression of 'Envy, Pride, Avarice and Ambition'. Principle is negotiable, but conflict and self-interest are inevitable. Furthermore, it is not really plausible to suggest that the stigma of this perversity is kept on one side of politics/religion. The 'factious Distinctions' include both sides explicitly – 'High and Low Church, of *Whig* and *Tory*, *Presbyterian* and *Church-of-England*' – and only the most rigorous bias could confine the criticism to one half of the parties. The reflexivity of the irony asserts itself further down when the titles '*Margaritians, Toftians*, and *Valentinians*' are proposed as substitute titles by which to distinguish between Whigs, Tories, and Trimmers, and we see that such a ridiculous translation of formal loyalties from principles to singers would do little to alter the structure of politics in the age of Anne. Moreover, the dangerous thread of irony will run further, for, in this bitter and witty deconstruction of the connection between word and moral idea, the terms of possibility for sincerely held principle are placed pessimistically beyond the realm of human political effort. Their very possibility is denied in an equation that offers only the alternatives of hypocrisy and amorality. One could reject the terms of the equation, and suggest, for example, that Swift opens a Pascalian space which must necessarily be filled by the revelation of an enigmatic God. But to imagine such a solution is not to interpret the text in any meaningful sense. It is to reject it.

The pattern of dangerously escaping ironies is so similar in the discussions of the practical virtues of nominal religion and of the mechanical and inevitable operation of the 'Spirit of Opposition' that these passages do not need separate attention. Only by strict and anti-interpretative adherence to an orthodoxy not directly figured in the text can the process of parodic erasure be bound to pious goals in these instances. Any lapse of discipline in reading allows the ironies to reflect implications not imaginable by the High-Church preacher. More surprisingly, if we worry less about biographical imperatives to see Swift as a particular sort of churchman, passages in the essay become more readily comprehensible in terms of Whiggish, libertine discourses, though these can never be said to be innocently (let alone indulgently) entertained.

The clearest emblem of this open and anarchic potential occurs in the dual function of this metaphor: 'Let the Mastiffs amuse themselves about a Sheep-skin stuffed with Hay, provided it will keep them from worrying the Flock.'[13] This striking perception of religion as the opiate of the people, and particularly the savage image of the 'Sheep-skin stuffed with Hay', breaches pious decorum. Labelling this as the errant utterance of an idiot Latitudinarian apologist for infidelity is not enough to master its power to suggest that all religion is convenient hypocrisy. The only way to dignify such an image is to reject its terms utterly, and that is not what happens in parody. The anarchy of parody stems from the fact that no monological voice can completely subdue the vestigial language of the other. The trace left in the process of erasure shapes the reader's response so that the meta-text can only transform the victim-text (or discourse), not remove all memory of it from our minds. The slippage here is all the more suggestive because, in this text, there is no unequivocal force explicitly determining the meaning. Thus this image is allowed to resonate damagingly against the text's broad meta-textual thrust. The 'Sheep-skin stuffed with Hay', like the

---

[13] Ibid., p. 35.

Tub in *A Tale*, runs with allegiances that are very much on the Whiggish, city, anti-clerical side. The fact that these affiliations frustrate the unified suasive interpretation is a natural function of parody and, I suspect, a deliberate and subversive aspect of the volatility of Swift's writing. Let us now see how far these affiliations will run in the text.

The *Argument* as an essay in Shaftesburian ridicule

We finished the previous section agonising over nodes of irony in the *Argument* and coming to the conclusion that their implications could not be confined to the narrow purposes of suasive parody. It could be argued that I am making a couple of minor inconsistencies and breaches of decorum carry a very great deal of weight in my determination to represent the essay as anarchic, so let us look to another way of justifying my assertion. There is, as we have observed, a broad ironic space opened in the text between a confused Whiggish, Latitudinarian mode and a High-Church Tory meta-text. As can be seen by the relatively stable process of parodic conversion figured in the *Abstract* of Collins' *Discourse* or Defoe's *Shortest Way*, this space need not be a problem if there are enough authoritative, ideologically marked bridges with the direction of flow of meaning marked on them clearly. In the *Argument*, however, the nature and direction of these bridges is disputable. It is easy to recognise that we are reading a parody (we are for-ever being thrown out of the Arguer's discourse) but it is not always obvious what we are supposed to learn from this dislocation. What I want to do here is to show in an extensive way that the proposed lesson is not necessar-ily Tory loyalism. As we trace another meta-text of implications and affilia-tions around another centre, we will discover a deep and radical duplicity in this pamphlet, which suggests a persistence of hermeneutic anarchy far more disturbing than the occasional paradox. This duplicity is not exactly an opposition, but it does suggest irreconcilable cultural loyalties, for, while the *Argument* is clearly readable as a piece of High-Church polemic, it is also readable as an essay in a notably distant discourse, 'polite' Shaftesburian ridicule.[14]

---

[14] Shaftesbury's cultural identity and significance have recently been excellently described in Lawrence E. Klein, *Shaftesbury and the Culture of Politeness: Moral Discourse and Cultural Politics in early Eighteenth-Century England* (Cambridge: Cambridge University Press, 1994). While this book arrived too late to have a significant influence on this study, I am relieved to report that it gives my reading of Shaftesbury a much firmer base and does not contradict me in any substantial way. Another recent book (Ian Higgins, *Swift's Politics: A Study in Disaffection* (Cambridge: Cambridge University Press, 1994)) fits less well with this Shaftesburian reading of Swift's early rhetorical modes. Higgins makes an extensive but (to my mind) not compelling argument that Swift was a lifelong Tory, who often wrote in Jacobite codes; one can interpret Swift's ironies this way, but one need not do so, as I hope to demonstrate by mapping out the plausibility of a dissident Shaftesburian reading of the *Argument* and, in following chapters, of *A Tale*.

This is an unusual claim to make for the work of 'the great Tory satirist', so we must first investigate the terms of its biographical, bibliographical, and historical possibility. Though not published until 1711, the *Argument* was written in 1708. Biographically, this is an important lapse of time for, while Swift was 'coming out' as a Tory Anglican loyalist in 1711, his credentials and circles of friendship were solidly Whiggish in 1708. Indeed, though he was in England as a representative of the established Church of Ireland, he had not been chosen to pursue the matter of the First Fruits because of his commitment to High-Church principles, but precisely because of his Whiggish connections, particularly with the circle of wits (including Steele and Addison) around the notably free thinking and free living minister, Lord Somers.[15] It could be argued that Swift had merely inherited these affiliations from Sir William Temple, that they were much against his natural temperament, and that he was in the uneasy process of casting them off and cleaving to his fundamental allegiances.[16] However, if we reject the benefit of hindsight and try to imagine how all this would have appeared in 1708, it is possible to imagine a Swift whose convictions were not fully formulated and whose ambitions were propelling him towards the main chance. Certainly, it would have struck a dispassionate observer of the world of letters in 1708 as surprising that the author of *A Tale*, the *Discourse of the Contests and Dissensions in Athens and Rome*, and the Bickerstaff hoax was, in fact, a secret and passionate defender of High-Church principles and pieties. The common reader of 1708 expected work of quite another kind from 'the Author of *A Tale of a Tub*'. She or he expected work like the *Letter Concerning Enthusiasm*.

Relying on circumstantial and internal evidence, Ehrenpreis can date the writing of the *Argument* no more accurately than 'probably mid-1708'.[17] Shaftesbury's *Letter* can be dated more precisely. On 12 July 1708, he wrote to Somers justifying his decision to allow his essay to appear in print and including a copy of the work which (like *A Tale*) was dedicated to Somers.[18]

---

[15] This assessment of Somers's character follows that of Robert M. Adams, 'In Search of Baron Somers', Perez Zagorin ed., *Culture and Politics from Puritanism to the Enlightenment* (Berkeley: University of California Press, 1980), pp. 165–202. Adams' essay, depicting Somers as the very image of modern Whiggery, is an essential corrective to the hagiography perpetrated by his morally self-conscious friends (Burnet, Tillotson, and Addison) and enthusiastically perpetuated by nineteenth-century constitutional historians and his most recent biographer, William L. Sachse, *Lord Somers: A Political Portrait* (Manchester: Manchester University Press, 1975).

[16] Indeed, this is very much the line Adams takes. While his reasoning is extremely suggestive, it does not seem *necessary* to assume that Swift's career was figured at this stage around covert attacks on Somers and all he stood for.

[17] *Swift*, II, p. 276.

[18] Richard B. Wolf, 'The Publication of Shaftesbury's Letter Concerning Enthusiasm', *Studies in Bibliography*, 32 (1979), 236–41. The letter cited by Wolf is Public Record Office, Shaftesbury Papers, PRO 30/24/22, no. 4, pp. 86–87. See also Robert Voitle, *The Third Earl of Shaftesbury, 1671–1713* (Baton Rouge: Louisiana State University Press, 1984), p. 324.

He had published only to forestall the publication of a pirated edition which some opportunistic member of Somers' circle intended to foist upon the world 'with a Title-Page bearing yr Ldps Name: a notable help to ye Book-Seller, especially when joynd with that of your pretended good Friend the Author of ye *Tale of a Tub*'.[19] This remarkable confusion between the work of the deist philosopher and that of the Tory satirist, even in the very circles where both authors were moving, might be explicable as a mere local per-versity, a *lusus naturae*, except for the fact that it was a widespread error when the *Letter* appeared in print. As Richard Wolf explains:

No evidence of contemporary attribution [of the *Letter*] to Shaftesbury survives, and the printed work, like the manuscript, was apparently believed by many to be the product of the Author of *A Tale of a Tub*. Swift indeed felt obliged to deny his authorship privately to three different correspondents as well as publicly in the Apology first printed with the fifth edition of the *Tale*.[20]

Though he denied the work repeatedly, Swift does not seem to have been particularly annoyed or surprised by the attribution. None of his epistolary denials captures the mood of Samuel Parker's savage denunciation of the *Letter* as:

Nine or ten Sheets full of such flagrant Buffoonery, Raillery and Ridicule upon all Religion, Natural as well as Reveal'd, as are enough to shock an ordinary Atheist...When I read it, almost every Period seem'd to come like a Flash from Hell. And at this time I can't look into't without trembling.[21]

Compared to this, the criticism Swift expresses in his letter to Phillips is remarkably muted:

There has been an essay of Enthusiasm lately published, that has run mightily, and is very well writ. All my friends have me to be the author, *sed ego non credulus illis*. By the free Whiggish thinking I should rather take it to be yours: But mine it is not; For tho I am every day writing my Speculations in my Chamber, they are quite of another sort.[22]

Certainly Swift seeks to distinguish Shaftesbury's 'free Whiggish thinking' from his own opinions and present labours, but he seems flattered that his

---

[19] Shaftesbury to Somers, March 1707–8, PRO 30/24/22, no. 4, p. 69; quoted Wolf, 'Shaftesbury's Letter', p. 238. Though anyone with pretensions to gentility in the world of letters always insisted that she or he published only to forestall a deformed pirated edition, Wolf is inclined to believe Shaftesbury in this instance.

[20] Wolf, 'Shaftesbury's Letter', p. 239. Swift's three correspondents were Ambrose Phillips (14 September 1708; *Corr.*, I, p. 100), Charles Ford (12 November 1708; *Corr.*, I, p. 110), and Robert Hunter (12 January 1708–9; *Corr.*, I, p. 122).

[21] *Censura Temporum 1* (1708), p. 244; quoted by Wolf, 'Shaftesbury's Letter', pp. 239–40. This was not Marvell's Samuel Parker, who had been dead for more than two decades, but another intem-perate High Tory clergyman of the same name.

[22] *Corr.*, I, p. 100.

friends should identify such a popular and 'well writ' piece as his, and he is willing to play along with the polite compliments by attempting to reflect the glory of authorship (under the cover of a mild piece of raillery) on to Phillips. In the letter to Ford he seems no more enraged than before that 'all my Friends would persuade me to have been the Author'[23] and he makes no attempt to criticise the book's opinions. He was still trying to shift the credit of authorship on to another friend and correspondent, Robert Hunter, in January, and it becomes quite clear that either he did not see the *Letter*'s notorious infidelity or it did not greatly concern him. Even two years later in the 'Apology' to the fifth edition of *A Tale*, when he was much more concerned to clean up his credentials as an orthodox Church of England man, the words he found to deny the *Letter* were not harsh:

Yet several have gone a farther Step, and pronounced another Book to have been the Work of the same hand with this; which the Author directly affirms to be a thorough mistake; he never having so much as read that Discourse, a plain Instance how little Truth, there often is in general Surmises, or in the Conjectures drawn from a Similitude of Style, or way of thinking.[24]

Swift is lying here. As his private correspondence indicates, he had read the *Letter*, with a degree of admiration. However, what is remarkable for our present purposes is not that Swift denies the fact of reading, but that he acknowledges fellowship ('a Similitude of Style, or way of thinking'), and makes no shift to reject the burden of the *Letter*'s message, a message whose threat to the fabric of society had been described by Mary Astell thus:

[It was] industriously spread in the Nation; put by way of ABC, into the hands of every young Fellow, who begins to speak great swelling Words, against what he Will not Understand, because he is Resolv'd not to Practice: And sent, by way of Mission, into Foreign Parts, upon that *hopeful Project!* which is now *the Heroick Passion of exalted Spirits, the saving of Men's Sense*, by the Damning of their Souls![25]

This is exactly the sort of dangerous enervation which Swift seems to be attacking in the *Argument* when he suggests (we presume sarcastically) that the wits need Christianity to display their cleverness against, or when he ridicules the man:

Who had heard of a Text brought for Proof of the Trinity, which in an antient Manuscript was differently read; he thereupon immediately took the Hint, and by a sudden Deduction of a long *Sorites*, most logically concluded; Why, if it be as you say, I may safely whore and drink on, and defy the Parson.[26]

---

[23] Ibid., p. 110.
[24] *A Tale*, p. 6; the *Letter* is identified by name in the margin.
[25] *Bart'lemy Fair: or, an Enquiry after Wit* (1709), p. 23; quoted by Wolf, 'Shaftesbury's Letter', p. 240.
[26] *PW*, II, p. 38.

Yet Swift seems to have been cautiously pleased to be identified with a text which was received by writers we tend to think of as his natural allies as a patent pretext for infidelity. The biographical space for a distinctly impious meta-text is clearly open.

To this point we have demonstrated three things: (1) that Shaftesbury's *Letter* was published at about the same time that Swift was writing the *Argument* (which was possibly one of the 'Speculations...quite of another sort' mentioned in the letter to Phillips); (2) that the *Letter* attained a degree of notoriety; and (3) that the *Letter* was linked to 'the Author of *A Tale of a Tub*', who was not displeased to have the work fathered on him. Beyond this, it is possible to speculate (and impossible to verify) that Swift may have had access to the *Letter* during its manuscript circulation, through the agency of his and Shaftesbury's common friend, that fulcrum of Whiggish culture, Somers.[27] Thus he may have had access to Shaftesbury's ideas while his own mind was turning to the issues which inform the *Argument*. On the other hand, it is also possible to speculate (and equally impossible to verify) that Swift's essay is an immediate reaction to the literary theory suggested in the *Letter*. As we know from the *Abstract* of Collins' *Discourse*, Swift could write rapidly and well on the latest thing, and it is possible that he may have been provoked by the publication of the *Letter* into making his own essay in Shaftesburian wit. We cannot know for sure whether either of these speculations be empirically true, but that they are historically and temperamentally possible is enough to license a reading of the *Argument* in Shaftesburian terms, to see if it works.

It is particularly necessary to avoid the unwisdom of hindsight in this instance. Swift held strongly partisan Tory convictions by 1714, but he did not seem to hold such views in his earlier career. It is no better than pious obfuscation to insist that Swift, being a Great Writer and a Great Moralist, must have had consistent and unified principles from puberty to the grave, and it seems to be on such dubiously hagiographical grounds that the insistence that Swift must have been either always a Whig or always a Tory rests. In 1708, at least, Swift and Shaftesbury were close enough practically and intellectually for it to be possible that the *Argument* might be a response to or a working out of implications within the *Letter*, and there is a sufficient quantity of circumstantial evidence to add force to this suspicion. I do not

---

[27] Harold Love, *Scribal Publication in Seventeenth-Century England* (Oxford: Clarendon Press, 1993) provides a fresh appraisal of the manuscript business through into our period, and demonstrates that it was a far more extensive form of publication than has usually been imagined. Shaftesbury's writings certainly did circulate in manuscript (though the method was becoming outmoded in the world at large, it suited Shaftesbury's ideal of polite aristocratic conversation perfectly) and Swift (as Temple's secretary and literary executor) was connected to these circles. Consequently, the possibility of his acquaintance with Shaftesbury's writings is very real, though nothing can be proved.

mean to insist that the *Letter* occasions the *Argument* in the way Collins' *Discourse* occasions Swift's *Abstract*. The relationship is neither so direct nor so directly oppositional. Rather than positing the *Letter* as Swift's victim-text (a text being directly and hostilely parodied) I propose rather to treat it as a key to the *Argument's* ethos. It may be an ethos entertained rather than fully accepted, but it is possible to read Shaftesbury's essay as a meta-text on the level of rhetorical function equivalent (but parallel) to the doctrinal meta-text of audibly absent High-Church loyalism proposed above.

The essential key is Shaftesbury's suggestion that:

> In short, my lord, the melancholy way of treating religion is that which, according to my apprehension, renders it so tragical, and is the occasion of its acting in reality such dismal tragedies in the world. And my notion is, that provided we treat religion with good manners, we can never use it with too much freedom and familiarity. For if it be genuine and sincere, it will not only stand the proof, but thrive and gain advantage from hence; if it be spurious, or mixed with any imposture, it will be detected and exposed.[28]

This is precisely the mode of the *Argument's* engagement with religious and moral error. Though Shaftesbury's naivety would sound disingenuous coming from Swift, it is clear that the *Argument* seeks to further the cause of the 'genuine and sincere' in religion while exposing the 'spurious'. The language employs 'freedom and familiarity', yet (at least by Swift's standards – consider the *Modest Proposal*) maintains 'good manners'. Certainly it avoids any suspicion of being a 'melancholy way of treating religion'. There is an inevitable slippage between mode and message, as the method of Shaftesburian ridicule theory comes to influence the logic and implications of the *Argument's* positions. Viewed in this way, Swift's text becomes part of the discourse of Whiggish wits and gentlemen, the sort of text likely to please a Somers, an Addison, or a Steele. Consequently, the light touch of the conversation enjoyed by aristocrats of the spirit becomes its essential aspect. Within this freemasonry of taste, the substance of opinions becomes immaterial, subordinate to the ideal of polite discussion which, in turn, ensures that truth will out. Hence it matters little whether real or nominal Christianity appears to be *advocated*; men of wit and taste will understand that the play of ridicule has scourged the false and purified our sense of what is true. Thus aristocratic utterance attains a reserved idiolect, where authority is implicit in the relationship between author and adept audience and hence appears in the text as a kind of silence, under erasure. It is socially as well as intellectually exclusive, as 'the vulgar, indeed, may swallow any sordid jest, any mere drollery or buffoonery; but it must be a finer

---

[28] *Characteristics of Men, Manners, Opinions, Times, etc.*, John M. Robertson, ed., 2 vols (Gloucester, Mass.: Peter Smith, 1963; reprint of 1900 edn; 1st edn, 1711), I, p. 24.

and truer wit which takes with men of sense and breeding'.[29] In his *Sensus Communis: An Essay on the Freedom of Wit and Humour*, Shaftesbury describes this conversational space positively as 'that sort of freedom which takes place among gentlemen and friends, who know one another perfectly well'.[30]

On this reading, therefore, while the *Letter* advocates tolerance and the *Argument* appears to oppose it, this kind of difference is less important than the texts' modal fellowship. It is the fellowship that readers of the time recognised immediately when they took the *Letter* to be by the same hand as *A Tale*, to Swift's flattered amusement and Shaftesbury's intense frustration. Shaftesbury attacked:

> That detestable writing of that most detestable author of the *Tale of a Tub*, whose manners, life, and prostitute pen and tongue are indeed exactly answerable to the irregularity, obscenity, profaneness, and fulsomeness of his false wit and scurrilous style and humour.[31]

Such virulence is quite extraordinarily out of character for Shaftesbury, whose general demeanour of polite magnanimity seems to have been both sincere and deliberately maintained. However, the horror of this identification remained Shaftesbury's problem, because (in a pose Swift also maintained throughout his life) the aristocrat of wit never exposes himself publicly as an author. Having erased himself from his own work – for example, he did not even openly admit his authorship of the *Letter* to Somers in the private letter accompanying the dedication copy[32] – he can only differentiate his utterance from *A Tale*'s by calling it the wrong kind of writing.

This self-erasure has benefits as well as frustrations, for it allows the possibility of entirely ironic utterance. In the *Argument*, Swift seems to have grasped the potential within Shaftesburian wit for rhetorical disguise. Let us take the lead from Shaftesbury again:

> If men are forbid to speak their minds seriously on certain subjects, they will do it ironically. If they are forbid to speak at all upon such subjects, or if they find it really dangerous to do so, they will then redouble their disguise, involve themselves in mysteriousness, and talk so as hardly to be understood, or at least not plainly interpreted, by those who are disposed to do them a mischief.[33]

This describes exactly the radical duplicity implicit in the irony being

---

[29] Ibid., I, p. 10.

[30] Ibid., I, p. 53.

[31] Letter to Pierre Coste, 25 July 1712; quoted in *The Life, Unpublished Letters, and Philosophical Regimen of Anthony, Earl of Shaftesbury, Author of the Characteristics*, Benjamin Rand, ed. (London: Swan Sonnenschein, 1900), p. 504.

[32] Letters to Somers of March 1707–8 and June 12 1708; quoted and discussed in Wolf, 'Shaftesbury's Letters', pp. 238–39.

[33] *Characteristics*, I, p. 50.

employed in the *Argument*. Within its terms, we can postulate interpretations of Swift's intended meaning that are, to put it unemphatically, alternative. We can see it this way: responsible to his Church in the matter of the first fruits, Swift could not afford to endanger his position with the relatively godless Whigs by writing straightforwardly on the rights of the Church, so he vents his frustrations under a guise of irony, writing 'so as hardly to be understood, or at least not plainly interpreted'. Or, looked at from the other direction, he employs a super-structure of limp pieties to disguise his desire to write freely and impiously on religion, knowing that he will have a willing audience for his true intentions among his Whiggish friends and a good explanation if questioned by his more orthodox Anglican masters. Nor, as words can entertain contradictions of intention, is it necessary that the situation be entirely one way or the other.

One of the most remarkable facts about the *Argument* is the disparity between the context in which it was first intended to be, and that in which it finally was, published. We have noted above that it appeared in the 1711 *Miscellanies* between the *Sentiments of a Church-of-England Man* and the *Project for the Advancement of Religion*, both eminently orthodox documents, and surmised that the context indicates that this essay should be read as part of Swift's demonstration of his pre-existing Church principles and hence of the integrity of his turn to the Tories. However, had the *Miscellanies* appeared in 1708 or 1709 with an introduction by Steele (as Swift had originally intended), the *Argument*'s Shaftesburian mode would easily have carried the burden of such free Whiggish connections as Swift was cultivating at that time.[34] What we have here is a text claimable for radically different (and essentially antagonistic) ideologies then current in literary culture.

This ironic openness of affiliation is both disturbing and playful, and it is easy to see its usefulness in the context of Swift's career as it was then developing. The rhetorical disguise of irony allows him to say several things at once, to play at being a wit while preaching piety and obedience. The parody arouses threads of quotation, erasure, and implication, but it does not tie them incontestably to a single meta-text, so the result, from a hermeneutic point of view, is anarchic. This may frustrate methodical readers, but it is hardly unimaginable as an example of writerly playfulness. Furthermore, the large degree of deniability had obvious professional benefits for Swift himself. It is a measure of his optimism at this time that (even after the hostile reception given *A Tale*) he could write a parody open to deeply antagonistic interpretations and expect different readers only to see what they liked and to ignore (fail to see) what they found offensive. It is also a measure of

---

[34] The same cannot be said for the *Sentiments* and the *Project*, which are moralistic works of Swift's right hand. Ehrenpreis (*Swift*, II, pp. 422–23) suggests that the tenor of these two tracts caused Swift to not publish the whole collection in 1708–9 when it would have annoyed his current Whig friends. This need not imply that the *Argument* would have had the same effect, however.

his experience that he did not allow the essay to be published until its field of implication had been restricted by context and overt (but extra-textual) intention. In the *Miscellanies* of 1711, it seems obvious that the *Argument* must be an orthodox church tract, but had it been published in 1708 as an anonymous pamphlet its affiliations would have been radically and conveniently negotiable.

5

Authority and the author: the disappearing centre in Swiftian parody

It could be argued that in the previous chapter on the *Argument against Abolishing Christianity*, I have proposed a false polarisation, warping my readings of the text around two equally unlikely interpretations. In that essay, it could be said, Swift advocates a balanced and practical middle way of public piety, something like the message deciphered by Philip Harth:

> There is no reason to believe that Swift is trying to win over the reader to the view that real Christianity is incompatible with any genuine civilisation. In reality, there is nothing the least rigoristic about any of these allusions to real Christianity. They simply suggest a state of affairs, unmarked by either enthusiasm or indifference, in which people attend church on Sundays, reverence the Christian religion, and are influenced in their belief and actions by the system of the Gospel.[1]

The fallacy here is not in the interpretation, but in the idea that there is only one authoritative Swift and that he can be placed reliably behind this single interpretation. The text can be read as a fundamentalist, moderate, or libertine tract. Its implications can be construed to support real or nominal Christianity. We can view the Shaftesburian mode positively as quotation (a playful essay in an essentially libertine and rationalist enterprise), or negatively as parody (an ironic exposure of the absurdity, irresponsibility, and immorality of that enterprise). We cannot know which of these alternatives is correct. The text is finally opaque because none of these interpretations can claim an overwhelming authority. None, in other words, can uphold its claim to be exclusively centred on Swift.

Obviously, the *Argument*'s narrator does not offer any reliable perspective on the text he imagines he is dominating. Nor does the idea of a persona offer any magic key, as the narrator holds to no consistent character and no determinate distance from truth. Rather, as in *A Tale* and *Gulliver's Travels*, the *Argument*'s narrator is a contested site for the articulation of blindness and insight, and certainly not a psychologically real character. What we come to realise as we attempt to decipher the parody and come up with remarkably discordant alternatives, is that the text has no centre, that authorship (the

---

[1] 'Ehrenpreis's Swift,' p. 278.

integrating impression of present, authoritative intention) is erased. This is in the nature of anarchic parody. The parodic process of quotation and erasure activates plural and contradictory narratives, which, in turn, imply plural narrators, and with them plural centres of authority. The voices mediate degrees of absence, error, and erasure. There is no necessary connection between them and a fully present, authoritative voice, only various degrees of difference. Swift has withdrawn from determinate meanings behind a veil of irony, leaving only traces of privileged discourses, perspectives, and opinions among the erasures and ridicule. In the previous chapter, I followed a couple of the threads that might plausibly be hypothesised as falling within the ambit of Swift's historical and biographical intentions in the *Argument*. The trouble is that these constructions of author-ity, which aim to solve and therefore dissolve the text as if it were a riddle, are at least as much the inter-preter's as the text's. The High-Church Anglican meta-text illustrates this point best, for it figures a coherent and dogmatic reading of audible absences and the barest of hints in its transformation of the negative image into posi-tive truth. It is not so much a negative interpretation of the parodied words on the page as a positive interpretation of words that are not there at all.

We can call our string of decipherment Swift's or the text's, but the assertion is a matter of faith rather than fact. Anarchic parody is not monological. Rather, it rejoices in language's power to say many things. Parody can only be held to determinate satiric purposes when it both refers to and obeys a strict code, when parodic statement A corresponds only to judgement B. Of course, by so strict a definition, pure suasive parody cannot exist, because (at least since Babel) such perfect correspondences cannot occur in language. However, my point is that anarchic parody does not even aspire to such purity of refer-ence. The *Argument* is not a botched attempt to encode a simple message. It is not a text looking to be solved. Rather, it embraces the power of parodic lan-guage to entertain plurality and mixed motives. We can imagine Swift to be the orchestrator of this inexhaustible play of conflicting implications, but we cannot place him as single centre of authority within the text. As a determi-nant of meaning, Swift has disappeared, leaving behind a text which has the brilliance and complexity of paradox rather than the vigour of resolution.

Bickerstaff and authority

The Bickerstaff controversy shows this collapse of authority from another angle. Through it, Swift stages the disappearance of a real author (John Partridge) and launches a fake author (Isaac Bickerstaff, Esq;) on the path to glory as the Tatler and the Censor of Great Britain.[2] While the *Argument*

---

[2] *The Tatler* was published and advertised as 'the Lucubrations of Isaac Bickerstaff, Esq;', and the title of Censor of Great Britain was first claimed in *The Tatler* no. 144 (17 March 1710), after which it was used widely by other pamphleteers in connection with Bickerstaff.

shows us what it is like to have the author as centre of meaning disappear, the Bickerstaff papers make it clear what an artificial thing narrative authority is. I have discussed the controversy at length elsewhere,[3] and so will give only a summary of its implications here. What Bickerstaff's career demonstrates is that, if the right rhetorical moves are made by a narrator, readers will assent to the authority of the most patent fictions. This assent may be more a willing suspension of disbelief than a considered agreement, but it is scarcely less powerful for that. When the narrator takes on the position of the temperate individual author, readers are inclined to become gullible.

And this is what happens with Bickerstaff. While, I assume, few have ever actually believed in his biological existence, many have been inclined to trust his judgement. The first reason for this is that the *Predictions for the Year 1708* do not parody the language of astrology so much as translate it into the more authoritative register of Modern, reformed science. Bickerstaff proclaims his abhorrence of the bastardised and fraudulent populism his science has fallen into, in which William Andrews could (without apparent irony) predict for July 1708:

Some places may now be in a more setled posture than in some Months past, and some Friendship and Amity may appear amongst some People and Countries, formerly disaffected to one another: and there may be now (or not long since have been) many things in agitation in some places, for the composing of some National Controversies, perhaps some New Leagues, or Negotiations tending thereto: yet, War may still afflict some *Foreign* People, and Martial Actions *Eastward*, and in some other Parts of the World.[4]

Bickerstaff seeks to reform the corrupted science of judicial astrology into a Modern discourse of appropriate neutrality and exactness. This was merely to take astrologers at their word,[5] making their science conform to the canons of linguistic verification required by Sprat in his *History of the Royal-Society*, a 'close, naked, natural way of speaking; positive expressions; clear senses; a native easiness: bringing all things as near the Mathematical plainness as they can'.[6] While astrological prediction would not bear such precision (and came to look ridiculous in the parodic mirror held up to it by Bickerstaff), the discourse of plainness proved very convincing. As Neil Saccamano points out and Bickerstaff demonstrates, 'style fabricates the person of the author'.[7]

---

[3] Robert Phiddian, 'A Name to Conjure With: Games of Verification and identity in the Bickerstaff Controversy', *Reading Swift: Papers from the Second Münster Symposium on Jonathan Swift*, Richard H. Rodino and Hermann J. Real, eds. (Munich: Wilhelm Fink Verlag, 1993), pp. 141–50.

[4] *Extraordinary News from the Stars: Or, An Ephemeris for the Year 1708* (London, 1708), p. [21].

[5] See Bernard Capp, *English Almanacs, 1500–1800: Astrology and the Popular Press* (Ithaca: Cornell University Press, 1979), particularly ch. 5 (i), 'The Controversy over Religion' (pp. 131–44), and ch. 6, 'Astrology, Science and Medicine' (pp. 180–214). As it happens, Partridge's was one of the loudest voices for the scientific reform of astrology.

[6] Sprat, *The History of the Royal-Society*, p. 113.

[7] 'Authority and Publication: The Works of "Swift"', *ECent*, 25 (1984), 241–62; quote, 260.

This is also clear in *The Accomplishment of the First of Mr Bickerstaff's Predictions*, where we have only the personality of the anonymous but urbane narrator to trust. He exudes impartiality, wisdom and polite scepticism in a manner prophetically suggestive of Mr Spectator:

On his Death-Bed he declared himself a Nonconformist, and had a fanatick Preacher to be his spiritual Guide. After half an Hour's Conversation, I took my Leave, being almost stifled by the Closeness of the Room. I imagined he could not hold out long; and therefore withdrew to a little Coffee-House hard by, leaving a Servant at the House with Orders to come immediately, and tell me, as near as he could, the Minute when *Partrige* should expire, which was not above, two Hours after; when looking upon my Watch, I found it to be above five Minutes after Seven: By which it is clear, that Mr. *Bickerstaff* was mistaken almost four Hours in his Calculation. In the other Circumstances he was exact enough.[8]

Compared to his impressive combination of tact and circumstantial realism, Partridge's protestations of his own continued existence look shrill, canting, and dubious:

You may remember there was a Paper published predicting my Death on the 29th of *March* at Night 1708, and after the day was past, the same Villain told the World I was dead, and how I died; and that he was with me at the time of my death. I thank God, by whose Mercy I have my Being, that I am still alive, and (excepting my Age) as well as ever I was in my Life, as I was also at that 29th of *March*. And that Paper was said to be done by one *Bickerstaffe*, Esq; But that was a sham Name, it was done by an *Impudent Lying Fellow*. But his Predictions did not prove true: What will he say to excuse that? For the Fool had considered the *Star of my Nativity* as he said. Why the Truth is, he will be hard put to it to find a *Salvo* for his Honour. It was a bold Touch, and he did not know but it might prove true.[9]

The game played between discourse simulating integrity and brute existence is fascinating. Partridge's scarcely coherent bluster, with its spite and frustration apparent through a particularly inept attempt at magnanimity, is hardly a triumphant assertion of integrity. Furthermore, there were perfectly good grounds for not believing that this denial was Partridge's legitimate utterance. Almanac buyers were creatures of habit, and the Stationers' Company often kept a name running long after the astrologer had died.[10] The *Accomplishment*'s attractively credible author had nothing to gain from proclaiming a mere fact, whereas the proprietor of Partridge's name had a reputation and a market to protect. Indeed, the first reply to Bickerstaff, *Mr Partridge's Answer to Esquire Bickerstaff's Strange and Wonderful Predictions for the*

8 PW, II, p. 155.
9 Merlinus Liberatus: Being an Almanack for the Year of our Blessed Saviour's Incarnation 1709 (London, 1709), pp. [46–47].
10 In fact, this occurred with Partridge once he died in 1715 – almanacs continued to appear under Partridge's name for the rest of the century.

Year 1708, is clearly not by Partridge, which shows that print can take a name promiscuously without any guarantee of authenticity. So we are thrown back upon our resources as readers, and here the counterfeit appears to win because it works harder at simulating the proper sources of verification; viz. proper credentials and proper method. It is not hamstrung by any naive belief in its own existence.

The Swiftian point is that personality, however plausible, is no valid basis for textual authority. As we can see in the *Vindication of Isaac Bickerstaff, Esq;*, Bickerstaff begins to become unreliable when he attains *too much* personality rather than too little. He loses the impersonality necessary for authoritative utterance and slides by way of partiality into the hopeless solipsism which always defeats the projecting dreams of Swift's narrating fools. Thus the extravagant deconstruction of Partridge and his charlatan's discourse is meant to be accompanied by a gentler deconstruction of that wayward figment of the imagination, Bickerstaff, and his authenticating styles. The disintegrating narrator remarks that 'perhaps a Name can make an almanack, as well as it can sell one'.[11] Name, signature, reputation are all words for a false, personally 'verified' appearance of authority and authenticity. The parody erases these claims: Bickerstaff is as empty a sound as Partridge, or Steele, or Mr Spectator.

But that was not the lesson taken by the literary culture of 1708–9, for in it personality was in the ascendent. Authority based on the author as a private, psychologically and rhetorically coherent individual was on the way to becoming the central tenet of public language, and Bickerstaff played a not insignificant part in this development. Having started in the very marginal sphere of astrology, he became a general signifier of sense and judgement at the heart of Augustan culture. As author of *The Tatler*, he attained an unprecedented authority as he provided information, opinions, and canons of taste for all, and was generally believed merely on the strength of his plausible style. Yet even at Bickerstaff's first appearance, we can see the latent insubstantiality of any claim to personal integrity in print:

I can this Year produce but a Specimen of what I design for the Future; having employed the most part of my Time in adjusting and correcting the Calculations I

---

[11] Davis follows Faulkner's text of 1735 and thus prints this phrase only as a textual variant (*PW*, II, p. 288). It appears in the three early (1708) editions of the pamphlet that I have seen, and the original text is readily available to modern readers in *Jonathan Swift: Satires and Personal Writings*, William Alfred Eddy, ed. (London: Oxford University Press, 1932); *Jonathan Swift*, Angus Ross and David Woolley, eds. (Oxford: Oxford University Press, 1984); and *The Writings of Jonathan Swift*, Robert A. Greenberg and William Bowman Piper, eds. (New York and London: W. W. Norton, 1973). The differences between the 1708 and 1735 texts are quite significant and, while there is good reason to believe (as Davis clearly did) that the Faulkner text represents a final authorised version, for my purposes of studying a controversy as it occurred, the earlier text is clearly preferable.

made for some Years past, because I would offer nothing to the World of which I am not as fully satisfied as that I am now alive.[12]

We are generally inclined to trust authors who give oaths on their own lives – it is a powerful trope of sincerity – but, of course, Bickerstaff was not alive and never had been, so the power of this ostensibly impressive assurance of integrity is completely dispelled. The ramifications are more serious, however, because anybody who can master the style of personal authenticity can thus 'verify' the greatest frauds of fact or opinion. Indeed, this is one way of viewing the 'rise of the novel', especially the novel as practised by Defoe. In the anonymous medium of print, authority can seem to come from the circumstantial plausibility of the narrator, but it is only a trick of language and technology. If the voice is authentic personal communication, there is no reason not to assume that an unmediated 'I' is either lying or misguided by its own partiality – it could be the voice of a knave or a fool. And if the voice is a counterfeit there is no knowing what ulterior purposes might be being served. Either way, 'I am telling you...' is no grounds for trust in communication. Individual utterance is not inherently authoritative.

An unsuccessful infanticide: Swift at the birth of the author

It is another Pattern of this Answerer's fair dealing, to give us Hints that the Author is dead, and yet to lay the Suspicion upon somebody, I know not who, in the Country;...[13]

Whatever the ideology informing a particular parody, parody as a method is anti-authoritarian. It is (as they say in Houyhnhnmland) 'the thing which is not' – a text defining itself by *not* being its pre-text. It queries the grounds of discourses and demystifies their claims of self-contained validity by pointing in one direction to sources and in the other to implications. The apparent unity of a text is divided against itself, and its claim to authoritative utterance has the critical and deconstructive supplement of parody grafted on to it. The danger posed by this supplement is apparent even today in our fragmented and self-consciously pluralist age, but it becomes even more dramatic if we exercise our historical imagination to see it occurring in a society committed to authoritarian modes of thought. It is a systematic querying of a text's or discourse's terms of construction, and, to the extent that it demonstrates their artificiality, it renders those terms ironic; hence the text's appearance of unity and validity are placed under erasure. It is not only an erasure (or multiplication) of utterances, however, but also an

---

[12] *PW*, II, p. 143.
[13] *A Tale*, p. 16.

erasure (or multiplication) of utterers. Modern authority is centred on and generated by the modern author, whose unique combination of experience, expertise, genius, sincerity, and intentionality mediates the validity of her or his work. In previous chapters we have seen several ways in which Swiftian parody problematises this 'innocent' transfer of wisdom from author to audience, and now it is time to draw some conclusions.

Bickerstaff's birth was, as we have seen, little more than a series of unpredictable accidents, but the terms of its possibility are far more significant. It occurred at the right moment to stand as an ironic synecdoche for the birth of the author. Though fleshless, Bickerstaff incarnated canons of authorial integrity and originality which were coming into cultural history at the time. These canons subsequently became so dominant that they became invisible, and only in recent decades has the modernity and contingency of the idea that the author stands at the authoritative centre of her or his text been recognised. Roland Barthes, his attention focused on the author's end, historicises the beginning cavalierly:

The author is a modern figure, a product of our society insofar as, emerging from the Middle Ages with English empiricism, French rationalism and the personal faith of the Reformation, it discovered the prestige of the individual, of, as it is more nobly put, the 'human person'. It is thus logical that in literature it should be this positivism, the epitome and culmination of capitalist ideology, which has attached the greatest importance to the 'person' of the author.[14]

Michel Foucault is more specific:

The author-function does not affect all discourses in a universal and constant way...There was a time when the texts that we today call 'literary' (narratives, stories, epics, tragedies, comedies) were accepted, put into circulation, and valorised without any question about the identity of their author; their anonymity caused no difficulties since their ancientness, whether real or imagined, was regarded as a sufficient guarantee of their status...A reversal occurred in the seventeenth or eighteenth century...Literary discourses came to be accepted only when endowed with the author-function. We now ask of each poetic or fictional text: from where does it come, who wrote it, when, under what circumstances, or beginning with what design?[15]

'The seventeenth or eighteenth century' is not a particularly precise date, but it comfortably encompasses the period of restoration enterprise in Britain. Also obvious is the fact that Swiftian parody enters a disjunctive (and hostile) relationship with this slippage in authority from impersonality

[14] 'The Death of the Author', Image – Music – Text, pp. 142–43; Bruissement, pp. 61–62.
[15] 'What is an Author?', Textual Strategies: Perspectives in Post-Structuralist Criticism Josue Harari, ed. (Ithaca: Cornell University Press, 1979), pp. 141–60; quote, p. 149. The English translation is a substantially revised version of an essay which appeared in the Bulletin de la Société Français de Philosophie, 63 (1969).

to personality. Recalling a plurality of discourses, parody inevitably multiplies possible origins and creates plural identities at the supposedly unified signifying heart of texts. It deconstructs the characteristic monovalency on which faith in the 'author-function' depends.

Taking his lead from Foucault, and bringing us directly into the English and Swiftian contexts, Neil Saccamano seeks to flesh out Foucault's high level of generalisation with more empirical detail by tying the birth of the author to the ascendancy of print:

Whether or not the notion of the author emerged at a specifiable 'moment,' as Foucault suggests, it certainly derives from the same principle on which eighteenth-century philosophical psychology, latitudinarianism, political liberalism, and aesthetics are based – the principle of individualization, which places the discrete subject at the center of all inquiries. What should be stressed here is that the conception of the author as the source of a work's meaning arises in conjunction with the conception of the author as the producer and proprietor of a printed text. With the transition from circulating manuscripts among a courtly audience to publishing these works for a growing reading public, the author comes not only to exercise power over the meaning of his work but also to claim legal rights to his printed copy. The Statute of Anne of 1709, which was introduced and passed primarily at the request of book-sellers seeking to control piracy, juridically defined for the first time the author as a person with rights to his literary property. Thus as works began to be considered the predicate and property of individual authors, ancientness in itself could no longer guarantee value and meaning. Instead of transmitting venerable commonplaces of universal wisdom, books express the opinions of individuals who become authors through publication. In this modern view of authorship and the work, the evaluation of a text must begin with the name of the author.[16]

Print and a name are the essential conditions of Bickerstaff's dissemination – print is the opaque and unreliable medium in which his individuality and authenticity can appear to be reliably figured. The style is the man. Elsewhere, the Swiftian presentation of the author openly deconstructs this ascendant form of authority, figuring narrators less reliably by entertaining multiple and fragmented styles. This only makes the satiric animus clearer. Swift is running counter to a literary–historical movement identified by Martha Woodmansee:

Moments of inspiration move, in the course of time, to the center of reflection on the nature of writing. And as they are increasingly credited to the writer's own genius, they transform the writer into a unique individual uniquely responsible for a unique product. That is, from a (mere) vehicle of preordained truths – truths as ordained either by universal human agreement or by some higher agency – the *writer* becomes an *author* (Lat. *auctor*, originator, founder, creator).[17]

---

[16] 'Authority and Publication', pp. 247–48.
[17] 'The Genius and the Copyright: Economic and Legal Conditions of the Emergence of the "Author"', *ECS*, 17 (1983–84), 425–48; quote, 429.

The metaphor of inspiration is particularly apt, pointing to this statement's unconscious status as a description of the messianic role claimed (but not earned) by the narrator of *A Tale*. It also returns us to another important parodic potential in Foucault's portrait of the 'author-function', the issue of origin and originality. Here Foucault demonstrates the contingency as well as the novelty of the assumption that the originator of a text both determines its meanings and is somehow retrievable, by stating the questions we 'naturally' ask: 'We now ask of each poetic or fictional text: from where does it come, who wrote it, when, under what circumstances, or beginning with what design?' This distances us from 'common-sense' critical manœuvres so that we can recognise the terms of their arbitrariness and identify the centrality of a sense of origin to our construction of literary meaning. The 'author-function' needs to have a discrete and procreative history; a text now needs to come from somewhere (and someone) in particular, to be the legitimate product of a historically specific act of creation. As Foucault makes clear, these are not the eternal terms of reference. Language always looks beyond itself for validity – that is the point at which parody and deconstruction strike – and at this historical moment it was turning meaning into a matter of private intellectual property. Thomas Docherty notes a significant semantic shift in the resonance of the word 'original':

> The very word 'original', of course, undergoes some semantic change at this time. Whereas it meant 'with reference to an anterior origin', and thus 'old-fashioned', it now begins to echo with its more contemporary meanings of 'new', 'novel', 'a departure from the norms of the past'.[18]

He then procedes to specify 'this time' by quoting an example from Congreve's *The Way of the World* (1700) where both senses of the word are active. The mystical source of meaning is shifting from immemorial truth to individual productivity.

Thus we have given a brief genealogy of the birth of the author. It will surprise no reader of this book to discover that I consider this birth in its English manifestation to be a major restoration enterprise, a swerve away from fractured unities of authority towards more cautiously conceived sites of authenticity. Swift is clearly a hostile midwife at this birth, demonstrating that the child is unreliable, falsifiable, and unverifiable. He shows that authors, far from being trustworthy centres of signification, can be fools, knaves, and shreds of artifice. Furthermore, an important lesson of Swiftian parody is that authors do not invent language and consequently cannot control the filiations of the words and discourses they are said to create. Though the narrators try to give the impression that they are using lan-

---

[18] *On Modern Authority: The Theory and Condition of Writing, 1500 to the Present Day* (Brighton: Harvester, 1987), pp. 219–20.

guage to express their potent and integrated selves, it is clear that language is constructing and disintegrating them. The selves which masquerade as the origins of authority in their texts are shown to have their origin in uses, ruses, and abuses of public discourse, so that the medium becomes the source and the source becomes a product. Finally, the intervention of print between reader and author multiplies the difficulties of the transfer of intellectual property. The idea of the authoritative author relies on the unstated assumption of a degree of residual orality which is entirely (and emptily) mythical in print. It seems natural for us to talk (!) of an author 'speaking' to us through her or his text, but this employs a metaphor, and a problematic one at that. Print makes no sound and betrays no identity, yet from its silence we construct a personality whose notional integrity shapes and authorises the implications of the marks on the page. Swiftian parody interrogates the terms of this metaphor and the silence it covers by multiplying centres of utterance in a single text. It becomes impossible to know who is 'speaking' and possible to posit a number of authorising voices even in the same group of words.

Clearly, the 'author-function' is being put under erasure in Swiftian parody, being marked as the hole in the heart of the modern textuality. Personal integrity and presence are shown to be abject failures as sites for totalising the meanings of texts. It does not follow from this, however, that Swiftian parody is entirely deconstructive. It is a commonplace of criticism, voiced most pungently, perhaps, by F. R. Leavis, that Swift's art 'is essentially negative...The intensity is purely destructive'.[19] However, while the parodies' immediate effect is obviously emetic, that is not the same as saying they are directionless or blankly monodirectional. Doctors, it is normally assumed, do not purge patients gratuitously, but rather with the intent of returning them to health, and the rationale of Augustan satire suggests just such a purpose of moral and cultural healing. Let us suspend judgement for a moment and try to imagine what a state of textual health at the end of the process begun by parodic diagnosis might look like. In other words, are any images of authority privileged in Swift's work?

Thackeray, Leavis, Rawson, and the rest of the negativists have their point, of course. It is much easier to see what Swift is against than what he is for. I do not intend, however, to place the full weight of Swift's personality and biography behind a single collection of opinions. My less ambitious purpose is to identify perspectives of authentic utterance within the parody, idiolects whose authenticity can at least be *argued* to be exempt from ironic erasure. The rhetoric of bourgeois, proprietorial self is deconstructed, but

---

[19] 'The Irony of Swift', *Scrutiny*, 2 (1934), 364–78; reprinted in *Swift: A Collection of Critical Essays*, Ernest Tuveson, ed. (Englewood Cliffs: Prentice-Hall, 1964), pp. 15–29; quote, p. 17.

two other possible sites of textual validity are at least arguably proposed, and attain some partial authority. Paradoxical though the coupling is, the two partially affirmed grounds of authenticity are the impersonal voice of properly constituted authority and the entirely personal idiolect of aristocratic wit. The one mediates institutional presence and is entirely devoid of irony, while the other mediates a freemasonry of readerly and writerly talent among 'Men of Wit and Tast'[20] whose mode is pure irony without content.

This is a Swift as preacher and jester kind of distinction,[21] but I want to keep the terms of that distinction as far as possible in the realm of textual rather than biographical meaning. In my discussion of the *Argument against Abolishing Christianity* I discussed the way these two discourses suggest themselves, though finally inadequately, as meta-texts which might solve the essay's impasses, and it seems to me that they enshrine *potentially* legitimate registers of language in Swiftian parody in ways personalised, Modern, projecting discourses do not. Both claim to be pure forms of language, with unproblematic sources and resonances unmarked by innovations. From the point of view of stylistics, this is just an egregious (and enabling) mystification of the terms of their own construction, but this eternal hermeneutic 'fact' should not be allowed to obscure an important difference of kind. Parody, like deconstruction, decentres discourses, but it by no means follows that a particular parody (or corpus of parodies) will therefore decentre all discourses equally. If parody can be allowed to have any practical or ideological function, and obviously it does on occasion, the possibility must be entertained that some discourses (patterns of language use) can be privileged in it. Furthermore, as parody is a reflective medium rather than a monological utterance, it is possible that it can reflect positively on (or towards) multiple discourses. These need not be homogeneous so, while the voice of the instrument of undivided authority is not the same as that of aristocratic *jouissance*, both can be figured in a parodic text as ideals. Their cohabitation will necessarily entail a degree of irony, which will render either ideal problematic to an extent, but it is not pointless to attempt an assessment of the traces each leaves.

The first image of legitimate discourse in Swiftian parody is the austere and authorised language of the preacher, advocated in the *Letter to a Young Gentleman, Lately Entered into Holy Orders* and practised in the *Sermons*. It is a rhetoric of potent and impersonal institutional presence where language is simple and monovalent, conveying precepts to the readers with undivided authority. Here language should not betray the writer's identity or preoccupations because it comes from the top of the chain of obedience, which is to say from God, via his earthly embodiments, the church or the state. It is

---

[20] *A Tale*, p. 20.
[21] Steele, *Jonathan Swift: Preacher and Jester* explores the potential of this distinction most extensively.

unproblematic in the strictest sense of not being open to criticism, because it enshrines a rigid subordination of reader or hearer to text. In theory, it is the tongue of Houyhnhnm ratiocination which unavoidably compels consent, but in the postlapsarian world it is the synecdoche of God, requiring the assent of obedient and self-effacing faith. Ideally it is without irony and beyond criticism, strictly monological in something very like Bakhtin's sense of the term. It is a fantasy of absolutism, only partially erased in the texture of Swiftian parody by the inconvenient fact that its immediate presence is suggested only by its absence, by its rigorous and obvious exclusion from the parodic texts. The discourses parodied inhabit a public sphere which is flawed by definition. The legitimate, unitary discourse cannot enter this sphere because it cannot be mingled with the languages of error, or it loses its purity. Consequently, its validity can only be reflected by its absence from the deconstruction of error. Though this is a tenuous argument, it is not a wholly invalid one, and it allows for the claimability (at a biographical/historical level) of Swift's carnivalesque texts for the sober purposes of the excoriation of vice and the inculcation (by reflection) of virtue.

The biographical paradox, which can be entertained in parody as in life, is that Swift also wanted to be able to claim his writing as the work of an aristocratic wit, a kind of contentless and vertiginous irony appreciated by the brilliant and the talented. This is something very like textual freeplay, except in that it is highly exclusive concerning the players. There is a fugitive sense in which Swiftian parody is dedicated, as Stendhal dedicated *La Chartreuse de Parme*, 'to the happy few'. Base illiterate scribblers and mechanical pedants, for example, cannot hope to understand and need not apply for membership of this club. The ideal of this discourse is conversation rather than script, and print is an almost unforgivably ignoble field of utterance for it.[22] Exponents of this deliberately casual, unsystematic, and elegant discourse include Temple and Shaftesbury, and it is clear that Swift's social and temperamental conditions place him in a position of creative tension rather than simple assent to this aristocratic playfulness. However, such a discourse of social and intellectual exclusivity, retaining (as it does) some of the 'authentic' residual orality of conversation, offers one important (and at least partially privileged) perspective for the hostile anti-typographic parody which occurs.[23] From this perspective, print and its characteristic tropes of discourse, form, and identity inhabit a bastardised public sphere which

---

[22] See Kernan, *Printing Technology, Letters and Samuel Johnson*, and Love, *Scribal Publication* on the persistence into the eighteenth century of the amateur and aristocratic ideals of manuscript circulation and casual production, defined against the growing print-based independence of the professional writer personified by Samuel Johnson. Terry Castle, 'Why the Houyhnhnms Don't Write: Swift, Satire, and the Fear of the Text', *Essays in Literature*, 7 (1980), 31–44, considers the issues of orality's clash with print at a more abstract level.

[23] Clive Probyn expands on this in 'Swift and Typographic Man'.

threatens the integrity of the aristocratic sphere of conversation, manuscripts, and patronage. The aristocratic author never discloses her or his
identity, publishing anonymously and 'involuntarily'. The purpose is com-
munion with like-minded souls rather than dispute or the dissemination of
information. In fact, this is very close to being a poetic of pleasure, of the
silent laughter of total irony.

Authorised, preacherly discourse is, of course, hostile to such nearly-liber-
tine pleasantry, but it does share aristocratic conversation's anti-typographic
animus. It, too, relies on a residual orality, though of a different kind, which
mediates prescriptive presence through the voice of the priest or the
monarch. This is an impersonal and objective voice that depends entirely
on the office of the utterer and not at all on his or her individual identity.
Moreover, the decentred authority of modern print (where meaning
becomes a form of private property dependent on the author-function)
allows for a proliferation of textual and discursive possibilities towards
which the preacherly ideal of a small, clean, obedient world is deeply hostile. Hence print can be seen to attack both textual ideals hinted at in
Swiftian parody, and the new identity of the author-function is, though for
different reasons, a false centre of signification for both.

The problem, of course, is that all this is not enough to stop the rot of
irony in Swiftian parody. I can claim (I do claim) that preacherly instruction, a rhetoric of unified presence that is only discoverable in the texts in
the faintest traces and the most rigorous interpretation of erasures that
amount almost to absences, is a goal of the parodies. However, they are not
(or not completely) self-effacing in this pious and simple way. The claims
made for *A Tale* in the 'Apology for the &c.' are not finally convincing:

There are three or four other Passages which prejudiced or ignorant Readers have
drawn by great Force to hint at ill Meanings, as if they glanced at some Tenets in
Religion; in answer to all which, the Author solemnly protests he is entirely
Innocent, and never has had once in his Thoughts that any thing he said would in
the least be capable of such Interpretations, which he will engage to deduce full as
fairly from the most innocent Book in the World.

I believe there is not a Person in *England* who can understand that Book, that ever
imagined it to have been any thing else, but to expose the Abuses and Corruptions
in Learning and Religion.[24]

These assertions are not simply misleading lies attempting to cover infidelity. There is partial truth in them, but only a very tactical part of the
truth, because they attempt to obscure parody's dangerous supplement. It
appears that Swift does little to suppress or direct the deconstructive playful-

ness released in the process of parody in his more anarchic works such as *A Tale*. Furthermore, even this case of special pleading admits that, for meaning to be discovered, the language needs to be converted by those 'who can understand that Book', which rather restricts its capacity to achieve a sermon-like didacticism. These readers who understand are like the aristocratic few who converse sympathetically with the author, but their image is distorted as well. Here they are presented as wise censors of morality who recognise the author's good intentions and approve his success in achieving them, yet the judicious censors figured by the text also require the converting imaginations of wits. There is a series of disjunctions here: even if we accept that the text's aims belong to piety, its fabric belongs to the discourse of wits, and, to complicate matters further, its component discourses are taken (and parodied) from the textual manifestations of error. This initial engagement with error makes it hard to maintain a positive decorum – it is very difficult (indeed, not finally possible) to discover a solving perspective within or without the parodies. The logics of the preacher and the aristocratic wit are not thought through or rendered compatible, and they only leave traces of authority.

We can, therefore, be more confident of the negative lesson (the deconstruction of the author-function) than of any positive construction of authentic utterance. We can see the hostility even in this passage from the 'Apology', where the narrator (whose identity with Swift should not be exaggerated) slips into the dubious rhetoric of the author-function. He constitutes himself as the centre of his text and declares 'the Author solemnly protests he is entirely Innocent, and never has had once in his Thoughts that any thing he said would in the least be capable of such Interpretations'. This sounds like protesting too much and, though I take the uneasiness to derive in this instance from anxiety rather than conscious irony, it illustrates the emptiness and counterfeitability of the trope of originating self. The novel trope of self draws much of Swift's parodic fire as he attempts to murder the infant author-function in the cradle. This should not, however, be allowed to obscure the important concurrent facts that it is origins and originality in general that parody deconstructs and that it was origins and originality that were the chief desiderata of restoration enterprises. We are about to turn to *A Tale*, which can be described as a comic extravaganza based on the confusion and simulation of origins and their filiations. It is important, therefore, to recognise the significance of this issue at the literary and historical levels.

The logic of reading assumes that discourse comes from somewhere, that utterance has an origin the markings of which are apparent and authentic. The validity of this origin is assumed rather than justified or explained, and often it is allowed a degree of fecund mystery. These were the sort of timelessly legitimate roots restoration enterprises were attempting to (re-) establish, and it is just these notionally valid and unified roots (and their consequent univocal discourses) which Swiftian parody managed to divide, demystify, and deconstruct. A self-consciously secondary form of language, Swiftian parody points to the fallibility and plurality of sources in general, as well as undertaking an extensive critique of the contradictions underlying the nascent author-function in particular. Parody is language after Babel, and it insists that all other discourses which attempt to obscure their fellowship in this linguistic fall be exposed as artificial constructions of validity rather than its natural emanations. It is the distorted image of imitation, for it enacts the activation, frustration, fracture, and entanglement of attempts to return to authentic origins. The origin is erased while the provisional centre (the narrator) is rendered plural and remote (eccentric). Even so, there is a final twist for, thus decentred and deconstructed, the Swiftian author dies writing.

6

Entrance to *A Tale of A Tub*

Whether a Tincture of Malice in our Natures, makes us fond of furnishing every bright Idea with its Reverse...[1]

How can we begin to make sense of *A Tale of A Tub*? If all else fails, and it generally does, we might try reading the instructions:

The most accomplisht Way of using Books at present, is twofold: Either first, to serve them as some Men do *Lords*, learn their *Titles* exactly, and then brag of their Acquaintance. Or Secondly, which is indeed the choicer, the profounder, and politer Method, to get a thorough Insight into the *Index*, by which the whole Book is governed and turned, like *Fishes* by the *Tail*. For, to enter the Palace of Learning at the *great Gate*, requires an Expence of Time and Forms; therefore Men of much Haste and little Ceremony, are content to get in by the *Back-Door*. (p. 145)

There are problems with this as a key to all mysteries, both in the incongruity of its appearing almost exactly at the volume's centre,[2] and in the clear satirical comment it makes on Modern ignorance and superficiality. The obvious implication is that opening at either end is a highly irresponsible way of 'using Books'. However, *A Tale* pre- and dis-figures so many interpretative strategies that no entrance into the text can claim complete innocence, and the '*Back-Door*' has at least an ironic authority. So let us employ the second way, 'which is indeed the choicer, the profounder, and politer Method', and observe 'the wise man's *Rule* of *Regarding the End*' (p. 145). To commence at the end is an appropriate enough technique to apply to a book so paradoxically obsessed with origins, because *A Tale* labours intently to subvert narrative sequence and integrity. It exposes the perversion of the apostolic succession in religion, it enacts learning's loss of connection to the authoritative and authenticating

---

[1] *A Tale*, p. 158; references in parentheses in this and subsequent chapters will refer to this text.

[2] In Guthkelch and Smith's edition on p. 145 of 289 pages of text and in Angus Ross and David Woolley's (Jonathan Swift, *A Tale of a Tub and Other Works*, (Oxford: Oxford University Press, 1986)) on p. 70 of 141 pages; these figures do not include editorial material such as introductions, appendices, and indices. In the early editions the placement of this passage is less precisely central but still close: in editions 1–4 (1704–5) it appears on pp. 138–39 of 322 pages, and in the fifth edition (1710) on pp. 150–1 of 344 pages. It is not at all clear that Swift had extensive editorial control over any edition of *A Tale*, but this passage is always going to be near the centre of the book unless the order of the parts is altered.

sources of ancient knowledge, and finally it sheds doubt on the possibility of intelligent communication. Michael Seidel makes a similar point: 'In all respects, the *Tale* is about satirically weakened lines of descent: fathers to sons, ancients to moderns…The putative subject of the *Tale* is the inability to transmit donated value across historical and generational boundaries.'[3] If anything, this underestimates the impact of lost origins, and the way they infiltrate the book's textuality and parodic logic at every level. The lines of descent are not only weakened; they are routinely broken.

In *A Tale*'s discursive world, language has lost touch with the creating word of Genesis and John. To the post-modern reader, this is an obvious fact, scarcely worth mentioning, but in the late Stuart context the idea was shocking. Within *A Tale*'s uprooted textuality, the true origins of authentic utterance have been lost, so we are left with few options but to be good, obedient Moderns and turn to the last words, forgetting for the moment that we have learnt this trick from the middle of the book. With indices, appendices, glossaries, notes, advertisements, and other necessary supplements to this bewildering text, modern scholars have obscured the ending which we are here told is the '*Tail*' which turns the '*Fish*'. In its early editions the last words of *A Tale*, apart from the printer's conventional 'FINIS', are the last words of *The Mechanical Operation of the Spirit*, an apocalyptic message which runs, '*Pray, burn this Letter as soon as it comes to your Hands*' (p. 289).[4]

Of course, this might be taken to be merely a play on the epistolary convention *The Mechanical Operation* parodies so woodenly, but in a book so aware of its physical printedness, it would be a brave reader who would insist that no further meaning is available. Swift was certainly aware of the inflammable potential of texts, as his comment in a letter to Pope in 1731 suggests: 'I write pamphlets and follies merely for amusement, and when they are finished, or I grow weary in the middle, I cast them into the fire, partly out of dislike, and chiefly because I know they will signify nothing.'[5] This is only a casual coincidence. However, *A Tale* goes to such lengths to thwart both its own declared aims and the best efforts of its readers that there can be no logical bar to treating *The Mechanical Operation*'s concluding phrase as a final trope of self-destruction, neatly spliced with an image of masturbatory procreation.[6] The book begs to be consumed by flames rather than read by readers, and it is a case of

[3] *Satiric Inheritance: Rabelais to Sterne* (Princeton: Princeton University Press, 1979), p. 169.
[4] I have seen copies of the first five editions (1704–10) and miscellaneous later editions printed in Swift's lifetime. Not until the pirated Dutch edition of 1720 entitled *Miscellaneous Works, Comical & Diverting: By T. R. D. J. S. D. O. P. I. I.* (for full bibliographical detail, see Guthkelch and Smith, *A Tale of a Tub*, p. lxx.) is there any divergence from this exact typographical form, and the original conclusion remained standard at least until the 1750s.
[5] *Corr.*, IV, p. 194.
[6] As *The Mechanical Operation* has never to my knowledge (and at least not during Swift's lifetime, according to Guthkelch and Nichol Smith's 'List of Editions', pp. lxv-lxxvii) been published separately from the other elements of the volume (though a couple of pirated editions have changed the order), it is not unreasonable to attribute to its last words a deliberate ultimacy in the whole enterprise.

'rather than', not 'subsequent to', for the words of the request do not allow for even one reading: '*as soon as it comes to your Hands*' means immediately, before the act of reading. This ultimate twist of self-laceration is a trap sprung in several ways and an emblem of the reader's plight.

Obviously, the dramatic statement '*Pray, burn this Letter as soon as it comes to your Hands*' operates under several erasures that undermine the positiveness of its apocalyptic tone. The heaviest of these has already been mentioned – its hollowness in its immediate context in *The Mechanical Operation* as an epistolary convention in a treatise that is only posing as a letter and leaves off even that pretence for most of its body: 'AND now, Sir, having dispatch'd what I had to say of Forms, or of Business, let me intreat, you will suffer me to proceed upon my Subject; and to pardon me, if I make no farther Use of the Epistolary Stile, till I come to conclude' (p. 263). Furthermore, within the logic of the convention, this request does not express a sincere desire for privacy, being little more than a trope of modesty. When measured against the monstrous appetite for self-promotion displayed by the hack-like narrator of the volume, this seems little more than a transparent ploy. Finally, even if we accept the words as sincere and resonant utterance, they remain a last exclamation of a lunatic contriver of texts in whom we have entirely lost faith. Thus we can erase the self-immolating artefact's final message. It is more interesting, however, to stress that message and see how, from its tyrannical position of ultimacy, it erases all that has gone before it. It is particularly disconcerting for the responsible reader, who has started at the beginning and worked her or his way through to the end, to find that the text she or he has just read is so dangerous that it should have been burnt before a page had been turned. An explanation of this revisionary moment might be that it illustrates Swift's satirical point about Modern writing, which is that we read books which should have been burnt before we could have read them. The problem with this is that the barb's reference cannot be so innocently reflected in a parodic mirror as to apply only in general terms to the worthless Modernism *A Tale* parodies. It cannot shake off its specific malediction of the preceding text, a text which is generally recognised as the masterpiece of Swift's literary youth. We are being told to burn the book itself as well as what it parodically represents, but if we had done this at first we would have destroyed the book that teaches us to destroy the books that are truly detrimental to our intellectual well-being (including the one we have just read) and hence we fall into a *mise en abîme* which renders the text in our hands logically insupportable.

A further irony lies in the fact that the irresponsible Modern readers figured in our opening quotation will have avoided this impasse by the natural exercise of their intellectual sloth. The first group will have read only the title and will have been unaffected by whatever dangers follow; the second will have gone straight to the back in search of an index only to find the inflammatory instruction, and can be assumed to have consigned their copies to the fire. By a trick of internal logic, these can claim to be ideal readers and readings, and the methodical readers who search every word for meaning can be depicted as violators of the text. And yet, if we eat of the forbidden fruit, the text demands the closest and most imaginative attention. What the emblem captures so well is that faithful attention, as much as any wayward unravelling of discourses and meanings, remains radically anomalous and fundamentally transgressive. There is no solid ground on which we can set up as interpreters which is not cut out from under us somewhere in the text, and it is hopeless to try to escape the fallen nature of interpretation in such a context. *A Tale* has escaped systematic explanation not because it employs a fiendishly difficult system which we have yet to isolate, but because it centres on contradictions, paradoxes, indeterminacies, reflections, shatterings, and redoublings. Here precisely is the 'Tincture of Malice' in its nature which makes it 'fond of furnishing every bright Idea with its Reverse' (p. 158). It transgresses itself, attacking itself from the margins and misaligning its parts, and throughout it maintains a hostility (sometimes amused, sometimes savage) towards its readers whom it will not let rest assured. The book's self-lacerating nature can be seen again near its other end, in the 'Preface':

I have observ'd some Satyrists to use the Publick much at the Rate that Pedants do a naughty Boy ready Hors'd for Discipline: First expostulate the Case, then plead the Necessity of the Rod, from great Provocations, and conclude every Period with a Lash. Now, if I know any thing of Mankind, these Gentlemen might very well spare their Reproof and Correction: For there is not, through all Nature, another so callous and insensible a Member as the *World's Posteriors*, whether you apply to it the *Toe* or the *Birch*. Besides, most of our late Satyrists seem to lye under a sort of Mistake, that because Nettles have a Prerogative to Sting, therefore all *other Weeds* must do so too. (p. 48)

A Tale does all these things, of course. It vindicates its aggression, lashes calloused and insensible posteriors, flings thistles and many other weeds, and generally rejoices in its helplessness either to control itself or the world around it. It even indulges so far in self-annihilation as to have the narrator describe himself as 'having neither a Talent nor an Inclination for Satyr' (p. 53) and proclaim the text 'so elaborate and useful a Discourse without one grain of Satyr intermixt' (p. 48). The text repudiates itself in so many ways that the job of interpretation (at least in anything remotely resembling an objective sense) is rendered impossible, even while it is most urgently required.

The monitory image of the Modern 'True Critick' hovers over all our hermeneutic endeavours to such an obvious and invasive extent that any criticism of this text is placed under erasure. It is manifest that we cannot 'solve' *A Tale*, but that does not mean that we cannot read it. I propose to interpret openly, to seek to exercise meanings rather than to determine meaning. Thus, rather than search for the key to all mysteries, I will commit the enabling misprisions necessary to allow us to wander usefully in the fertile fields of Error. The meaning of Error which I hope to activate is not the natural one of being simply wrong, but closer to its etymological root in the Latin *errare*, to wander. This allows for creative indeterminacy, for unguidedness as well as misguidedness. I do not expect to escape from *A Tale*'s complexities and contradictions into some privileged field of certainty, and so, as a sign of this, I take my cue for each section of exposition from a statement in the text that ironises the process I am about to undertake.[7] I have started by finding great significance in *'Regarding the End'* and will proceed from here to try to imagine the commonplace book of fragments from which *A Tale*'s parodic fabric is constituted. In the next chapter, I will discover irreconcilable differences of interpretation for a passage in the 'Digression on Madness' all 'manifestly deduceable from the Text' (p. 185), and will further discuss this book whose author commissions the bookseller to father on 'which ever of the Wits shall happen to be that Week in the Vogue' (p. 207) as an orphaned text. In the last chapter, I will attempt to describe *A Tale*'s anomalous relationship to Swift's career and self-image. The analysis will be self-parodying but not, I hope, useless, as I try to participate in this prismatic text rather than to escape it.

The pre-textuality of *A Tale of A Tub*

I believe one of the Authors Designs was to set curious Men a hunting thro' Indexes, and enquiring for Books out of the common Road. (p. 187)

As I indicated in the previous section, *A Tale* is pre-eminently about origins and the frustration of their filiation to the present. In this it shares the concerns of its age for patterns of restoration and legitimacy. The word 'original' and its variants recur constantly throughout the text (appearing forty times) and the text is full of fantastic fabrications of authoritative origin and pedigree.[8] Furthermore, it is also a commonplace book spinning out of control, (almost) every phrase of which points to an origin outside the present text in other discourses. Obviously, however, the relationship between these origins and their manifestation is not a simple one. Connections are constructed by fabrication, ridicule, fiction, misprision, fantasy, misunderstanding, blindness, and distortion. In short, the relation-

[7] This is not an original technique. It has been used often for articles and most concertedly in Frederik N. Smith, *Language and Reality in Swift's A Tale of a Tub* (Columbus: Ohio State University Press, 1979).
[8] See Harold D. Kelling and Cathy Lynn Preston, *A KWIC Concordance to Jonathan Swift's A Tale of a Tub, The Battle of the Books, and A Discourse Concerning the Mechanical Operation of the Spirit, a Fragment* (New York: Garland Publishing, 1984), pp. 582–83. In a text as miscellaneous as *A Tale*, this concordance (or 'Index') is an indispensable tool which I have had recourse to on many occasions. I would like to record my heartfelt thanks to the editors and publishers for making it available.

ship between the text and its multiplicity of origins is parody. When, for example, the authentic meaning of a word is searched for in the seminal authority of an etymology, only a succession of puns is discovered. The way the bench is excluded from the company of oratorical engines shows this:

Neither can the *Bench* it self, tho raised to a proper Eminency, put in a better Claim, whatever its Advocates insist on. For if they please to look into the original Design of its Erection, and the Circumstances or Adjuncts subservient to that Design, they will soon acknowledge the present Practice exactly correspondent to the Primitive Institution, and both to answer the Etymology of the Name, which in the *Phoenician* Tongue is a Word of great Signification, importing, if literally interpreted, *The Place of Sleep*; but in common Acceptation, *A Seat well bolster'd and cushion'd, for the Repose of old and gouty Limbs: Senes ut in otia tuta recedant.* (pp. 56–57)

Though 'primarily' a barb aimed at the law in general and judges in particular, this parody of a search for an authentic source catches the tone and mood of restoration enterprise in its language as well as its form. As with all disputes on the constitution, it claims 'to look into the original Design'; the Anglican discourse of primitive christianity is precisely recalled in the triumphant discovery that 'the present Practice [is] exactly correspondent to the Primitive Institution'; and the new philological scholarship resonates comically through the mock etymology and definition in the passage's final clauses. The original meanings of words are privileged as having some sort of luminous significance, yet they are received only through an extremely unreliable dissemination. It is along these disseminating threads of error and obfuscation that the parody runs, and it runs freely.

In *A Tale*, more than anywhere else in Swift's writing or eighteenth-century writing at large (except, perhaps, *Tristram Shandy*), the author renounces property rights over meaning and the filiation of meaning through prior texts. Even in the *Battle of the Books*, for example, the mock heroic style operates as a (fairly) stable structure for parody. It provides a valued discourse wherein the virtues or pretended virtues of the combatant books/authors can be placed and measured with reasonable confidence. What is truly heroic in style and conduct remains unscathed while only those with baseless pretensions to heroic grandeur find their faces reflected in the mirror of satire. The catch is that we are probably among them. An equal and opposite interpretative bracing occurs in the *Abstract* of Collins' *Discourse of Free-thinking*, where the text parodied is treated as patently perverse and beneath contempt. We can be confident that, whoever and whatever else is drawn into the parodic ridicule, the primary targets remain Collins' text and the programme it advocates. In *A Tale*, we can never be so sure where we stand.

A working model of *A Tale of A Tub*'s pre-textuality

There are many ways of engaging in *A Tale*'s instability of signification, several of which we will pursue in later sections. However, the most conservative method of literary scholarship, the search for sources, remains a very useful strategy for the elucidation of this text. *A Tale* revels in the 'pre-loved' status of language, and a systematic approach to its pre-textuality is indispensable to reading it as parody. The textuality informing the book is profuse and the divisions within it are extremely fluid, so I do not claim that this model is either comprehensive or definitive, but something like it is necessary. I suggest that there are three kinds of pre-text for *A Tale*: Ancients, good Moderns, and bad Moderns.[9] Given the complexities of Swift's cultural affiliations and the alterity of the learned culture of the late seventeenth century, these terms are not self-explanatory. Indeed, they require careful explanation before they become much use to us.

By Ancients I do not mean merely the classical writers of Greece and Rome who, in fact, exert an extremely distant normative influence on *A Tale*. Rather, I mean the accrued moral and literary wisdom of the ages, a fusing of orthodox and aristocratic traditions in wit and learning. This stems from a sense of (or, more darkly, a perceived need for) received cultural authority, authorising certain messages and forms of expression, marking all others as innovation and error. The discussion in previous chapters of restoration enterprises and their underlying anxious desire to rediscover and reassert foundations feeds into this cultural preoccupation and the form it takes in late Stuart England. The archetypal authoritative text in this sense is the Bible, for it has absolute prescriptive validity. However, there is not a big book to be made in a study of Swift's use of the Bible.[10] If its presence is to be felt in *A Tale* (and Swiftian parody at large), it is as an absence, an audible erasure of authentic utterance countering the errant excess of the discourses being deconstructed. Scripture appears as a dead (a murdered) letter, as the will of the father in the allegory. It is undeniably true but closed and silent, imprisoned by the interpretation of those for whom its chaste dictates are too inconvenient. This inscrutable, unexpounded

---

[9] The important sources are the Guthkelch and Nichol Smith edition of *A Tale*; Miriam Kosh Starkman, *Swift's Satire on Learning in A Tale of a Tub* (Princeton: Princeton University Press, 1950); Phillip Harth, *Swift and Anglican Rationalism: The Religious Background of A Tale of a Tub* (Chicago: University of Chicago Press, 1961); Joseph M. Levine, *The Battle of the Books: History and Literature in the Augustan Age* (Ithaca: Cornell University Press, 1991); and Kenneth Craven, *Jonathan Swift and the Millennium of Madness: The Information Age in Swift's A Tale of a Tub* (Leiden: E. J. Brill, 1992). *A Catalogue of Books belonging to Dr Jonathan Swift, Dean of St Patrick's, Dublin, Aug. 19. 1715*, William LeFanu, ed. (Cambridge: Cambridge University Library, 1988) is highly suggestive as well, but altogether a blunter instrument, as we cannot know exactly when Swift bought (or otherwise received) the books there listed. Unfortunately, we lack what would be the most important book-list of all, an accurate description of Sir William Temple's library.

[10] Sixty-eight pages, to be exact: Beaumont, *Swift's Use of the Bible*.

will/testament/Bible symbolises the place of positive teaching in *A Tale*: it is presumed to be simple and obvious, but it remains unexplained, outside the discourses of the text.[11]

The 'Ancients' who inform the parody with normative comic values and rationales are of quite a different kind. In the first place, most of them are not ancient in the strict literary historical sense. *A Tale* belongs most naturally among the great comic texts of the European Renaissance, more particularly in the tradition of paradox. It is a praise of folly, a Menippean satire, a comic scourge of overproud seriousness, to be placed beside the writings of Erasmus, Rabelais, Thomas More, Montaigne, Cervantes, Burton, and Thomas Browne; it explores the comedy of human intellectual ambition thwarted by human limitation and exposed as delusion.[12] These 'Ancients' do not supply Swift with verbal material for parody to any great extent – they are sources for moral and intellectual stances, perspectives on how to understand folly rather than fools drawn into the fabric of ridicule. In short, they are not parodied so much as imitated, and they are imitated only in the loose sense of imitating the spirit.

A very different and rather anomalous group of Ancients behind *A Tale* are the Fathers of the early church. As I have indicated above, Anglican the-

---

[11] Apposite to this point is Jay Arnold Levine's discussion of *A Tale* as anti-Scripture in 'The Design of *A Tale of a Tub* (With a Digression on a Mad Modern Critic)', *ELH*, 33 (1966): 198–227. More recently, Marcus Walsh, 'Text, "Text", and Swift's *A Tale of a Tub*', *MLR*, 85 (1990): 290–303, has demonstrated that there are positive echoes of the Restoration Anglican apologetic for the validity and recoverability of scriptural text and meaning against the Catholic criticism that only the long-standing tradition of doctrine (incarnated in the institution of the church) could promise security for individual believers. There is no denying that such pious and positive threads persist in *A Tale*, but even Walsh admits that 'Clearly the meaning or meanings of *A Tale of a Tub* are not straightforwardly given by, or in any simple way controlled by, the context of intellectual debate I have outlined' (303).

[12] See Rosalie Colie, *Paradoxia Epidemica: The Renaissance Tradition of Paradox* (Princeton: Princeton University Press, 1966) for a survey of this tradition. John R. Clark, *Form and Frenzy in Swift's 'Tale of a Tub'*, (Ithaca: Cornell University Press, 1970) studies this tradition as it applies to *A Tale*, ch. 7 (pp. 181–230); and Frank A. Palmeri explores its generic implications in '"To write upon Nothing": Narrative Satire and Swift's *A Tale of a Tub*', *Genre*, 18 (1985): 151–72. Eugene R. Hammond, 'In Praise of Wisdom and the Will of God: Erasmus' *Praise of Folly* and Swift's *A Tale of a Tub*', *SP*, 80 (1983), 253–76, makes an impressive (if, at times, overenthusiastic) case for the proposition that 'There is no better key to the ironic method, the mock encomium structure, and the thematic concerns of Swift's *A Tale of a Tub* than Erasmus' *Praise of Folly*' (p. 254). Everett Zimmerman, *Swift's Narrative Satires: Author and Authority* (Ithaca: Cornell University Press, 1983) also proposes *The Praise of Folly* as *A Tale*'s 'formal model' (p. 72), and agrees (pp. 52–57) with Ronald Paulson, *Theme and Structure in Swift's Tale of a Tub* (New Haven: Yale University Press, 1960), on the pre-textual importance of Montaigne (p. 8). Harth's assertion (*Swift and Anglican Rationalism*, p. 5) that the satire on religion is free of any connection to this tradition only holds if one is prepared to accept the absolute separation he makes between the satire on religion and that on learning. *A Tale* is simply too deeply enthralled in matters of the multiplication, falsification, and transgression of margins for such tidy-minded distinctions to be more than pious fictions. Irvin Ehrenpreis, 'The Doctrine of *A Tale of a Tub*', *Proceedings of the First Münster Symposium on Jonathan Swift*, Hermann J. Real and Heinz J. Vienken, eds. (Munich: Wilhelm Fink Verlag, 1985), pp. 59–71, allows Harth's bifurcation of the text, but maintains the importance of paradoxical encomium in the books.

ology of the late seventeenth and early eighteenth centuries was remarkable for the stress it placed on patristic teaching and the example of the early church. The presumption was that these ancient discussions of doctrine and ecclesiastical polity were in uncorrupted apostolic succession from Christ's institution of his church. Thus they prescribed an inspired pattern for the church for all time, and this pattern was quaintly alleged to be almost identical with that of the reformed and therefore truly Catholic Church of England. Anglican theologians understood reform to mean the stripping away of innovation, the return to the original, essential, and therefore perfect form of the early church. The allegory of the coats in *A Tale* assumes this vision of reform, and also mirrors the way Anglicans displaced biblical theology to focus on authorised form, be it intellectual (doctrine), ceremonial (liturgy), or administrative (ecclesiology). However, it is not the positive patristic teachings that most inform the satiric logic of *A Tale*. On the title page we are alerted to Irenaeus' great second-century attack on heresy, *Adversus Haereses*, and, in the midst of the parody, there is often a sense of militant combat with error. The problem is that no seamless orthodoxy is asserted, as should have been the case had Swift been a proper disciple of Irenaeus, Origen, Tertullian, and the rest of the ancient preceptors. Instead, there is a dangerous openness about the exploration of gnostic or enthusiastical modes of thought and expression that casts doubt on the validity of orthodox strictures, even if it falls a long way short of blessing inspiration as higher wisdom. Still, the stern Fathers are around, in the pre-textuality. They may be disapproving and subverted ancestors, but their informing presence is more immediate than that of the God they claim to represent.

The orthodox homiletic tradition had its origins with the Fathers and appeared in Swift's time in attacks on enthusiasm and deism, which could loosely be described as 'good Modern'.[13] It provided Swift with much ammunition for his parody of bad Modernity, including some important patterns of imagery, particularly in the descriptions of Jack and the cult of Aeolism. Burton's *Anatomy of Melancholy* (1621) can be seen to straddle the division between Renaissance Ancient and good Modern, for it was the source for seventeenth-century analysis of enthusiasm as well as being a normative comic treatment of human inadequacy to the demands of imagination. It inaugurated the psychopathology of imagination, inspiration, and fantasy for the seventeenth century (at least in England) by treating its many manifestations under the idea of melancholy. A sense of urgency was introduced to these issues by

---

[13] Harth, *Swift and Anglican Rationalism*, and Thomas L. Canavan, 'Robert Burton, Jonathan Swift, and the Tradition of Anti-Puritan Invective', *JHI*, 34 (1973), 227–42, survey this material as it relates to *A Tale*; Michael Heyd, 'The Reaction to Enthusiasm in the Seventeenth Century: Towards an Integrative Approach', *Journal of Modern History*, 53 (1981), 258–80, reviews research into enthusiasm more generally; and for Swift's most direct source on enthusiasm, see Robert Crocker, 'Mysticism and Enthusiasm in Henry More', Sarah Hutton, ed., *Henry More (1614–1687), Tercentenary Studies* (Dordrecht: Kluwer, 1990), pp. 137–55.

the unthinkable ideological and military conflicts of the middle of the century, when orthodox thinkers were required by events to try to imagine what sort of madness could sponsor the destruction of order in religion, politics, and culture. For Burton, melancholy was ubiquitous (a natural if perverse function of being human) but for his ideologically motivated followers it became 'other' in a more threatening sense. Meric Casaubon, *A Treatise Concerning Enthusiasme* (1655) and Henry More, *Enthusiasmus Triumphatus; Or, A Brief Discourse of the Nature, Causes, Kinds, and Cure of Enthusiasm* (1656) identified religious enthusiasm as an intellectual and pathological aberration, using Burton's analysis of melancholy as a pattern to explain a phenomenon that could no longer be written off as merely a hypocritical mask. They depicted personal inspiration without the support of institutional teachings of traditional dogma or hermeneutics as having a dangerous potential for delusion and subversion. At the Restoration, with the Puritans excluded from political culture and orthodox religion to become Dissenters, the rhetoric of attacks on enthusiasm rapidly became more extreme and scurrilous – Butler's *Hudibras* (1663) is a notable early example. The Dissenters and their distinctive forms of intellectual aberration came increasingly to bear the blame for the collapse of good order in the Cromwellian period, and they were depicted increasingly as dangerous lunatics and/or insidious subversives by the High-Church rhetoric of the day. Whereas More and Casaubon were liberal and reasonably tolerant proto-latitudinarians, temperate analysis of enthusiasm rapidly gave way to increasingly shrill criticism as it became a High-Church loyalist property, attaining colourful extremities in the writings of Samuel Parker and Roger L'Estrange earlier in our period and Charles Leslie, George Hickes, and Henry Sacheverell later.

The mood of *A Tale* on the subject of enthusiasm most closely mirrors More's, as we can see in this passage:

The *Spirit* then that wings the *Enthusiast* in such a wonderful manner, is nothing else but that *Flatulency* which is in the *Melancholy* complexion, and rises out of the *Hypochondriacal* humour upon some occasional heat, as *Winde* out of an *Aeolipila* applied to the fire. Which fume mounting into the Head, being first actuated and spirited and somewhat refined by the warmth of the Heart, fills the Mind with variety of *Imaginations*, and so quickens and inlarges *Invention*, that it makes the *Enthusiast* to admiration *fluent* and *eloquent*, he being as it were drunk with new wine drawn from that Cellar of his own that lies in the lowest region of his Body, though he be not aware of it, but takes it to be pure *Nectar*, and those waters of life that spring from above.[14]

The imagery and diction of this semi-serious pathology of inspiration are very Swiftian, and the connection with *A Tale*'s Aeolism is obvious, particularly in the materialist insistence on the literal meaning of inspiration and in its location at the nether end of the alimentary canal. This is a more violent

---

[14] Henry More, *Enthusiasmus Triumphatus; Or, A Brief Discourse of the Nature, Causes, Kinds, and Cure of Enthusiasm*, M.V. De Porte, intro. (Los Angeles: Augustan Reprint Society, 1966; reprint of 2nd edn, 1662), p. 12.

reaction than Casaubon's, but it betrays a horrified fascination and appalled imaginative engagement which does not correspond to the more orthodox High-Church retaliation to Dissent of total rejection. Like More, Swift found a literary and imaginative resource in the language and logic of enthusiasm which transformed condemnation into parody.

Swift provides the *Battle of the Books* to name the happy few he considers good Moderns in the fields of secular learning. Their natural leader was Sir William Temple, and they shared his distaste for the small-mindedness and unfounded pride of the Moderns who claimed their dwarfish labours as improvements on the great work of the Ancients, with all its formal elegance, wealth of appropriate detail, and breadth of vision. One tends to assume that the author includes the gentle reader in this natural aristocracy of talent but it is hard to feel confident of this. Swift, as a mere private secretary and/or a minor cleric at the time of composition,[15] could not by right affect such assured aristocratic confidence as Temple, Somers, or Shaftesbury, much though he may have wanted to. Also, as he was such a restlessly inventive writer, it is hard to believe that he would have been happy to restrict his possible role to that of ancillary embroiderer on a preformed and self-sufficient fabric of learning. Like a Bloomian strong poet, he sought to appropriate and transform the textual past. The part of Swift that wanted a small, clean world might have been capable of such a self-lacerating gesture of submission. However, there is sustenance in the text for the 'Milton's God' argument, that Swift was of the Moderns' party without knowing it, or a modification of Leavis' argument concerning Yahoos and Houyhnhnms along the lines that the good Moderns have all the politeness, while the bad Moderns have all the life, a lunatic life though it be. Poise and elegance are, after all, nouns notably absent from the lexicon of Swift studies. So, whatever Swift's exact attitude

---

[15] I do not propose to enter into the complex debate about exactly where, when, and by or with whom which bits of *A Tale* were written. In a text which is a tissue of quotations, questions of origin and originality will of necessity remain vexed, but questions even of authorship in *A Tale* remain stubbornly open. No one agrees any longer with William Wotton's opinion that Temple was the true author, but the evidence concerning whether and, if so, to what extent Swift's cousin, Thomas Swift, collaborated on the project remains inconclusive. Recent treatments of this material include Robert M. Adams, 'Jonathan Swift, Thomas Swift, and the Authorship of *A Tale of a Tub*', *MP*, 64 (1967), 198–232, and his 'The Mood of the Church and *A Tale of a Tub*', *England in the Restoration and Early Eighteenth Century: Essays on Culture and Society*, H. T. Swedenberg, Jr, ed. (Berkeley: University of California Press, 1972), pp. 71–99; David Woolley, 'Joint Authorship and *A Tale of a Tub*: Further Thoughts [A hard look at Tom Swift]', *Monash Swift Papers I*, Clive T. Probyn and Bryan Coleborne, eds. (Melbourne: Monash University, 1988), pp. 1–25. Adams has added further to the possibilities by unearthing plausible but hardly conclusive evidence to suggest that an ur-text of the allegory might have been concocted as an exercise in wit by the lords Somers, Shrewsbury, and Shaftesbury, deposited with their mutual friend, Temple, to be picked up in his library by the cousins Swift and elaborated towards its 'final' form; see Robert M. Adams, 'In Search of Baron Somers'. I have nothing to add to this controversy, and will treat *A Tale* (according to literary historical tradition) as a text pieced together largely by Jonathan Swift, at various times in the 1690s, published in 1704, and significantly revised in 1710.

toward aristocratic wit in the *Battle*, and whatever his covert reservations, we can at least assert that in *A Tale* itself such polite and witty gentlemen do not exercise overwhelming influence. Their image, particularly as we as readers are wont to imagine it as identical with our own, might be said to project a sensible absence. They provide an image of paragons ignored, subverted, and therefore (perhaps) affirmed when we as readers realise in ourselves the ideal of rejecting hackish tom-foolery and cleaving to authoritative wisdom.

However, if this were the text's true image of an author, then, like Sir William Temple, the author is dead. All that remains are traces of a style, of manners and conventions mocked up into a debased image by a Grub Street Hack trying to appropriate his authority. While positive models are hard to reconstitute from the hints and absences left in the text, bad Modernity is undeniably present, and it is useful to employ the term 'the Hack'[16] as a collective noun for the narrating voices parodied in *A Tale*. While it is quixotic to try to form a unified mock narrator as real as Robinson Crusoe (or even Gulliver) from these shards of narrative presence, to assume that we hear the voice of Swift using the occasional piece of ventriloquy seems equally fallacious. Modernity takes many feral forms in *A Tale*, but they exhibit enough in the way of family resemblances to be ascribed a corporate identity. The hackish grouping of exposed voices includes Rosicrucians, textual critics, freelance writers, scientists, poets, Dissenters, deists, Epicureans,[17] Catholics, and sundry others. This may seem somewhat indiscriminate to a sanguine reader, but all these writers/writings are associated in a primal guilt. The guilt is error, and it manifests itself in unauthorised utterance as madness, pride, transparent propaganda, greed, self-delusion, and bad writing. Whereas the ancients might be said to exercise structural and temperamental influences on *A Tale*, and the good Modern enemies of error to appear as tell-tale traces of imagery and implied analysis, the body and fabric of the text is overwhelmingly made up of Modern, errant textuality. The discourses of Modernity have been taken into the parody to such an extent that positive, external points of reference cannot be confidently assumed. There is not, for example, the reliable mock-heroic style of Pope's *Rape of the Lock*, ever-present to remind us how far modern life falls short of the normative high seriousness imputed to classical art.

---

[16] For the case for personae, see William Bragg Ewald, Jr, *The Masks of Jonathan Swift*, (Cambridge, Mass.: Harvard University Press, 1954); Charles A. Beaumont, *Swift's Classical Rhetoric* (Athens, Ga.: University of Georgia Press, 1961); Robert C. Elliott, *The Literary Persona* (Chicago: Chicago University Press, 1982); and, particularly, Paulson, *Theme and Structure in Swift's Tale of a Tub*. The dispute over Swiftian personae has been ably summarised by Veronica Kelly, 'Following the Stage-Itinerant: Perception, Doubt, and Death in Swift's *Tale of a Tub*', *SECC*, 17 (1987), 239–58; 256–57, n. 3.

[17] Just as Ancient means 'deservedly lasting' and can include Renaissance authors under its banner, so there is no statute of limitations on Modernity. As Starkman (*Swift's Satire on Learning*, pp. 33–44) points out, Epicurus was undoubtedly a Modern, particularly as he was seen to be the forerunner of Modern materialism and Hobbes. It is indicative of Swift's fascination with error that he read Epicurus' disciple, Lucretius thrice in 1697 (*A Tale*, introduction, p. lvi.).

Rather we are reading a Modern text (or a miscellany of Modern texts loosely
co-ordinated) which we know, from abundant external and internal evidence,
are self-destructive. In chapter 1, I discussed the commonplace book theory of
textual construction outlined in *A Tale* (pp. 209–10), and the book itself is an
extraordinary collocation of deluded late seventeenth-century voices/styles.
While the validity of these hackish voices is undoubtedly questioned, they are
still all we have to be getting on with, so let us uncover a few of the 'Seven
Hundred Thirty Eight *Flowers*, and *shining Hints* of the best *Modern* Authors,
digested with great Reading, into my Book of *Common-places*' (p. 209) that go
to make up *A Tale*, and see how they work.

Imitating an identity: John Locke, Thomas Vaughan, and the Hack

Even at its most breathlessly and inventively lunatic, the Hack's discourse
is not unique. For all its extravagance, it is always collecting and disseminating the words and errors of others. Those characteristics which seem to be
most typical of him – the confessional tone and intimations of the enduring
revelatory power of his writing – find parallels in such apparently disparate
pre-texts as Thomas Vaughan's hermetic writing and the philosophy of John
Locke. Consider the measured casualness of the opening paragraph of
'The Epistle to the Reader' which prefaces the *Essay Concerning Human
Understanding* (1690):

Reader,
I Here put into thy Hands, what has been the diversion of some of my idle and
heavy Hours: If it has the good luck to prove so of any of thine, and thou hast but
half so much Pleasure in reading, as I had in writing it, thou wilt as little think thy
Money, as I do my Pains, ill bestowed. Mistake not this for a Commendation of my
Work; nor conclude, because I was pleased with the doing of it, that therefore I am
fondly taken with it now it is done. He that hawks at Larks and Sparrows, has no
less Sport, though a much less considerable Quarry, than he that flies at nobler
Game: And he is little acquainted with the Subject of this Treatise, the UNDER-
STANDING, who does not know, that as it is the most elevated Faculty of the Soul,
so it is employed with a greater, and more constant Delight than any of the other.
Its searches after Truth, are a sort of Hawking and Hunting, wherein the pursuit
makes a great part of the Pleasure. Every step the Mind takes in its Progress towards
Knowledge, makes some Discovery, which is not only new, but the best too, for the
time at least.[18]

---

[18] John Locke, *An Essay Concerning Human Understanding*, Peter H. Nidditch, ed. (Oxford: Oxford
University Press, 1975), p. 6. W. B. Carnochan, 'Swift, Locke, and the *Tale*', *Swift Studies*, 1 (1986),
55–56, remarks on parodic family resemblances between Locke's fawning 'Epistle Dedicatory' and
Swift's 'Bookseller's Dedication', and between Locke's 'Epistle to the Reader' and Swift's 'Epistle to
Prince Posterity'.

We know, of course, that this self-protective play on gentlemanly tropes of amateurishness and humility is meant to reassure the reader that the author is in full control of his faculties and aware of his limitations. The logic of the strategy suggests to the reader (already flattered by being addressed directly, as a friend) that a writer who is not fooling himself is unlikely to be trying to fool us. We may find the ploy a little cloying, but it works well enough here to inspire confidence. What, then, is the effect of the opening of the Hack's 'Epistle Dedicatory to His Royal Highness Prince Posterity'?

SIR,
I here present *Your Highness* with the Fruits of a very few leisure Hours, stollen from the short Intervals of a World of Business, and of an Employment quite alien from such Amusements as this: The poor Production of that Refuse of Time which has lain heavy upon my Hands, during a long Prorogation of Parliament, a great Dearth of Forein News, and a tedious Fit of rainy Weather: For which, and other Reasons, it cannot chuse extremely to deserve such Patronage as that of *Your Highness*, whose numberless Virtues in so few Years, make the World look upon You as the future Example to all Princes.   (pp. 30–31)

I do not mean to suggest that this 'Epistle' is a direct parody of Locke's – the parallels are by no means close enough for this to be asserted with any plausibility. It seems far more likely, given the monstrous proliferation of prefatory material in the late seventeenth century, that the parody is of a style of writing rather than of any specific text, and for my present purposes one of Dryden's more ingenuous prefaces would do as well.[19] However, if we do read the Swift passage as a parodic quotation of Locke's (and it is the nature of intertextuality that we may – parody of a group becomes specific when a member of that group is identified) implications flow both ways. The relation of the later epistle to its pre-text is fairly obvious: Locke shows us the conventions that structure the Hack's increasingly breathless poses. We sense how close to acceptable diction the later text is. Reading from the parody to the pre-text we see a shadow of doubt cast on the pre-text's conventions, particularly its unifying principle, the unique and humble writing self. The Hack's self-depiction has more circumstantial detail than Locke's, and yet this circumstance only serves to undermine his reality. Locke's description of his *Essay* as 'the diversion of my idle and heavy hours' allows an off-hand and melancholy mysteriousness to the creative process which is rendered ridiculous when a similar creative moment is further described as 'a very few leisure Hours, stollen from the short Intervals of a World of Business...that Refuse of Time which has lain heavy upon my Hands, dur-

---

[19] It is important, however, that this comparison be done with an author who is still considered significant, if only to demonstrate that Swift does not restrict himself to a Pope-like demolition of dunces. The modesty tropes in these authors are by no means unique; Starkman, *Swift's Satire on Learning*, pp. 118–19, illustrates their popularity among Sir Richard Blackmore, Robert Boyle, and several other members of the Royal Society.

ing a long Prorogation of Parliament, a great Dearth of Forein News, and a tedious Fit of rainy Weather'. The convention of pretending to have casually tossed off a treatise is exploded by more specificity than it will bear, and we might even begin to wonder why Locke had idle time to spend.

Were his idleness and his desire to write excited by circumstances bearing any resemblance to these in the Hack's less than candid later admission (from the 'Preface')?

> The shrewdest Pieces of this Treatise, were conceived in Bed, in a Garret: At other times (for a Reason best known to my self) I thought fit to sharpen my Invention with Hunger; and in general, the whole Work was begun, continued, and ended, under a long Course of Physick and a great want of Money.   (p. 44)

Armed with scholarly biographies of John Locke, great philosopher and political theorist, friend of the great and the dangerously liberal, we know that the *Essay Concerning Human Understanding* was not written by a mad, starved scribbler in a garret. That is not the point. The point is that the tropes of sincerity and the self constructed by introductory epistles are literary artifices, recyclable without the content and eminently open to parody (which is to say, deconstructible). They are exposed in *A Tale* as hollow formal writing, suggesting the possibility of 'unsuspected Faults' (like those of the beau whose carcass is later stripped in the 'Digression on Madness') to explain what increasingly looks like subterfuge. Once one starts to think along these lines, the parody proceeds to unravel its pretexts and to deconstruct their rhetorical assumptions rapidly. There is a disconcerting family resemblance shared by Locke's description of 'searches after truth' as 'a sort of hawking and hunting' and the Hack's sense of himself as 'a Person, whose Imaginations are hard-mouth'd, and exceedingly disposed to run away with his *Reason*, which I have observed from long Experience, to be a very light Rider' (p. 180). The Hack's fuller exploration of the metaphor of hunting truth is a distortion of Locke's intent, presumably, but a plausible one. And – appropriate though the sense of provisionality is to Locke's subjective epistemology – when we come to the last sentence of his paragraph, 'Every step the mind takes in its progress towards knowledge makes some discovery, which is not only new, but the best too, for the moment', we are reminded forcefully though 'inappropriately' of the Hack's claims to currency and the temporary absolute:

> I profess to *Your Highness*, in the Integrity of my Heart, that what I am going to say is literally true this Minute I am Writing: What Revolutions may happen before it shall be ready for your Perusal, I can by no means warrant.   (p. 36)

> But here I think fit to lay hold on that great and honourable Privilege of being the *Last Writer*; I claim an absolute Authority in Right, as the *freshest Modern*, which gives me a Despotick Power over all Authors before me.   (p. 130)

Such is the demoralisation *A Tale* can wreak on so sober and circumspect a writer as Locke, and his conventions of self-presentation and self-image. What happens when the pre-text is a truly mad Modern? Robert Day has argued impressively that the Hack's jumbled and lively style is Swift's prescient recognition of the appearance of typographic man in this early stage of print culture.[20] He suggests that the great classical scholar, Richard Bentley, and the Grub Street hack, John Dunton, were typographic men in that they had lost the sense of the printed word as controlled or shaped discourse, and allowed their unregulated thoughts to spill into public view without making any conscious attempt to create order in them. *A Tale* is certainly readable as *skaz* (a Bakhtinian term that Day applies to this style), but no identification excludes other possibilities, and another strange voice in this tissue of quotations is that of the hermetic visionary/propagandist, Thomas Vaughan.

The extent of hermetic 'influence' (in the traditional sense) on *A Tale* is impossible to quantify. Guthkelch and Nichol Smith provide as an appendix 'Notes on Dark Authors' (pp. 353–60) which suggests various connections to the hermetic tradition. In a looser sense we can often identify a hermetic or mystical turn to the way the Hack exercises his 'converting Imagination' (pp. 189–90) – a phrase which suggests acquaintance with the Latin term central to the hermetic tradition, *ars combinatoria*. However, our present attention is on surfaces rather than profundities, or, to put it another way, on converting quotation. Were we searching for intellectual influences, Paracelsus would have a good claim to our attention, as he is mentioned by name on four occasions (and twice more in the *Battle*);[21] we also know that Swift owned an edition of his *Opera omnia medico-chemico-chirurgica*.[22] Thomas Vaughan is also recognised explicitly in the text, and his claim on our present attention is stronger, not merely because he wrote in English, but because he wrote like this:

To the Reader.

NOW God defend! what will become of me? I have neither consulted with the *stars*, nor their *Urinals*, the *Almanacks*. A fine Fellow, to neglect the *Prophets*, who are read in *England* every Day! They shall pardon me for this [oversight]. There is a *Mystery* in their *profession*, they have not so much as heard of: *Coelum stellatum Christianum*; a *new Heaven* fansied on the *old Earth*. Here the *Twelve Apostles* have surpris'd the *Zodiak*, and all the *Saints* are rang'd on their *North*, and *South-sides*. It were a pretty vanity, to preach when Saint *Paul* is *ascendent*, and would not a *Papist* smile to have his *Pope elected* under Saint *Peter*? Reader, if I studied *these Things*, I should think my self worse imployed than the *Roman Chaucer* was in his *Troilus*. I come out as if there were no *Houres* in the *Day*, nor *Planets* in the *Houres*: neither do I care for any thing, but that *Interlude* of *Perendenga* in *Michael Cervantes*: *Let the old Man my Master live, and Christ be with us all*. Thou wilt wonder where this drives, for I have neither a

[20] Robert Adams Day, 'Richard Bentley and John Dunton: Brothers under the Skin', *SECC*, 16 (1986), 125–38.
[21] See Kelling and Preston, *A KWIC Concordance*, p. 597.
[22] LeFanu, *A Catalogue*, p. 25; he also owned an English translation of *Nostradamus*, *The True Prophesies*.

Conde de lemos, nor a *Cardinal* to pray for. *I pray for the Dead*, that is, I wish *him* a *fair Remembrance*, whose *Labours* have *deserv'd* it.[23]

This extraordinary, extroverted diction, with its sudden changes of direction, breathlessly conversational style, miscellaneous attention, and relish for ludicrous imagery, is clearly similar to (though, we assume, less consciously ironic than) Swift's carnivalesque display. The exact nature of the relationship is vexed by the perennial problem of the balance between ridicule and engagement in parody. When Vaughan's earlier treatise, *Anthroposophia Theomagica* (1650), is mentioned in the 'Digression in the Modern Kind', a degree of ambiguity is opened up. The narrator, who at this point is very Hack-like, is clearly impressed by its wisdom, and arraigns Homer for his shallow reading of this and other Modern masterpieces: 'his Account of the *Opus magnum* is extremely poor and deficient; he seems to have read but very superficially, either *Sendivogius, Behmen*, or *Anthroposophia Theomagica*' (p. 127). Simultaneously, by a trick of typography, the anonymous annotator offers another assessment from another centre of authority in a footnote, describing the treatise as '*a Piece of the most unintelligible Fustian, that, perhaps, was ever publish'd in any Language*' (p. 127). With a high degree of probability, we can assume that the footnote represents Swift's considered opinion, but its status, hanging from the bottom of the text keeping company with such luminaries as Wotton, remains problematic and keeps its authority on edge. Vaughan is clearly being attacked, but the terms of that attack and the extent to which they involve a creative engagement remain negotiable.

As the passage above suggests, Vaughan wrote virtuoso fustian which could on occasion attain considerable lunatic beauty and intense vision. This gives his narratorial presence an extremely Hackish complexion – the outrageous propriety of describing almanacs as 'the *stars...Urinals*' captures *A Tale*'s tone brilliantly. Vaughan's work provides a discursive base for the quicksilver rhetorical and conceptual excess we most admire about *A Tale*. Even Marvell, when he is mixing metaphors with abandon in *The Rehearsal Transpros'd*, retains a degree of dispassionate analysis which gives the reader a sense of security and responsible judgement. Vaughan's enthusiasm carries her or him beyond these checks and balances, into a kind of lunacy nearly free of self-regard or self-control, and a part of Swift (the left-handed Swift) is willing to go there with him.[24]

---

[23] *Anima Magica Abscondita: Or A Discourse of the universall Spirit of Nature, With his strange, abstruse, miraculous Ascent, and descent, The Works of Thomas Vaughan*, Alan Rudrum and Jennifer Drake-Brockman, eds. (Oxford: Clarendon Press, 1984), p. 99. For a more extensive survey of the connection between Vaughan and *A Tale*, see N. J. C. Andreasen, 'Swift's Satire on the Occult in *A Tale of a Tub*', *TSLL*, 5 (1963–64), 410–21.

[24] Anselment, *'Betwixt Jest and Earnest'*, argues for *A Tale*'s place in a carefully controlled tradition of religious ridicule wherein the cause of truth was served by well regimented wit and humour. Certainly we do well to remember that religious dispute in seventeenth-century England did have its humorous tropes, but to depict *A Tale* as orthodox, well-meaning piety with jokes is to perpetrate a pious fraud. It ignores contemporary reactions and suppresses the wildness.

Vaughan writes his fustian without poise or balance or premeditation, which is exactly the impression given by the Hack. We know that the historical Swift would have disapproved of such incontinence, and we know that he worked carefully and consciously to make his text from the odds and ends of the intellectual life of his time, but if we look *at* the text rather than *through* it, we cannot say that it repudiates Vaughan entirely. The parody makes an example of him, but not merely in the judicial sense, for without him (or other appropriate enthusiasts and fools) there could be no text. And, in the end, Vaughan is treated (or reflected) with no *less* respect than is Locke.

Parody of the outer form: Dryden's *Virgil*

We now proceed from textual traces and local identifications of parody in echoes of stance and rhetoric – the products of a commonplace book theory of quotation – to more significant (or at least more comprehensive) parodic engagements between *A Tale* and other books. It is no discovery to find Dryden's *Virgil* and Marvell's *Rehearsal Transpros'd* in the background of *A Tale*,[25] but it is useful to see how they inform Swift's work, extensively but at quite different levels. Dryden's place in the scheme of things is less complex than Marvell's, in that he is clearly considered a bad Modern, a midget cowering in gigantic Virgilian armour (as the *Battle* suggests), and so his work is (almost) persistently subverted in *A Tale*. The *Rehearsal Transpros'd*, on the other hand, shows up the limitations of my taxonomy by belonging to all groups, ancients and moderns, good and bad.

As far as we can guess, *A Tale* and Dryden's *Virgil* were closely contemporary. *A Tale*'s second dedication is dated 1697, and the major literary event of that year was the publication by subscription of the *Virgil*. Dryden's actual words in the translation have proved to be very enduring, running to nearly a hundred editions since the first, and only being superseded as the standard translation in the second half of our own century.[26] Even Swift seems to acknowledge its literary value by using it to gloss his (or the Hack's?) Virgilian tag in a footnote on the first page of 'Section I' (p. 55). It is also

---

[25] Recent critics have suggested other fundamental pre-texts, notably Erasmus' *Praise of Folly* (Eugene R. Hammond, 'In Praise of Wisdom'), the controversy in Dublin over the works and visit of the deist John Toland (Kenneth Craven, '*A Tale of a Tub* and the 1697 Dublin Controversy', *Eighteenth Century Ireland*, 1 (1986), 97–110), a selection of late seventeenth- and early eighteenth-century writers (Craven, *Swift and the Millennium of Madness*), and dispute over the validity and recoverability of biblical authority (Walsh, 'Text, "Text", and *A Tale*'). These suggestions are interesting, but are paths not taken by the present book. I am not so mad as to aim for comprehensive elucidation of *A Tale*'s pre-textuality, and do not consider that Dryden and Marvell have been displaced as important forerunners by these subsequent discoveries.

[26] *The Works of John Dryden: Poems, The Works of Virgil in English*, 1697, William Frost and Vinton A. Dearing, eds. (Berkeley: University of California Press, 1987), vols V and VI of the California Dryden; quote, VI, p. 886.

mentioned in the 'Dedication to Prince Posterity' as a Modern work likely to have left some trace even months after its publication:

I do therefore affirm upon the Word of a sincere Man, that there is now actually in being, a certain Poet called *John Dryden*, whose Translation of *Virgil* was lately printed in a large Folio, well bound, and if diligent search were made, for ought I know, is yet to be seen.   (p. 36)

Faintly approving though this is (and who is doing the approving, anyway – this is the Hack defending his own party of scribblers), it conceals a barb that leads us to the more important role of Dryden's *Virgil* in *A Tale*'s pre-textuality, its exemplary status as a flagrant piece of Modern typographical excess and idiosyncrasy. By the innocent words 'well bound' hangs a strange tale well told by Dryden's most recent editors, Frost and Dearing:

The folio first edition of Dryden's Virgil, lavishly illustrated and sold by subscription as well as offered for regular sale, remains a fascinating piece of bookmaking...The book was sold unbound, and constituted a sort of kit complete with assembly instructions, a set of *Directions to the Binders how to place the Several Parts of this Book.* These directions, bewildering in their seeming illogic, are placed, prophetically, at the bottom of a page otherwise devoted to errata, which were testily drawn up by Dryden himself. Unsurprisingly, not all copies are bound in accordance with the directions, perhaps because some first owner yearned for a better, or any, logic in the ordering of parts, or perhaps because the directions were not encountered until the end of the book's fourth part.[27]

They go on to explain the further complications caused by the placement of the 101 plates, which were issued separately. These were the same engravings which had adorned the Ogilby translation of 1654, here with dedications to Dryden's subscribers added, and often assigned to different places in the text. In short, the book as it came from the bookseller was not well bound at all, but confusingly fractured into loose collections of pages. Nearly all books were sold disbound at this time, so the fact that it appeared in sheets was hardly surprising. However, the fragmentation of this particular text, with its array of dedications, notes, illustrations, a life of Virgil, and a postscript, rendered this method of presentation unusually vexatious to the purchaser, and the order proposed by the author/translator was palpably eccentric. It is probable that Swift was taking a jab at the book's physical lack of integrity and suggesting that it mirrored a mental scrappiness.[28]

---

[27] Ibid., V, p. vii.

[28] Of course, the *Virgil* was an expensive and important book, and would therefore generally have been 'well bound' by its original purchasers or even by enterprising retailers. It is unlikely, however, that Swift is referring to this common experience of the book, but to its original form(lessness). If, as Frost and Dearing suggest, 'Large-paper subscription copies may...have been available by mid-July, and regular copies were probably on sale to the public by 10 August', (VI, p. 846) the book can hardly have had sufficient time to have filtered through at least to the second-hand market by 'Decemb. 1697', the notional date of the 'Dedication to Prince Posterity'.

There may even be a suggestion that such a work of Modern disintegration needs to be 'well bound' to disguise its fundamental disunity. Indeed, the presence of 'Directions to the Binders' as one of the *Virgil*'s many parts seems almost to admit as much, and the idiosyncrasy of the suggested order further illustrates the point. For example, the directions insist that the dedication of the *Pastorals* to Lord Clifford should come at the very beginning of the volume, separated from the *Pastorals* themselves by a biography of Virgil, a preface, commendatory poems, errata, directions to the binders, and two lists of subscribers. Dryden seems to be attempting to proclaim order in confusion, and thus betrays his Modern incapacity to master his text in a way that is more anxious and dishonest than the Hack's candid admission at the end of the 'Digression in Praise of Digressions':

The Necessity of this Digression, will easily excuse the Length; and I have chosen it for as proper a Place as I could readily find. If the judicious Reader can assign a fitter, I do here empower him to remove it into any other Corner he pleases.   (p. 149)

The Hack admits what Dryden attempts to hide, that there is no necessary form to the fragments he indiscriminately generates (or collects?). The reader need have no reverence for the Modern text because its integrity is merely (and fragilely) an illusion of typography.

A Tale also uses Dryden's *Virgil* as a base for an attack on the venality of Modern authorship. Dryden's extraordinary multiplication of prefaces, dedications, illustrations, and other formal mechanisms offers an obvious model for the external structure of *A Tale* and a target for Swift's snide suggestion that any 'very considerable Addition to the Bulk of the Volume' is '*a Circumstance by no means to be neglected by a skilful Writer*' (p. 132). *A Tale* is swollen to nearly three times its essential size (that is, the space taken up by the story of the Brothers) by the proliferation of 'unnecessary' digression, introduction, annotation, and the appending of two other treatises. It is a text which continuously destabilises and transgresses 'natural' boundaries and decorums of integrity, and there are few texts for which the further accretions of the 'Apology', Wotton's notes, Curll's key, independent sequels such as the 'History of Martin', indices, and the whole subsequent paraphernalia of eighteenth- to twentieth-century scholarly apparatus could be more perfectly appropriate and ludicrous at once. Dryden's folio swells in a similar manner, and (we begin to suspect) for similarly cynical reasons. Not only does his *Virgil* have three full-dress dedications to different lords of the realm (one for the *Pastorals*, another for the *Georgics*, and a third for the *Aeneid*), but there is also a name and coat of arms of one of the major subscribers, 'Each Subscription being Five Guineas',[29] attached to each of the 101 plates, and a list of 250 '*Names of the second SUBSCRIBERS*'.[30] When you

---

[29] Frost and Dearing, V, p. 67.
[30] Ibid., V, p. 69.

consider this vigorous merchandising, there is poignancy as well as a point in the Hack's lament that:

Our famous *Dryden* has ventured to proceed a Point farther, endeavouring to introduce also a Multiplicity of *God-fathers*; which is an Improvement of much more Advantage, upon a very obvious Account. 'Tis a Pity this admirable Invention has not been better cultivated, so as to grow by this time into general Imitation, when such an Authority serves it for a Precedent. Nor have my Endeavours been wanting to second so useful an Example: But it seems, there is an unhappy Expence usually annexed to the Calling of a God-Father, which was clearly out of my Head, as it is very reasonable to believe. Where the Pinch lay, I cannot certainly affirm; but having employ'd a World of Thoughts and Pains, to split my Treatise into forty Sections, and having entreated forty Lords of my Acquaintance, that they would do me the Honor to stand, they all made it a Matter of Conscience, and sent me their Excuses.
                                                                            (p. 71–72)

The whole begging process of patronage is exploded, and Dryden's natural affiliation with the necessitous Hack is exposed. If the joke has a positive point, it is probably that the lords should have 'made it a Matter of Conscience' not to support the earlier work as well. This would have saved them their money and, at the same time, discouraged the highwaymen of literature.

And that highwayman, Dryden, was also a politician throughout his life, even in the supposedly neutral activity of translation. Virgil's works, particularly the *Aeneid*, were the classic touchstone for images of civic virtue and the providential history of an emerging nation, yet (in defiance of recent history) Dryden's dedicatees were all, and the subscribers were overwhelmingly, Tory. As Steven Zwicker has demonstrated, even the placement of plates in the *Virgil* had political overtones,[31] and scorn for such hypocrisies comes out in *A Tale* when Dryden's confessional mode is parodied:

THESE Notices may serve to give the Learned Reader an Idea as well as a Taste of what the whole Work is likely to produce: wherein I have now altogether circumscribed my Thoughts and my Studies; and if I can bring it to a Perfection before I die, shall reckon I have well employ'd the poor Remains of an unfortunate Life. This indeed is more than I can justly expect from a Quill worn to the Pith in the Service of the State, in *Pro's* and *Con's* upon *Popish Plots*, and *Meal-Tubs*, and *Exclusion Bills*, and *Passive Obedience*, and *Addresses of Lives and Fortunes*; and *Prerogative*, and *Property* and *Liberty of Conscience*, and *Letters to a Friend*: From an Understanding and a Conscience, thread-bare and ragged with perpetual turning; From a Head broken in a hundred places, by the Malignants of the opposite Factions, and from a Body spent with Poxes ill cured, by trusting to Bawds and Surgeons, who, (as it afterwards appeared) were professed Enemies to me and the Government, and revenged their Party's Quarrel upon my Nose and Shins. Four-score and eleven Pamphlets have I

---

[31] See Zwicker, *Politics and Language in Dryden's Poetry*, pp. 177–205, especially pp. 188–96.

written under three Reigns, and for the Service of six and thirty Factions. But finding the State has no farther Occasion for Me and my Ink, I retire willingly to draw
it out into Speculations more becoming a Philosopher, having, to my unspeakable
Comfort, passed a long Life, with a Conscience void of Offence.   (pp. 69–71)

In the 1710 edition the anonymous annotator (Swift) made sure that the
readers would not miss the point by glossing the passage with '*Here the Author
seems to personate* L'Estrange, Dryden, *and some others, who after having past their
Lives in Vices, Faction and Falshood, have the Impudence to talk of Merit and Innocence
and Sufferings*' (p. 70). It is, of course, a corrosive parody of many a self-righteous apologia from these two great proponents of Restoration Toryism, but
it sits particularly accusingly beside Dryden's 'Postscript to the Reader'
which almost[32] brings his *Virgil* to an end:

What *Virgil* wrote in the vigour of his Age, in Plenty and at Ease, I have undertaken
to Translate in my Declining Years: strugling with Wants, oppress'd with Sickness,
curb'd in my Genius, lyable to be misconstrued in all I write; and my Judges, if they
are not very equitable, already prejudic'd against me, by the Lying Character which
has been given them of my Morals. Yet steady to my Principles, and not dispirited
with my Afflictions, I have, by the Blessing of God on my Endeavours, overcome all
difficulties; and, in some measure, acquitted my self of the Debt which I ow'd the
Publick, when I undertook this Work. In the first place therefore, I thankfully
acknowledge to the Almighty Power, the Assistance he has given me in the beginning, the Prosecution, and Conclusion of my present Studies, which are more happily perform'd than I could have promis'd to my self, when I labour'd under such
Discouragements. For, what I have done, Imperfect as it is, for want of Health and
leisure to Correct it, will be judg'd in after Ages, and possibly in the present, to be
no dishonour to my Native Country; whose Language and Poetry wou'd be more
esteem'd abroad, if they were better understood...Here [i.e. the faults of English
poets and translators] is a Field of Satire open'd to me: But since the Revolution, I
have wholly renounc'd that Talent. For who wou'd give Physick to the Great when
it is uncall'd: To do his Patient no good, and indanger himself for his Prescription?
Neither am I ignorant, but I may justly be Condemn'd for many of those Faults, of
which I too liberally Arraign'd others.[33]

The relationship is clear and hostile. Both authors complain of ill health
and persecution while proclaiming their steadfast support of the public
interest. Swift only discards the concluding *mea culpa* and exaggerates the
symptoms of culpability, so as further to expose the Drydenic Hack's protestations concerning the cleanliness of his conscience.

Thus the moral stance, physical appearance, political allegiance, rhetorical
structure, and marketing strategy of Dryden's *Virgil* are all harshly reflected in
the parodic mirror presented by *A Tale*. What further indignity could Swift

---

[32] It is followed only by the 'Notes and Observations'.
[33] Frost and Dearing, VI, pp. 807–8.

visit on his familial and literary ancestor's most ambitious work? Only to base
the whole process of his book around that of translation and its close cousin
plagiarism. In a loose sense that is nearly useless as a hermeneutic tool, parody can be imaged as a miscellaneous and faithless form of translation.
Different texts are translated in the literal sense from one context to another,
and are transformed in the process. In the case of honest translation, this
transformation should ideally be neutral, making one text available to an
audience unequipped to read it in the original. In parody the transformation
distances us from the original text or texts, confusing or distorting or simply
shedding light on their unspoken assumptions, and setting up a sort of intertextual critique. In sublunary reality, no translation is or can be perfect and so
all translations participate in a degree of parody of their model, howsoever
faithful they aspire to be. This very general proposition takes on corrosive
meaning when we consider the specific limitations of translating into English
heroic couplets and Dryden's attempts to overcome them. Unlike French with
its 'feminine' rhymes, good rhymes are not prolific in English and the possibilities for expressing particular phrases in much translated works like Virgil's
were well canvassed by Dryden's time. To put it bluntly, the great poet stole
words and phrases on a large scale from previous translators. Even such
indulgent critics as Frost and Dearing are at one point moved to suggest that
'Lauderdale is the most significant single predecessor: to such an extent that it
might not be unfair to call Dryden's translation, at least of the *Aeneid*, the
Dryden-Lauderdale'.[34] Nor was Lauderdale alone as a quarry for verbal
forms; he was only the most liberally plundered. Thus Dryden's text was not
simply a translation of an original text, but had also silently picked up a collection of fragments from intermediate texts along the way. It is probably not
a fair expectation of translation to require originality, but Swiftian parody
tends to be pertinent rather than fair. *A Tale* is, therefore, a grotesque patchwork of quotation claiming inspired originality which reflects poorly on the
status of its most significant formal progenitor, a more decorous patchwork of
quotation which does little to proclaim its derivativeness. We begin to look on
Dryden as an author who would be completely at a loss if, like his descendant
the Hack, he found his 'Common-Place-Book fill[ing] much slower than I
had reason to expect' (p. 54), for it is through the petty larcenies of commonplace book production as much as in the inspiration of the poetic muse that
the *Virgil*'s origin is to be traced.

Marvell and the practice of ridicule

The letter killeth, but the spirit giveth life. Swift kills the letter (verbal, physical, and political form) in Dryden's *Virgil*, but lets the spirit of Marvell's

[34] Ibid., VI, p. 867.

Rehearsal Transpros'd (1672) give his work life. Marvell's satire on Archdeacon (later Bishop) Parker's absolutist propaganda is a crucial imaginative resource for *A Tale*. Indeed, Ricardo Quintana goes so far as to suggest that it is 'as good a key as any to the methods employed in the *Tale*'.[35] Guthkelch and Smith express their sense of the intertextuality shared by the two books thus:

> The style of Swift is Swift himself, a style which has never been imitated successfully, and could not be formed by imitation. But when we read Marvell after reading Swift we feel the kinship in the muscular strength, the simplicity that is fraught with meaning, and the seemingly careless ease that comes from perfect confidence.
> (pp. lix–lx)

While the critical terminology may seem old-fashioned, the aptness of the judgement has not been dulled by our passing to newer and better modernities.

The *Rehearsal Transpros'd* provides an immediate source for Swift's title in the description its second part provides of the first: 'I only threw it out like empty Cask to amuze him, knowing that I had a *Whale* to deal with, and least he should overset me; he runs away with it as a very serious business, and so moyles himself with tumbling and tossing it, that he is in danger of melting his *Sperma Ceti*.'[36] But ultimately Marvell's text shares much more with the later satire than a radically dismissive self-image. Its brilliant verbal wit and imagery, its hilarious exploitation of puns' destructive (or anarchic) potential, its manipulation of intertextuality, and its deft control of ridicule all prepare us for the gyrations of *A Tale*. A crucial difference is that the *Rehearsal Transpros'd* is not primarily parody: it is an overt attack on an author and his texts wherein the narrator and his text are not distanced from authority by participating in the lunacy being exposed. The narrative voice is basically Marvell speaking *in propria persona*, so error is depicted vividly but from a position of control, rather than enacted in a context of ever receding controls. In a moment of exasperation at Parker's dangerous lunacy the *Rehearsal Transpros'd* marks *A Tale*'s stepping off point:

> It were a wild thing for me to *Squire* it after this *Knight*, and accompany him here through all his Extravagancies against our *Calvinists*. You will find nothing but *Orthodoxy*, *Systems*, and *Syntagms*, *Polemical theology*, *Subtilties* and *Distinctions*. *Demosthenes*; *Tankard-bearers*; *Pragmatical*; *Controversial*: General terms without foundation or reason assigned. That they seem like words of Cabal, & have no significance till they be

---

[35] *Swift: An Introduction* (Oxford: Oxford University Press, 1955), p. 47.
[36] Andrew Marvell, *The Rehearsal Transpros'd, and The Rehearsal Transpros'd, The Second Part*, D. I. B. Smith, ed. (Oxford: Clarendon Press, 1971), p. 198. As Guthkelch and Smith point out (p. xxx), the phrase 'a tale of a tub' was proverbial and the seamen's custom well known. However, the turn given to the image in both the *Rehearsal Transpros'd* and *A Tale* is so similar that an intertextual connection can hardly be denied, even if it be not exclusive of other connections.

decipher'd. Or, you would think he were playing at *Substantives* and *Adjectives*. All that rationally can be gathered from what he saith, is, that the Man is mad.[37]

Swift does exactly this wild thing, squiring it after his mad Modern knight as a particularly slippery and malicious Sancho Panza into crazy 'Extravagancies...General terms without foundation...words of Cabal...playing at *Substantives* and *Adjectives*'; everywhere it is demonstrated, but nowhere is it plainly stated that 'the Man is mad'. Swift deconstructs a house of cards that Marvell would only have blown over.

Following through the caveats on Marvell's undoubted influence on *A Tale* is almost more use than acknowledging the more simple debts. Take the two books' approach to the implications of mass communication through print:

The Press (that *villanous* Engine) invented much about the same time with the Reformation, that hath done more mischief to the Discipline of our Church, than all the Doctrine can make amends for. 'Twas an happy time when all Learning was in Manuscript, and some little Officer, like our Author, did keep the Keys of the Library. When the Clergy needed no more knowledg then to read the Liturgy, and the Laity no more Clerkship than to save them from Hanging. But now, since Printing came into the World, such is the mischief, that a Man cannot write a Book but presently he is answered. Could the Press but once be conjured to obey only an *Imprimatur*, our Author might not disdain *perhaps* to be one of its most zealous Patrons. There have been wayes found out to banish Ministers, to fine not only the People, but even the Grounds and Fields where they assembled in Conventicles: But no Art yet could prevent these seditious meetings of Letters. Two or three brawny Fellows in a Corner, with meer Ink and Elbow-grease, do more harm than an *hundred Systematical Divines* with their *sweaty Preaching*. And, which is a strange thing, the very Spunges, which one would think should rather deface and blot out the whole Book, and were anciently used to that purpose, are become now the Instruments to make things legible. Their ugly Printing-Letters, that look but like so many rotten-Teeth, How oft have they been pull'd out by B.[irkenhead] and L.['Estrange] the Publick-Tooth-drawers! and yet these rascally Operators of the Press have got a trick to fasten them again in a few minutes, that they grow as firm a Set, and as biting and talkative as ever. O *Printing!* how hast thou disturb'd the Peace of Mankind! that Lead, when moulded into Bullets, is not so mortal as when founded into Letters! There was a mistake sure in the Story of *Cadmus*; and the Serpents Teeth which he sowed, were nothing else but the Letters which he invented. The first Essay that was made towards this Art, was in single Characters upon Iron, wherewith of old they stigmatized Slaves and remarkable Offenders; and it was of good use sometimes to brand a Schismatick. But a *bulky* Dutchman diverted it quite from its first Institution, and contriving those innumerable *Syntagmes* of Alphabets, hath pestred the World ever since with the *gross Bodies of their German Divinity*. One would have thought in Reason that a Dutchman at least might have contented himself only with the Wine-press.[38]

---

[37] Marvell, *Rehearsal Transpos'd*, pp. 32–33.
[38] Ibid., pp. 4–5.

The printing press appears here as a '*villanous* Engine', to put beside Swift's three 'Oratorial Machines', and its bogus genealogy is peculiarly Swiftian. The story of print's origin in the cruelty of branding deviants displays *A Tale*'s economy of horror exactly, and the surreal materialism in the collision of myth and sensation throughout is of a piece with Swift's most brilliant satire. Type is treated as a dangerous species of teeth, a more deadly use for lead than bullets, and its magical powers suggest a mutation of the story of Cadmus, the dragon's teeth sown to strife being nothing other than print. It is a form of super-teeth, having unnatural powers of regeneration, for when it is drawn from its setting by 'the Publick-Tooth-drawers' (that is, the censors), Birkenhead and L'Estrange, it can be refastened in minutes to 'grow as firm a Set, and as biting and talkative as ever'. The Swiftian collision of theory and practice is enacted in the image of 'an *hundred Systematical Divines* with their *sweaty Preaching*' being superannuated by a couple of mechanics and their machine. And to conclude with a tidy piece of chauvinism at the expense of German divines and Dutch printers hits the note exactly. This is the conceptual space of *A Tale*, where fantasy and physicality, language and limitation, mix in extraordinary images that are at the same time apocalyptically apt and hopelessly inappropriate.

Yet while there are similarities in texture, there are also differences of direction between the two texts. Marvell, a friend of the free press and an ally (at least) of the Dissenters, is clearly speaking with loaded sarcasm when he describes an Edenic time before the Reformation when knowledge was kept in manuscript under lock and key, guarded by a clergy only less ignorant than an almost unlettered laity. He believed that the free market of ideas would eventually expose error in its natural deformity, and consequently that the press was truth's ally. However, Swift's attitude towards this image of safety in ignorance is not as straightforward, for at least a part of him was drawn to the simple, obedient, and nearly empty world of the Houyhnhnms. While Marvell projected the press as a democratic force of almost magical potency which could be operated privately for the public good (a monster only in the eyes of those classes which benefit from holding a monopoly on information), Swift was capable of advocating suppression of heterodoxy in ideological patterns similar to (though generally less extreme than) Parker's. Thus the direct references to printing in *A Tale* treat the issue of freedom of information ambiguously. There is the oppressive sense of a crowded marketplace for texts in the 'Preface's' list of formulaic complaints about the congestion of the press, followed by a pregnant pun in the parable of the '*Mountebank* in Leicester-Fields' where the fat man is '*half stifled in the Press*' (p. 46). Then we have the ingenuous suggestion that we submit our critical faculties to typographic convention by accepting that 'whatever word or Sentence is Printed in a different Character, shall be judged to contain something extraordinary either of *Wit* or *Sublime*' (pp. 46–47). Indeed, it is possible to read what follows (the body of *A Tale*) as a fear-fulfilling extravaganza on the new found power of the press to disseminate error. When we reach the 'Conclusion', we have been given many reasons to distrust the assumption that words somehow attain 'Preferment and Sanction in *Print*' (p. 210).

Swift and Marvell were, however, in more perfect agreement concerning inspiration, differing only on the ideological commitments of those likely to indulge in such prideful fraudulence. There are many intimations of Aeolism in the pre-textuality of *A Tale*, but few as suggestive as this one:

And so thinking himself now ripe and qualified for the greatest Undertakings, and highest Fortune, he therefore exchanged the narrowness of the University for the *Town*...He follow'd the Town life, haunted the best companies; and to polish himself from any Pedantick roughness, he read and saw the Playes, with much care and more proficiency than most of the Auditory. But all this while he forgot not the main chance, but hearing of a vacancy with a Noble man, he clapp'd in, and easily obtained to be his Chaplain. From that day you may take the date of his Preferments and his Ruine. For having soon wrought himself dexterously into his Patrons favour, by short Graces and Sermons, and a mimical way of drolling upon the *Puritans*, which he knew would take both at Chappel and Table; He gained a great Authority likewise among all the domesticks. They all listened to him as an Oracle: and they allow'd him by common consent, to have not only all the *Divinity*, but more wit too than all the rest of the family put together. This thing alone elevated him exceedingly in his own conceit, and raised his *Hypochondria* into the Region of the Brain: that his head swell'd like any Bladder with wind and vapour ...[B]eing of an amorous Complexion, and finding himself (as I told you) the *Cock-Divine* and *Cock Wit* of the Family, he took the privilege to walk among the Hens: and thought it not impolitick to establish his new-acquired Reputation upon the Gentle-womens side. And they that perceived he was a Rising-Man, and of pleasant Conversation, dividing his Day among them into Canonical hours, of reading now the Common-prayer, and now the Romances; they were very much taken with him. The Sympathy of Silk began to stir and attract the Tippet to the Pettycoat and the Petticoat toward the Tippet. The innocent Ladies found a strange unquietness in their minds, and could not distinguish whether it were Love or Devotion. Neither was he wanting on his part to carry on the Work; but shifted himself every day with a clean Surplice, and, as oft as he had occasion to bow, he directed his Reverence towards the Gentlewomens Pew. Till, having before had enough of the Libertine, and undertaken his Calling only for Preferment; he was transported now with the Sanctity of his Office, even to extasy: and like the Bishop over *Maudlin Colledge* Altar, or like *Maudlin de la Croix*, he was seen at his Prayers to be lifted up sometimes in the Air, and once particularly so high that he crack'd his Scul against the Chappel Ceiling. I do not hear for all this that he had ever practised upon the Honour of the Ladies, but that he preserved alwayes the Civility of a *Platonick Knight-Errant*. For all his Courtship had no other operation than to make him stil more in love with himself: and if he frequented their company, it was only to speculate his own Baby in their Eyes. But being thus, without Competitor or Rival, the Darling of both Sexes in the Family and his own Minion; he grew beyond all measure elated, and that crack of his Scull, as in broken Looking-Glasses, multipli'd him in self-conceit and imagination.[39]

The pretence of biography here – the facts, such as they are, correspond to known events in Parker's life – only offers light cover for the real enterprise, which is personal abuse. The extensive efforts to imply sexual licence (a family of vices to which Parker was not prone), amounting even to vague suggestions of sexual ambiguity and, perhaps, masturbation in the phrase 'the Darling of both Sexes in the Family and his own Minion', are covered by a formal denial which is meant to sound hollow, even though it was the denial rather than the insinuation that was empirically true. The sheen of playful wit is merely a means of facilitating the attack. However, it is as a mythos of error that this fragment of biography feeds into *A Tale*'s pre-textuality. Read from the vantage point of the story of the three brothers, Marvell's Parker rises above his historical status to become a figure of pride, lust, ambition, charlatanry, hypocrisy, and temporising. Indeed, it would seem to be precisely this sort of ironic dignification that Swift has in mind in the 'Apology' when he comments: 'we still read *Marvel's* Answer to *Parker* with Pleasure, tho' the Book it answers be sunk long ago' (p. 10). Marvell's 'Rising Man' has collapsed to obscurity from his peak of inflation on the chapel ceiling, while Marvell has risen to immortality on his back, and this is what *A Tale* does to Modern textuality.

The depiction of Parker's inflation with a sense of his own importance mirrors in shape (and to some extent in detail) the description of the world's corruption of the three brothers, their 'Primitive Institution' (p. 56) in section II of *A Tale*, and Jack's subsequent lunacies of inspiration, as well as the description of Aeolism. We can detect a reshaping of verbal and metaphoric forms, but it is difficult to give the intertextual relationship a name. It is not so innocent as imitation, yet it falls well short of the hostility of parodic ridicule. Reading and attending plays as an education; delivering short, canting graces and sermons to ingratiate himself with a patron; the rising of hypochondria to the brain, there to manifest itself as a 'head swell'd like any Bladder with wind and vapour'; the phallic imagery of '*Cock-Divine*' and '*Cock* Wit', with attendant lasciviousness; the pursuit of and self-satisfied basking in flattery; the combination of pride, madness, and the fantastic in the image of a skull cracked by floating on its own self-esteem to a chapel's ceiling; the subordination of doctrine to convenience – all this is the world of *A Tale*'s allegory and pathology of enthusiasm. Swift only goes further, only combines words and images more bizarrely, only drags more knaves into the vortex of parodied modern madness, only blurs the distinction between fools and knaves more radically. The Swiftian satire could be imag-

[39] Ibid., pp. 29–31.

ined as in apostolic succession to Marvell's, the brilliant pupil improving reverently on the master's work and furthering the tradition of religious ridicule. But there is a catch. Swiftian parody consumes its pre-texts, even those it learns from most creatively. If we go back to the *Rehearsal Transpros'd* from *A Tale*, we will find it subverted, not only in the way that its anti-Anglican animus has been redeployed to attack the Puritan Jack. We will look back on the originating masterpiece and see it as a brilliant expression of the spirit of laughing 'Ancient' Renaissance Humanism, and we will see it as a brilliant 'good Modern' deflation of modern lunacy. But we will also see in it the image of *A Tale* itself, a mad expression of the 'bad Modern' proliferation of books and comment, fixed in the ephemerality of everyday controversy, aiming for extraodinary wit in language, image, and opinion, rather than for simple truth. It is a shallow game to be in and, while Marvell does it well, he does not do it as well as Swift. The earlier work is subordinated by its successor, which, in turn, is a very 'wild thing' indeed.

The final lesson of all this delving into pre-textuality is twofold. First, the relationships between texts in parody is not a simple one of priority/posteriority; the divisions between *A Tale* and its pre-texts are much more blurred than that. The process is not one of simple progress of an idea or image from a source to marmorealisation in great literature, but a dialogical interplay of recognitions and judgements. The Hack claims 'that great and honourable Privilege of being the *Last Writer*...an absolute Authority in Right, as the *freshest Modern*, which gives me a Despotick Power over all Authors before me' (p. 130), but his text shows that posteriority, particularly when incompetently exercised, accords no privileges. In the simultaneous moment of textuality, a ridiculous text can gain no special purchase just by being the latest. Though it claim uniqueness and integrity, its resonances are disseminated by parody and quotation through prior and subsequent texts, and status results only from this dialogue. *A Tale* does not just recall other texts, it refunctions them and is refunctioned by them in a process that only happens in the reader's perceptions. This leads to the second part of the lesson about pre-textuality, which is that it cannot be exhausted. The threads of quotation and parody are not determinate in number, but flow back and forth through *A Tale* and its pre-texts in a process fuelled by the reader's recognition. This does not mean that parody is a merely general process, castigating the general forms of errors, but that its particular implications can be multiple. In other words, even if we could recover Swift's specific intentions, that would not exhaust the possible readings. The same passage can recall and refunction the discourses of writers as miscellaneous as Locke, Vaughan, and Dryden, even if we maintain the convention of considering only temporally prior texts, and there is no very good reason why we should be forbidden from seeing reflections between the Hack's stance and those of Sterne's Tristram Shandy or Nabokov's Charles Kinbote. A connection made is a connection that exists, and an 'obvious' barb or implication does not preclude the possibility that other points can be seen to be made. *A Tale*'s pre-textuality is not finally a stable body of knowledge, and it will not stay in its place as merely ancillary to the act of reading. The text makes it a necessary participant in dialogue and reading makes it dynamic.

7

A Tale of A Tub as an orphaned text

At length we agreed upon this Expedient; That when a Customer comes for one of these, and desires in Confidence to know the Author; he will tell him very privately, as a Friend, naming which ever of the Wits shall happen to be that Week in the Vogue; and if *Durfy*'s last Play should be in Course, I had as lieve he may be the Person as *Congreve*.   (p. 207)

It is suggested in the 'Introduction' that 'Books [are] the Children of the Brain' (p. 71), and here the author renounces paternity of his book. He authorises the bookseller to father it indiscriminately, and purely for mercenary reasons, on whomever fashion most favours, be he a hack (Durfey) or a genius (Congreve). The book is orphaned, disowned by its proud but servile author, cut off from its origin, and sent seeking filiation into the world. Set loose in a culture orphaned from seminal origins of legitimacy by the wilfullness of its recent history, the orphaned text generates myths of origin and authenticity in a frantic attempt to claim or forge a legitimacy to which it has no natural claim. In *A Tale*'s parodic sphere, lines of authority have always already been subverted and the origin has always already been irrecoverably displaced. Authoritative utterance is impossible, and the wit and motion is the sound of the book-bastard's attempt to mock up the impression that it has a right to exist.

Fictions of desertion, attempts to engender a self

The orphaned text is a pregnant metaphor under which to discuss *A Tale*. What Hugh Kenner says of the counterfeit can simply be repeated for parody: '[It] does not claim a reality it does not possess, but only an origin – that is, an authorisation.'[1] Parody is about the implication, inference, construction, confusion, and complication of origins, and *A Tale* itself is laden with traces of such concerns. The excessive prefatory material, for example, is a medley of overdetermining attempts to place the book, to give it a context and an identity which it has not inherited, and to validate (at least pro-

---

[1] *The Counterfeiters: An Historical Comedy*, 2nd edn (Baltimore: Johns Hopkins University Press, 1985), p. 165.

140

visionally) the inherent illegitimacy of its presence in the public sphere. In the midst of these digressive and inconsistent postures, the 'Bookseller to the Reader' reads like a report from the orphanage to prospective foster parents. The Bookseller (not John Nutt speaking *in propria persona* – the part was undoubtedly written by Swift) can offer us no assurances of the book's source or authenticity:

As to the Author, I can give no manner of Satisfaction; However, I am credibly informed that this Publication is without his Knowledge; for he concludes the Copy is lost, having lent it to a Person, since dead, and being never in Possession of it after: So that, whether the Work received his last Hand, or, whether he intended to fill up the defective Places, is like to remain a Secret.   (p. 28)

The infant text has been mislaid or even abandoned by its progenitor, who imagines it lost to the world. Like the harrassed proprietor of a workhouse, the bookseller implores us to look upon this orphaned text indulgently and give it a good home on our book-shelf despite its defects and illegitimacy. The origin suggested here is obscure, but we are told that the book itself is blameless, and we are asked to buy a copy out of charity, to place ourselves *in loco parentis*.

There is a more explicit but no less furtive story of the text's origin in the 'Preface'. Here, instead of displaying the benign indifference towards open questions of authorship and the means of production recommended by the 'Bookseller', the author insists that we become the authors ourselves:

Whatever Reader desires to have a thorow Comprehension of an Author's Thoughts, cannot take a better Method, than by putting himself into the Circumstances and Postures of Life, that the Writer was in, upon every important Passage as it flow'd from his Pen; For this will introduce a Parity and strict Correspondence of Idea's between the Reader and the Author. Now, to assist the diligent Reader in so delicate an Affair, as far as brevity will permit, I have recollected, that the shrewdest Pieces of this Treatise, were conceived in Bed, in a Garret: At other times (for a Reason best known to my self) I thought fit to sharpen my Invention with Hunger; and in general, the whole Work was begun, continued, and ended, under a long Course of Physick, and a great want of Money. Now, I do affirm, it will be absolutely impossible for the candid Peruser to go along with me in a great many bright Passages, unless upon the several Difficulties emergent, he will please to capacitate and prepare himself by these Directions. And this I lay down as my principal *Postulatum*.   (pp. 44–45)

This predictive parody of biographical interpretation does not hide the orphaned text's low origins, though it does make feeble attempts to obscure them. 'Conceived in Bed, in a Garret', attended by hunger, disease, and poverty, 'this Treatise' has not come into the world by the high road. The growth of the author's mind has been a harsh affair, marked by indignities which he cannot bring himself to name but which can be easily inferred. All the metaphors and analogies suggest illegitimate utterance, a confluence of human and verbal frailties redolent of literal bastardising. Furthermore, readers who wish to understand the text fully are exhorted to engage in the author's debased conditions. The character of the ideal reader is no longer that of a sympathetic bystander – she or he is required to become a poor, hungry, diseased fornicator with words. This seminal passage links the act of writing to obscure origins, suspect motives, and a disturbing failure of authorial restraint.

A Tale is a text sorely and self-consciously in need of legitimation. These efforts to implicate the reader are self-protective gestures similar in kind (and perhaps in success) to a more outward-looking attempt to latch on to legitimising patronage. In the 'Introduction' the Hack confesses that he had hoped to follow the great example of Dryden and attach 'a Multiplicity of Godfathers' (p. 72) to his book. However, something went horribly wrong:

> But it seems, there is an unhappy Expence usually annexed to the Calling of a God-Father, which was clearly out of my Head, as it is very reasonable to believe. Where the Pinch lay, I cannot certainly affirm; but having employ'd a World of Thoughts and Pains, to split my Treatise into forty Sections, and having entreated forty Lords of my Acquaintance, that they would do me the Honor to stand, they all made it a Matter of Conscience, and sent me their Excuses.   (p. 72)

There is a desolation in this amounting almost to pathos. In this (fictional) scene, not one of the chosen Lords was prepared to be a patron, so the effort and iconoclasm involved in splitting the treatise's integrity into forty sections was completely wasted. The absolute lack of a response is flattening, tantamount to a complete rejection of the book's credentials by those entrusted by society with the roles of leadership and the maintenance of cultural standards. The image is of an orphan being frustrated in its attempt to align itself with legitimacy, and the correspondence can be identified more intricately, as something rather shameful. The Hack attempts to shift the blame for this failure of sponsorship on to the miserliness and hypocrisy of the Lords by allowing us to assume the worst interpretation of the connection between 'there is an unhappy Expence usually annexed to the Calling of a God-Father', and 'they all made it a Matter of Conscience, and sent me their Excuses'. The interdependence of 'Expence' and 'Conscience' suggests a satire on the Lords for their niggardly unwillingness to recognise genius, and solicits an attitude from the readers similar to that solicited by Johnson towards Richard Savage's 'mother', Anne Countess of Macclesfield in his 'Life of Savage' (1779). This self-aggrandising meaning cannot drive out all other implications, however. If we read against the grain we can uncover an explanation more damaging to *A Tale*, its author, and its fictitious authenticity. Strenuously though the text seeks to obscure the possibility, money is not the only motive for 'a Matter of Conscience'. At least as immediate a source of scruples against being publicly associated with a particular man and his book might be the actual illegitimacy of either. In short, the man-book might be a bastard which no man of honour could be seen to acknowledge.

But these are just episodes compared to the text's most ambitious attempt to ally itself with legitimating presence, 'The Epistle Dedicatory, to His Royal Highness Prince Posterity'. This amazing amalgam of sycophancy and self-congratulation is a savage assessment of the mortality of Modern texts:

'TIS not unlikely, that when *Your Highness* will one day peruse what I am now writing, you may be ready to expostulate with Your *Governour* upon the Credit of what I here affirm, and command him to shew You some of our Productions. To which he will answer, (for I am well informed of his Designs) by asking *Your Highness*, where they are? and what is become of them? and pretend it a Demonstration that there never were any, because they are not to be found: Not to be found! Who has mislaid them? Are they sunk in the Abyss of Things? 'Tis certain, that in their own Nature they were *light* enough to swim upon the Surface for all Eternity. Therefore the Fault is in Him, who tied Weights so heavy to their Heels, as to depress them to the Center. Is their very Essence destroyed? Who has annihilated them? Were they drowned by *Purges* or martyred by *Pipes*? Who administered them to the Posteriors of -----?   (pp. 31–32)

The '*Governour*' is obviously Time, and there is pointed satire in the only slightly exaggerated prediction that he will annihilate all the works of the current crop of Moderns. Though the ephemeral texts of Modernity be light enough to rest like scum on the surface, the filtering process of time will tie 'Weights so heavy to their Heels, as to depress them to the Center', and they will be lost, 'sunk in the Abyss of Things'. For all their claims to supplant the works of the Ancients, they do not attain primacy. They are merely posterior, or rather merely an adjunct, in the grossest sense, to the function of posteriors.

A Tale is riddled with such anxieties of insignificance and expropriation, and this passage continues with particularly fruitful reflection on the condition of orphanhood. It is the nightmare vision of Prince Posterity's Governour and his hostility to the works of the Moderns:

But that it may no longer be a Doubt with *Your Highness*, who is to be the Author of this universal Ruin; I beseech You to observe that large and terrible *Scythe* which your *Governour* affects to bear continually about him. Be pleased to remark the Length and Strength, the Sharpness and Hardness of his *Nails* and *Teeth*: Consider his baneful abominable *Breath*, Enemy to Life and matter, infectious and corrupting: And then reflect whether it be possible for any mortal Ink and Paper of this Generation to make a suitable Resistance. Oh, that *Your Highness* would one day resolve to disarm this Usurping *Maitre du Palais*, of his furious Engins, and bring Your Empire *hors de Page*.   (pp. 32–33)

There is comedy here in the clever parody of the eternal rebel's demand that the monarch come to his senses, free himself from his evil ministers, and enter a brave new world under the influence of the rebels. This comedy is doubled (and perhaps given a hint of tragedy) by the fact that the tyranny railed against is the unavoidable function of the natural order of things. Rebellion was, as we have seen, the primary anxiety of late Stuart culture, and local exemplars of this dangerous rhetoric of evil ministers included Monmouth's Rebellion and the pre-regicide phase of the 'Great Rebellion'. It is also possible to see in the Hack here an inept and impotent image of the greatest rebel of all, Milton's insinuating Satan.

However, it is the fractured imagery of family drama that I particularly want to remark on here; imagery fractured by the absence of nurturing parents and the terrifying presence of the figure of the evil guardian, replete with long, strong, sharp, hard teeth, bad breath, and a 'large and terrible *Scythe*'. This Dickensian plot is the orphan's malign fantasy of primal displacement, neglect, and persecution.[2] The intensity of the imagery of the guardian as terrible ogre and the imminence of annihilation betray the orphaned text's fear of being blocked, unable to connect with a legitimating source of authority. It is fearfully aware that the way of the world is malign and that, without the help of powerful affiliation or uncommon originality, the textual waif is more likely to finish wiping posteriors than reverenced by posterity. The immediacy of this anxiety is heightened by the binding together of human and textual images. '[A]ny mortal Ink and Paper of this Generation' is a remarkable anthropomorphosis, and the pun in the idea of wresting the empire of letters '*hors de Page*' enacts the doubleness of resonance between textual and human mortality perfectly. The 'literal' meaning is that the Prince should liberate himself from his guardian's malign regency to rule in his own person, but there is also a hint of the impossibly wishful idea of releasing literary virtue from the restrictive tyranny of the page of paper and print. This fantasy of liberation is typically Modern in its projecting desire to escape from common forms into a new, heightened (but inane and chimerical) state of being or mastery. Posterity without the recording page may be desirable in some esoteric way – it may obscure the sense of fear, shame, resentment, and aggression towards a scoffing world contingent on *A Tale*'s marginality. However, it is hopelessly sterile. It betrays a guarded, Uriah Heepish hostility towards the whole world for being so superior, and towards us, the actual readers, for being implicated in the plot. Whether this hostility is the Hack's or Swift's is a question forever left open by the irony at the heart of Swiftian parody.

---

[2] Without wishing to become mired in Freudian analysis, it is worth remarking that this attitude corresponds roughly to Swift's own opinion of his persecution under the care of his guardian, Uncle Godwin. The Hack's constant anxieties of belatedness have a correlative in Swift's resentment of his own 'posthumous' birth.

Appeals to authority: original rights and original systems

But this is enough chasing of images. The point has been sufficiently demonstrated, I hope, that *A Tale* figures itself as an orphan: marginal, belated, and friendless. Traces of myths of origin are generated almost randomly, and equally paradoxical appeals are made to farcical overriding systems. The deconstruction of these two kinds of claim to authentication expose different kinds of gaps and anxieties. Myths of mechanical system or transcendent mystery are attempts to constitute authority in the individual book or person; they displace issues of heritable legitimacy by an assertion of immediate connection between original order and present utterance. Myths of origin, on the other hand, attempt to create a façade of inherited legitimacy; they mediate (or appear to mediate) from the original (divine) authorisation to the present application. In *A Tale*, the two sorts of discourse collide and contradict each other, as well as themselves, in parody which betrays anxieties of difference, originality, belatedness, and relatedness. These are, as I have suggested in earlier chapters, the dominant rhetorical anxieties of late Stuart culture, and they provide the discursive fabric of the book. In a marginal space somewhere between pure textuality and the brute existence of books (as printed artefact) and writers (as emotional, physical, and economic units) *A Tale* tries feverishly to make a name for itself and, by failing, succeeds. Even its naming is emblematic of the confusion of the boundaries between word play and the phenomenal world. To have a legitimate name is to have a history and an identity, but this book's naming is provisional, entirely contingent on the needs of the moment. It is a tub in 'the literal Meaning' (p. 40). If we take 'literal' to mean actual and physical it indicates an empty, resounding, wooden barrel, and if we take 'literal' to mean 'to the letter' it is a verbal distraction, an empty cipher. Either way the tub is accidental, lacking intrinsic or inherited validity.

Let us look at some of the ways *A Tale* attempts to legitimate itself by appealing to systems which claim inspired originality. In a general sense, these are the claims of the Moderns to know, think, and do better than their Ancient forebears. The Moderns cut lines of authority, displacing received method and opinion in favour of their own original perception of truth. As the pun suggests, the knaves make origins of themselves and then attempt to attract disciples to make traditions of their hubristic errors. The parody portrays the processes and results of cleaving to error. It creates a cacophonous intertext where patterns of thought and language enact their own collapse and wear destructively against each other as if unaware that a proliferation of absolutisms undermines rather than aids certainty. Mechanistic systems, Aeolism, textual scholarship, and alchemy are all presented enthusiastically as simple and easy methods for appropriating control of all sorts of religious and intellectual endeavour. The shape of this sort of enterprise is exposed in

the 'Digression on Madness' in the persons of two great materialist philosophers, Epicurus and Descartes:

> For, what Man in the natural State, or Course of Thinking, did ever conceive it in
> his Power to reduce the Notions of all Mankind, exactly to the same Length, and
> Breadth, and Height of his own? Yet this is the first humble and civil Design of all
> Innovators in the Empire of Reason. *Epicurus* modestly hoped, that one Time or
> other, a certain Fortuitous Concourse of all Mens Opinions, after perpetual
> Justlings, the Sharp with the Smooth, the Light and the Heavy, the Round and the
> Square, would by certain *Clinamina*, unite in the Notions of *Atoms* and *Void*, as these
> did in the Originals of all Things. *Cartesius* reckoned to see before he died, the
> Sentiments of all Philosophers, like so many lesser Stars in his *Romantick* System,
> rapt and drawn within his own *Vortex*.   (pp. 166–67)

The appeal to personally apprehended system attempts 'to reduce the
Notions of all Mankind, exactly to the same Length, and Breadth, and
Height of [one's] own', but it succeeds only in impotently imposing an *idée
fixe* on the variety of the universe. Like Gulliver before he renounced all
visionary schemes of reforming humanity, Epicurus and Descartes are presented as fully expecting all human thought to warp around their revela-
tions of life's true substance. Their new materialisms allow anyone who can
master a few wayward notions to prove the greatest absurdities 'by uncontroulable Demonstration', (p. 34) and so to constitute himself or herself as
an 'uncontroulable' source of authority. This image of overweening fantasy
is itself constrained to act as a demonstration of the Hack's pet pseudo-phys-
iological hobby-horse, the motivating force of madness:

> Now, I would gladly be informed, how it is possible to account for such
> Imaginations as these in particular Men, without Recourse to my *Phaenomenon of
> Vapours*, ascending from the lower Faculties to over-shadow the Brain, and thence
> distilling into Conceptions, for which the Narrowness of our Mother-Tongue has
> not yet assigned any other Name, besides that of *Madness* or *Phrenzy*.   (p. 167)

The use of materialist rhetoric to undermine materialist system-makers is
not a simple irony, though it is a pervasive one. In the text, the question of
whether inner substances are preferable to surface appearances moves from
the field of moral philosophy into physiology, and a woman is proclaimed
distinctly worse for her having been flayed out of her skin. At the whim of
'systematic' materialism, the metaphor on which the idea of inspiration
depends is both analysed and analised in the pneumatic religion of the
Aeolists. So it goes – as is appropriate for parody, the systems that are being
exposed return to take over the text.

A pure illustration of this is the circular way an alchemical tradition is (or
can be seen to be) internalised into the parody's fabric. After hinting at the
presence in the text of 'a full Receit of the *Opus Magnum*' (p. 187), the Hack
claims to outline another great secret in the text:

Whoever will be at the Pains to calculate the whole Number of each Letter in this Treatise, and sum up the Difference exactly between the several Numbers, assigning the true natural Cause for every such Difference; the Discoveries in the Product, will plentifully reward his Labour. (p. 187)

The obvious meta-textual meaning is that the plentiful, or at least the appropriate, rewards for such numerological labour are wasted effort and frustration. The language seems to strain parody of alchemical discourse almost to the point of simple satiric denunciation. However, if we view the words 'innocently', without the presumption of irony, they can be interpreted as perfectly traditional alchemy. The brothers of the Rosy Cross were held to be a secret order.[3] They were not allowed to make their membership public, and were sworn to keep the mysteries hidden. The secrecy was so well maintained that it is not possible to determine if such a society ever existed formally, but people and texts associated with alchemical ideas were often not above a bit of playful and riddling half-exposure of secrets. One trick was to publish incomplete descriptions of experiments, the gaps in which could only be filled by the illuminated reader. If we pretend to take the method seriously for a moment, the effort proposed above fits this pattern perfectly and in a particularly ingenious manner. The direction 'to calculate the whole Number of each Letter in this Treatise' and perform a number of functions on them seems to be explicit and feasible enough for an *adeptus* to be able to proceed to the plentiful reward. However, in exactly the manner of the true Rosicrucian tease, the information given is radically incomplete. The treatise on which the mathematical process is to be based (*A Tale*) is incomplete, because there are hiatuses in the text. The gaps mean that there is an unknown number of letters the whole numbers of which cannot be known or reliably guessed at. Therefore, the parodic decorum has not been breached – the secret has been kept hidden while appearing to be told. We may suspect that the whole process is empty of meaning anyway, but it is also empty in an internally consistent way, and provides enough confusion to keep the apprentice *illuminatus* tantalised.

This small emblem of the paradoxical completion of empty processes is a tidy illustration of the way *A Tale* figures itself around patterns whose value it erases. The theory and practice of Aeolism, for example, clearly enshrine error, yet that religion's canons of sense and imagery, and its methods of communication come to dominate the book in crucial ways that cannot be apprehended purely as imitative satire. Modernism's many mechanisms are not simply exposed to ridicule: the book is in many ways a masterpiece of Modernity. Any impression of textual integrity is erased by the hiatuses and queried by the marginal terrorism of footnotes; fantasies of inspiration

[3] I take my information on Rosicrucianism in this period from Frances A. Yates, *The Rosicrucian Enlightenment* (London: Routledge & Kegan Paul, 1972).

impregnate all the text's propositions of religious (and intellectual) authority. Moreover, without the impersonations of mechanical modes of delusion *A Tale* would be a lifeless rant that would never have been '*light* enough to swim upon the Surface for all Eternity' (p. 32). We read it for the verbal brilliance of its transgression of the boundaries between sense and lunacy rather than for its profundity, and understand that the book is mad at least to the extent that it is shaped by the systematic forms of madness it attacks. It has little other foundation and no other material.

The Hack's systems collapse on themselves, on the vacuity at their centre which seeks to constitute itself as an original authority. Myths of origin recede into obscurity and error, so that even etymological origins are subverted. This can be done explicitly, as in the etymology of the judge's bench, 'which in the *Phoenecian* Tongue is a Word of great Signification, importing, if literally interpreted, *The Place of Sleep*; but in common Acceptation, *A Seat well bolster'd and cushion'd, for the Repose of old and gouty Limbs: Senes ut in otia tuta recedant*' (p. 57). However, it is most universally influential in the persistent punning that pervades the text. Punning is a playful writerly act, but it also destabilises language in important ways, particularly when it appears in a text deeply anxious about origins and the transmission of valued certainties. It fractures the connection between word and meaning and exposes a duplicity in the word's original form that makes the ideal of closed and exact communication impossible. In practice, it makes intended meaning keep bad (and low) company which often runs quite counter to the author's ostensible aims. A pun is a trace of false loyalties and false origins. It suggests indirections, frustrations, and forkings in the filiation of meanings which are analogous to the other bizarre genealogies promiscuously generated by the text.[4]

One of these is the account of the transmigrations of error's soul in the person of the '*True Critick*':

Every *True Critick* is a Hero born, descending in direct Line from a Celestial Stem, by *Momus* and *Hybris*, who begat *Zoilus*, who begat *Tigellius*, who begat *Etcaetera* the Elder, who begat *B--lly* and *Rym--*, and *W--ton*, and *Perrault*, and *Dennis*, who begat *Etcaetera* the Younger.   (p. 94)

This almost blasphemous parody of biblical genealogy is soon followed by a description of the critic's providential duty:

NOW, from this Heavenly Descent of *Criticism*, and the close Analogy it bears to *Heroick Virtue*, 'tis easie to Assign the proper Employment of a *True Ancient Genuine Critick*; which is, to travel thro' this vast World of Writings: to pursue and hunt those Monstrous Faults bred within them: to drag out the lurking Errors like *Cacus* from

---

[4] On Swiftian puns, see David Nokes, '"Hack at Tom Poley's": Swift's Use of Puns', *The Art of Jonathan Swift*, Clive T. Probyn, ed. (London: Vision Press, 1978), pp. 43–56.

his Den; to multiply them like *Hydra*'s Heads; and rake them together like *Augeas*'s Dung. Or else to drive away a sort of *Dangerous Fowl*, who have a perverse Inclination to plunder the best Branches of the *Tree of Knowledge*, like those *Stymphalian* Birds that eat up the Fruit.   (p. 95)

The Critick makes a strangely inverted Hercules. Cacus ('a vast, hideous, three-headed shepherd,...son of Hephaestus and Medusa, who was the dread and disgrace of the Aventine Forest, and puffed flames from each of his three mouths,'[5] but also in Latin '*caco, avi, atum, are*, to go to stool, to be at stool'[6]), lurks like error in his den and is dragged out into the open by the Critick, whereas in the ancient story the dragging had been done by Cacus and in the other direction. He had stolen six of the cattle of Geryon and dragged them backwards by the tail into his cave so that he might not be traced. In *A Tale*'s misunderstanding of the myth, the trajectory of error is outwards. Similarly inverted and scatological is the treatment of the Augean stables, which are no longer flushed clean and pure by the diversion of the rivers Alphaeus and Peneius (as in the traditional story) but rather have their contents raked together into a pile, a noisome image of the Critick's scholarship. Our hero perverts the task of criticism, transforming its search for sweetness and light into a pursuit of 'those Monstrous Faults bred within' writing. Furthermore, this Critick does not even pretend to be a purifier of the body literary, for once he has discovered his lurking errors he multiplies and collects them. A perverse kind of knight errant, he acts as Error's uncritical servant, doing his best to frustrate the transmission of value by driving away '*Dangerous Fowl*, who have a perverse Inclination to plunder the best Branches of the *Tree of Knowledge*'. I take these '*Stymphalian* Birds' (a kind of mythological crop-duster, 'brazen-beaked, brazen-clawed, brazen-winged, man-eating birds', which killed 'men and beasts by discharging a shower of brazen feathers and at the same time muting a poisonous excrement, which blighted the crops')[7] to be heavily armed equivalents of the *Battle*'s bee, modern Ancients who still pursue the proper end of letters, which is to learn from the best of the past and ignore what is pedestrian.[8] However, here again the narrator's misunderstanding of his sources is extensive and suggestive, for the fortified birds which he considers the Critick's natural enemies provide tidy symbolic equivalents to the Critick themselves, particularly in their proclivity for poisoning crops by excreting on them from a great height.

---

[5] Robert Graves, *The Greek Myths*, 2nd edn, 2 vols. (Harmondsworth: Penguin, 1960), II, p. 136; Graves is the source for the information on Hercules' labours.
[6] Charlton T. Lewis and Charles Short, *A Latin Dictionary Founded on Andrews' Edition of Freund's Latin Dictionary* (Oxford: Oxford University Press, 1879), p. 257.
[7] Graves, II, p. 119.
[8] A problem with this benign reading of the birds is that Adam and Eve plundered the tree of knowledge and got into no end of trouble. It is particularly Swiftian to use such a double-edged image.

Ultimately, this perverse concentration on dung rather than fruit illustrates the logical consequence of Modern enterprises which seek to establish their own primacy in a mythology of progress. Multiplying errors 'like *Hydra*'s Heads', raking them together in noisome piles, and persecuting the true disciples of learning, the true Critick attains the stature of a formidable anti-hero. He derails questions of value, using previous texts and ideas merely as grist to a mill which he turns mechanically in a pointless attempt to constitute himself and his system as the supreme source of wisdom. If he has roots, they are in error. Like his close acquaintance, the Modern Author, his claim to represent final, ultimate authority is groundless and is seen to founder, leaving him with only that most dubious form of ultimacy, proclaimed in the 'Digression in the Modern Kind': 'I here think fit to lay hold on that great and honourable Privilege of being the *Last Writer*, I claim an absolute Authority in Right, as the *freshest Modern*, which gives me a Despotick Power over all Authors before me' (p. 130). This posteriority is a pitiful primacy, arbitrary and impotent. Yet it is also dangerous in its puerile will to destroy the power of monuments of genuine value. Like parody, it suggests a confusion in (or, at least, a diversion from) the original order of things which exposes other, more damaging meanings than those 'intended'. It suggests the anxiety and seductiveness of error.

Error and the apostolic succession: the allegorical tale

It was necessary, that Corruption should have some Allegory as well as the rest

(p. 14)

A Tale of A Tub is an insistently topical book, and its most persistent topic is error. It figures itself as a tub in 'the literal meaning' (p. 40), tossed into the sea of controversy to distract the forces of Leviathan, the late seventeenth-century archetype of error. We can treat this as one of our text's self-advertising myths of significance, an attempt to disguise its rootless supplementarity. However, it also operates as a tidy allegory of its function as parody. As some theorists have recognised,[9] parody and allegory are intimately related genres, both concerned with the transformation of textual appearance into ramifying layers of significance. The relationship is not one of simple synonymy, but the differences between the genres – the sorts of meaning they are trying to convey and the ways they treat their pre-texts – offer an intriguing dialogue. At the point of greatest generalisation, where the largest and emptiest truths lie, the difference could be summarised in the proposition that allegory teaches its readers to see beyond appearance to

---

[9] Notably Quilligan, *The Language of Allegory* and Gay Clifford, *The Transformations of Allegory* (London: Routledge & Kegan Paul, 1974).

recognise truth while parody teaches it readers to see beyond appearance to recognise error. In allegory irony is instrumental while in parody it is critical, but both genres focus on the plurality of discursive (written) meaning and comment on its echoes and contingencies. Quilligan describes the point of similarity and divergence:

> If allegories are ideally the recreations of the forms of 'better' books, if they are lesser copies which lead the reader back to the values presented by the sacred book, then the status of the allegory will depend on the status of the sacred pretext. The same, however, is true for parody: the impact of *Shamela* depends upon what Henry Fielding can make us think of the status of *Pamela*. The difference, of course, is that the impact of an allegory is to reveal the privileged status of the pretext, while a parody aims at undermining the value of the original text, providing a true criticism, not a commentary.[10]

Though this may exaggerate the determinacy of the process of parodic criticism, at least for parody as complex and playful as *A Tale*, it marks space usefully. There is a family likeness between parody and allegory which *A Tale* exploits subtly and, in the tale of the three brothers, extensively. In what Clifford describes as a 'deliberate parody of the allegorical method, a brilliant palimpsest of irony',[11] the book offers a parody of church history as the frustration of the original will of the Father and the perversion of his institution on earth. There are unmistakable sectarian markings (more in the biting attacks on Popery and Dissent than in the notoriously limp advocacy of the Anglican alternative), but there is a larger story in play as well. This is a tale of origin lost, of the twisting away from the true though chaste pattern of conduct prescribed in the beginning into the empty attractions of error. After seven years (or centuries) of apostolic purity, the brothers break the thread which connects them to their father, and from then on the apostolic succession becomes the succession of error and corruption. Once the break has been made, perfect true religion is irrecoverable – even the most sincere and well informed attempt to re-establish primitive Christianity is doomed to keep some marks of corruption, while all enthusiasms are doomed to repeat the empty ambitions of Aeolism and the sect of the tailor-god.

The story starts, fairy-tale style, with an orphaning:

> ONCE upon a Time, there was a Man who had Three Sons by one Wife, and all at a Birth, neither could the Mid-Wife tell Certainly which was the Eldest. Their Father died while they were young, and upon his Death-Bed, calling the Lads to him, spoke thus...   (p. 73)

In this family drama of displacement the father (who represents authority) dies, and the mother (who would represent nurturing) is so completely

---

[10] Quilligan, *The Language of Allegory*, pp. 135–36.
[11] Clifford, *The Transformations of Allegory*, p. 49.

unimportant that her disappearance is not even commented on – we do not
know whether she died or simply absconded to Leicester. So, like Swift, the
brothers are cut off from biological origins at the beginning of the story.
They are left only with a Will which prescribes the rules they are to keep
and coats which will protect them from the elements. This is no religion of
the living God, but if it falls short of the Gospel promise of life in all its full-
ness, it seems likely that this is a limitation of Swift's theology – his temperamental preference for a harsh image of the Old Testament God – rather
than any deliberate criticism of the bleakness of the task set. The father's
last recorded words are monitory, betraying no sympathy and enjoining a
bare obedience to his dead hand:

Pray Children, wear them [the coats] *clean, and brush them often. You will find in my Will*
(here it is) *full Instructions in every particular concerning the Wearing and Management of your
Coats; wherein you must be very exact, to avoid the Penalties I have appointed for every
Transgression or Neglect, upon which your future Fortunes will entirely depend. I have also commanded in my Will, that you should live together in one House like Brethren and Friends, for then
you will be sure to thrive, and not otherwise.*   (pp. 73–74)

Thus the Will (or Scripture) is figured as a dead letter, defining and confin-
ing life, keeping it within the parameters prefigured by proper authority.
While it is obeyed, connection to the true source is maintained, and its later
subversion provides us with an allegory of misreading. The complementary
abuse of the living coats (the Church) provides an allegory of desire and corruption. Put together, we have an allegory of error, expressed in both its
intellectual and institutional forms. The orphaned brothers first lose the
presence of their guiding progenitor, and then frustrate the filiation of his
authority by their breach of apostolic obedience. They are left rootless with
only their fantasies and a few fugitive traces of the ideal to make their way
in the world, and, as always with Swift, they do not succeed in overcoming
these odds.

The story of the Will is not just any allegory of misreading, of course. It is
the parodic equivalent of the subversion of *the Word*, of God's Will as
expressed in Scripture,[12] and it is also (as Walsh and Harth demonstrate[13]) a
specifically Protestant and Anglican story. Initially, the Will has the power to
protect the brothers from their fallen nature, but slowly and insidiously the
relationship of masterful text and obedient interpreter is turned around. Led
by Peter, 'the distinguishing Brother' (p. 84), a subversive power is extended
over the Will by means of wilfully self-seeking interpretation. The notion of
'*Jure Paterno*' is abstracted from the simple, explicit dictates of the Will, and
twisted to serve as canonical sanction for such hermeneutic sleight-of-hand

[12] See Levine, 'The Design of *A Tale*', and Quilligan, *The Language of Allegory*, pp. 132–45 for a discussion of *A Tale*'s relationship to the infallible word of Scripture.
[13] 'Text, "Text", and *A Tale*', and *Swift and Anglican Rationalism*.

as justifying shoulder knots '*totidem literis*', with a special exemption for the letter K, which, being 'a modern illegitimate Letter' (p. 84), can be taken to be represented by C. A kind of hermeneutic Fall (a compact edition of the Tower of Babel) takes place whereby the connection between the Will's original meaning and its current interpretation is broken, so that the outer literal form is manipulated with complete disregard for its literal sense, let alone any idea of guiding intent. Once this Rubicon of misreading has been crossed there is no stopping the brothers. They still pretend to reverence the Will, but pursue such a wilful mastery over it that their coats are safe from no adornment of fashion. Gold lace, unmentioned in the Will, is 'remembered' to be enjoined by tradition (another word for conveniently fabricated hearsay, a furtive and illegitimate line of authority). Flame coloured satin is 'found' in a codicil to the Will, a dangerous supplement corresponding to the authority allowed apocryphal additions to Scripture. Silver fringe is desired, so the Will's specific command that it be shunned is avoided by etymological subterfuge; fringe is said to signify broom-stick, and the absurdity of a command forbidding the wearing of silver broom-sticks on overcoats is declared a sacred mystery. Embroidered images are forbidden, so they are excused by the sophistry that the new fashion in images is different from that of the father's time. Finally, the brothers (notably Peter, 'the Sholastick Brother' (p. 89)) tire of the game of repeatedly defeating a subverted text, so they lock it up (keeping it under erasure) in 'a *Strong-Box*, brought out of *Greece* or *Italy*, (I have forgot which) and trouble themselves no farther to examine it, but only refer to its Authority whenever they thought fit' (p. 90).

Reading with an eye to satire, all this makes some pointed, easily convertible, and traditionally Protestant criticisms of the corruptions of Popery. The '*Strong-Box*' is the Vulgate, and the embroidered images are religious art or graven images (depending on your point of view). The sartorial ostentation of silver fringe is justified by sophistry, that of flame coloured satin by appeal to the inauthentic (and delusive) authority of the Apocrypha,[14] that of gold lace by appeal to unreliable and unverifiable oral tradition, and that of shoulder knots by recourse to numerological anagram. In historical context, this vindication of the Reformation is the section's obvious meaning. However, there is also the more general dimension of an anatomy of wilful misreading – the conquest of logos by criticism. This parody of Popish interpretation shows the shifts made by corrupt desire to overthrow (or deconstruct) the Word's true, original authority. In ways too many to enumerate, *A Tale* is *about* the subordination of simple, apparent, and prescriptive utterance to perverse and self-serving interpretation.

---

[14] As the annotator suggests (p. 86), the satin can also be seen as the doctrine of purgatory, a place of fire and scourging, the only scriptural authority for which being a forced interpretation of the non-canonical 2 Maccabees 12, 43–45.

The story of the coats gives the institutional half of the equation. The subversion of the Church's fabric and mission demonstrates the fragility of apostolic institutions, because they rely on the persistence of an unbroken filiation to revealed order. The original coats have magical qualities of protection: '*with good wearing, they will last you fresh and sound as long as you live*' and '*they will grow in the same proportion with your Bodies, lengthening and widening of themselves, so as to be always fit*' (p. 73). Plentiful directions are given in the Will on how to keep them in this pristine and serviceable state, but their magical qualities do not extend to being able to protect themselves from modification or affray. They provide the fabric upon which the brothers work their errant wills as they become dedicated followers of fashion. Once modifications are made, and corruptions set in, the coats cannot be returned to their original condition even with the best will in the world. When Martin and Jack steal a copy of the original Will from Peter and determine to reform their coats in accordance with it, Jack's fundamentalist fury to '*Strip, Tear, Pull, Rent, Flay off all*' (p. 139) reduces his coat to rags, and even Martin, the sensible Anglican brother, cannot entirely return his coat to its primitive state. Instead, after an initial fit of fury (probably corresponding in Swift's private demonology to Henry VIII's attacks on the Church's rights and properties), he patiently picks out what he can and leaves what cannot be removed without damaging the remains of the original fabric. He can only make the best of a fallen thing.

Once the father's will has been subverted, the brothers have wandered into error and are left entirely to their own intellectual and moral resources. Martin's cautious and obedient piety is commended and he fades from the scene – the allegory loses interest in him and focuses on the double image of Peter and Jack. Frank Palmeri gives a clear analysis of the dynamics of this move:

Throughout the *Tale*, Swift suppresses potential middle terms and mediating categories in favour of a thoroughgoing doubleness that represents the brotherly dissimilarity of opposite extremes. The story of the three brothers depicts this pattern most clearly and least subtly: Martin drops out of the picture, and then the other two come to mirror each other.[15]

The two allegories of solipsism, Peter's self-promoting knavery and Jack's enthusiastic madness, form two images of error: the appeal to corrupted lines of authority and the appeal to an imagined original system. The semi-identical twins (in the mirror of irony, they are exactly complementary) illustrate the proliferation of error in the unrestrained and unguided human spirit.

Peter declares himself a sort of medium for the father's will, capable of

---

[15] '"To write upon Nothing"', p. 159.

declaring *ex cathedra* without reference to any verbal traces of intent locked in the Will. By forging a deed of conveyance,[16] he takes over a house and makes himself master of it above his brothers. He then proceeds to engender himself, first as the elder brother, then as Mr Peter, then Father Peter, then My Lord Peter, and ultimately Emperor Peter. His moods, actions, and sense of his own primacy become ever more extravagant as he gets carried away by the power of infallibility which he has conferred upon himself: 'Even in his lucid Intervals, [he] was very lewdly given in his common Conversation, extream wilful and positive, and would at any time rather argue to the Death, than allow himself to be once in an Error' (pp. 119–20). He makes the fundamental mistake of believing himself incapable of error, and his manners degenerate with his wisdom: 'He had an abominable Faculty of telling huge palpable *Lies* upon all Occasions; and swearing, not only to the Truth, but cursing the whole Company to Hell, if they pretended to make the least Scruple of believing Him' (p. 120). He becomes an absurd tyrant, infatuated with his usurped power, and demands that his brothers and followers submit to all kinds of hardship and crazy tests of faith. Finally, the cunning which served him so well in his early days as the distinguishing brother deserts him as he presumes too far upon his artificial authority:

IN short, *Peter* grew so scandalous, that all the Neighbourhood began in plain Words to say, he was no better than a Knave. And his two Brothers long weary of his ill Usage, resolved at last to leave him; but first, they humbly desired a Copy of their Father's Will, which had now lain by neglected, time out of Mind. Instead of granting this Request, he called them *damn'd Sons of Whores, Rogues, Traytors*, and the rest of the vile Names he could muster up. However, while he was abroad one Day upon his Projects, the two Youngsters watcht their Opportunity, made a Shift to come at the Will, and took a *Copia vera*, by which they presently saw how grosly they had been abused.   (p. 121)

Like the true tyrant he has become, Peter resorts to military force to expel his disobedient brothers from the house and fades out of the tale into a malevolent retirement behind the barriers of his self-importance (in Rome).

From this separation springs a second allegory of solipsism, figured in Jack's mad career. The two Protestant brothers have armed themselves for their independent (i.e. reformed) existence by going back to the source of authority, the father's Will. There has been little difficulty in making a *copia vera* of the authorising text,[17] but the task of using this copy as a means of

---

[16] A satiric barb aimed at the Roman Church's use of the Donation of Constantine to gain temporal power over Rome and that part of Italy which became the Papal States.

[17] As Walsh, 'Text, "Text" and *A Tale*', demonstrates, this was another specifically Anglican point, countering the Roman Catholic scholarship devoted to undermining confidence in the received or recoverable text of the Bible.

reforming their coats into a *copia vera* of their original state proves to be more difficult. Motivated by an extreme resentment towards Peter and a determination to make his own mind the measure of all things, Jack wrenches the will out of apostolic context, to treat it with idolatrous (but tyrannical) respect as a complete cure-all, an infallible system independent of history. This fantasy of immediate communication with the father's will through his rediscovered Will becomes merely another way of subduing the text and subverting proper obedience. Idolatry of the letter is exposed as a particularly virulent form of misreading, distorting 'obvious' meaning and justifying ratbaggery on a grand scale:

JACK had provided a fair Copy of his Father's *Will*, engrossed in Form upon a large Skin of Parchment; and resolving to act the Part of a most dutiful Son, he became the fondest Creature of it imaginable. For, altho', as I have often told the Reader, it consisted wholly in certain plain, easy Directions about the management and wearing of their Coats, with Legacies and Penalties, in case of Obedience or Neglect; yet he began to entertain a Fancy, that the Matter was *deeper* and *darker*, and therefore must needs have a great deal more of Mystery at the Bottom. *Gentlemen*, said he, *I will prove this very Skin of Parchment to be Meat, Drink, and Cloth, to be the Philosopher's Stone, and the Universal Medicine*. In consequence of which Raptures, he resolved to make use of it in the most necessary, as well as the most paltry Occasions of Life. He had a Way of working it into any Shape he pleased; so that it served him for a Night-cap when he went to Bed, and for an Umbrello in rainy Weather.   (p. 190)

The claims Jack makes for the Will's power are even more exorbitant than those made for bread in the parody of transubstantiation. Peter only declares his crust to be flesh and wine, whereas Jack proclaims the Will to be '*Meat, Drink, and Cloth, to be the Philosopher's Stone, and the Universal Medicine*'. The important thing about his relationship with the Will is that he exerts tyrannical and fanciful control over its signification. If communication is immediate, there are no inherent controls over signification, and the reader can make of texts – even sacred texts – what she or he pleases. There is no way of forbidding a situation where, if the reader's desires are perverse, consequent readings will be perverse, and interpretation will become meaningless except as a licence for wish-fulfilment.

Jack does not understand the difference between words and things, between fantasy and reality. In a parody of materialism, he makes a strange glide from faith in the efficacy of the word in a spiritual sense to the efficacy of the book in a physical sense. He uses pieces of parchment (which are physically removed from the original Will by being merely a copy – the magic is apparently transmissible through copyists) like a quack remedy, literalising the metaphor of the word as the bread of life. His perception has become a hostage to his converting imagination. Like Epicurus seeing the universe as clinamina and Descartes seeing it in terms of vortices, Jack has blind faith in his self-apprehended system. The parody materialises this metaphor explicitly when, systematically working through the proposition 'That a *Wise Man was his own Lanthorn*' (p. 192), 'HE would shut his Eyes as he walked along the Streets, and if he happened to bounce his Head against a Post, or fall into a Kennel (as he seldom missed either to do one or both) he would tell the gibing Prentices, who looked on, that...' (p. 192), whereupon he launches into a long sermon on the dangers of opening his eyes and the benefits of keeping them shut. With his vision notionally concentrated on the heavens, but actually turned inwards, he is often, like the philosopher in the *Mechanical Operation of the Spirit*, 'seduced by his *lower Parts* into a *Ditch*' (p. 289). Jack displays a wilful disregard for 'common sense' and extrapolates a canting hypocrisy from his lunatic precepts that goes well beyond the bounds of sanity, yet remains threatening. He turns his coat to rags, and insists that everybody follow his example. The danger is that the perversity might be contagious.

This returns us to the core of the allegorical tale, the nature of error and the essential homogeneity of its manifestations. Finally, these allegories of the displaced word (Jack) and the displaced succession (Peter) come together in a denouement in which family likeness is revealed where it is most denied:

IT was highly worth observing, the singular Effects of that Aversion, or Antipathy, which *Jack* and his Brother *Peter* seemed, even to an Affectation, to bear toward each other. *Peter* had lately done *some Rogueries*, that forced him to abscond; and he seldom ventured to stir out before Night, for fear of Bayliffs. Their Lodgings were at the two most distant Parts of the Town, from each other; and whenever their Occasions, or Humours called them abroad, they would make Choice of the oddest unlikely Times, and most uncouth Rounds they could invent; that they might be sure to avoid one another: Yet after all this, it was their perpetual Fortune to meet. The Reason of which, is easy enough to apprehend: For, the Phrenzy and the Spleen of both, having the same Foundation, we may look upon them as two Pair of Compasses, equally extended, and the fixed Foot of each, remaining in the same Center, which, tho' moving contrary Ways at first, will be sure to encounter somewhere or other in the Circumference.   (pp. 198–99)

The image of the compasses is crucial: no matter how it tries to distinguish itself, error is error. Jack bears 'a huge Personal Resemblance with his Brother *Peter*'; he is mistaken for him in the street by friends and bailiffs; despite constant efforts 'to grind away the Remnants of *Lace* and *Embroidery*' (p. 199) from his coat ('he rubbed every day for two hours, against a roughcast Wall' (p. 199)), his rags continue 'to bear a kind of mock Resemblance to Finery' (p. 200). Jack in his self-indulgent tatters is essentially the same as Peter in his bizarrely ornate finery. Both attempt to overpower truth by asserting a perverse *originality* in themselves, portraying this as true obedience to the will and Will of the father, but actually indulging in self-serving (and self-deconstructing) parodies of authenticity.

Throughout *A Tale*'s allegory of error, the insidious plasticity of corruption and the vulnerability of its opposite, obedience, are everywhere apparent. Corruption is powerful, flexible, seductive, and brilliant in its perversity. The devil gets all the good lines as well as all the good tunes. Yet the Blakean argument concerning Milton's God remains radically inadequate in this context, for the loss of value (and the ability to recognise value) are vividly rendered. All three brothers have lost the direct connection to the true source of certainty and safety, and two embrace error by trying to make themselves master in place of the father who has died and then been dishonoured by disobedience. Two parody authenticity, and only Martin has the humility to *imitate* authenticity in a pious and sensible manner. The subtlety of this distinction – how do we know where pious imitation ends and mad parody begins? – figures the pessimism of Swift's religious vision and his love of pushing propositions into the further reaches of paradox. Throughout Swift's writing, all human endeavour is either perched ironically on the edge of error, or it has fallen in.

Parodic self-exposure and the origin of the speaking voice

But the Reader truly *Learned*, chiefly for whose Benefit I wake, when others sleep, and sleep when others wake, will here find sufficient Matter to employ his Speculations for the rest of his Life. It were much to be wisht, and I do here humbly propose for an Experiment, that every Prince in *Christendom* will take seven of the *deepest Scholars* in his Dominions, and shut them up close for *seven* Years, in *seven* Chambers, with a Command to write *seven* ample Commentaries on this comprehensive Discourse. I shall venture to affirm, that whatever Difference may be found in their several Conjectures, they will be all, without the least Distortion, manifestly deduceable from the Text.   (p. 185)

The interpreter's role is deeply and ironically inscribed in *A Tale*, and these elusive clues, erased by irony yet vindicated by the motley history of interpretation generated by 'this comprehensive Discourse', are as close as we will get to a key. The narrator authorises promiscuity of interpretation – he declares that all will be 'manifestly deduceable from the Text' – but this slight effort to embrace the inevitable is not entirely satisfactory. Hermeneutics is, after all, the art of evacuating irony, of converting words into meaning. To be the propagator of one of 'several Conjectures' is not enough for us critics, because our investigations are 'surely' too profound and integral to the text to be mere conjecture. Thus criticism resists plurality as anxiously as late seventeenth-century culture did, so it seems probable that this passage remains as disconcerting as it ever was. While the strict adherence to patterns of seven has not been maintained, the prediction here has proved a more durable truth about the reception of *A Tale* than any of the commentaries it authorises. Let us, therefore, embrace the irony, and attempt a further 'Experiment' to discover why and how this plurality of signification comes to pass.

The thread we will follow is the text's tone of voice and the identity of the narrator(s) it suggests. This is in part a search for the sort of residual orality Swift identified in one of his *Thoughts on Various Subjects*: 'When I am reading a Book, whether wise or silly, it seemeth to me to be alive and talking to me.'[18] This is all very well as a principle, but who do we hear talking in *A Tale*? In the 'Apology', 'The Author farther asserts that the whole Work is entirely of one Hand, which every Reader of Judgment will easily discover' (pp. 20–21), but, apart from a prevailing sense of guiding genius, this fact is not as self-evident as 'the Author' would have us believe. At least on the surface of the text, we are likely to discover many hands and many voices, even in the same group of words. There are various parodies ('where the Author personates the Style and Manner of other Writers, whom he has a mind to expose' (p. 7)) and the text is riddled with cavities (even in the typography). Consequently, the single, unitary voice of authority is one of the most remarkable gaps. Not only are 'several Conjectures...manifestly deduceable from the Text', so are several narrators, and none of them speaks with full, authentic presence.

We will, in due course, analyse a passage from the 'Digression on Madness' with a view to demonstrating this hypothesis in detail. However, according to the terms of our enterprise, this is an experiment, so, before we go any further, we should apply a 'control'. That bastion of narratorial integrity, the Victorian Novel, offers the likeliest source. In *Bleak House*, Dickens employs two narrators. Esther Summerson writes a narrative from inside the story, betraying her hopes and fears, acting and trying to assimilate actions, and generally exuding the insufferable niceness which, Dickens liked to imagine, constituted female virtue. The other narrator has no name and no historical existence; it is a brooding rhetorical presence, Dickenslike, perhaps, but more objective and all-seeing than any single human could be; more like a god who can only record, or an objectification of conscience. Each narrator's chapters appear in a loosely paratactic structure governed, we willingly assume, by the historical Charles Dickens, whom we can see behind each narrator and in the ultimate shape of the novel. The demarcations between narrator and narrator are absolutely unbreachable. There is and can be no negotiation across the white spaces between the chapters, as the terms of each perspective are radically distinct. The result is a binocular view which gives the reader an enlightening depth of field. It is not particularly difficult to construct a sense of where the ultimate source of authority, the writer Dickens, stands. While he says nothing *in propria persona*, we can sense his shaping hand in the whole and decipher his authorised

[18] *PW*, IV, p. 253.

version of the meaning (within reasonably stable parameters) by negotiation of the perspectives available.[19]

The effect of all this is that we readers can be confident of the ground on which we stand. We may wish to interrogate the informing perspectives, but their discrete presences are not problematic. Compare such confidence to the reader's plight in this, the second most famous passage of the 'Digression on Madness':

For, the Brain, in its natural Position and State of Serenity, disposeth its Owner to pass his Life in the common Forms, without any Thought of subduing Multitudes to his own *Power*, his *Reasons* or his *Visions*; and the more he shapes his Understanding by the Pattern of Human Learning, the less he is inclined to form Parties after his particular Notions; because that instructs him in his private Infirmities, as well as in the stubborn Ignorance of the People. But when a Man's Fancy gets *astride* on his Reason, when Imagination is at Cuffs with the Senses, and common Understanding, as well as common Sense, is Kickt out of Doors; the first Proselyte he makes, is Himself, and when that is once compass'd, the Difficulty is not so great in bringing over others; A strong Delusion always operating from *without*, as vigorously as from *within*. For, Cant and Vision are to the Ear and the Eye, the same that Tickling is to the Touch. Those Entertainments and Pleasures we most value in Life, are such as *Dupe* and play the Wag with the Senses. For, if we take an Examination of what is generally understood by *Happiness*, as it has Respect, either to the Understanding or the Senses, we shall find all its Properties and Adjuncts will herd under this short Definition: That, *it is a perpetual Possession of being well Deceived.* And first, with Relation to the Mind or Understanding; 'tis manifest, what mighty Advantages Fiction has over Truth; and the Reason is just at our Elbow; because Imagination can build nobler Scenes, and produce more wonderful Revolutions than Fortune or Nature will be at Expence to furnish. Nor is Mankind so much to blame in his Choice, thus determining him, if we consider that the Debate meerly lies between *Things past*, and *Things conceived*; and so the Question is only this; Whether Things that have Place in the *Imagination*, may not as properly be said to *Exist*, as those that are seated in the *Memory*; which may be justly held in the Affirmative, and very much to the Advantage of the former, since This is acknowledged to be the *Womb* of Things, and the other allowed to be no more than the *Grave*. Again, if we take this Definition of Happiness, and examine it with Reference to the Senses, it will be acknowledged wonderfully adapt. How fade and insipid do all Objects accost us that are not convey'd in the Vehicle of *Delusion*? How shrunk is every Thing, as it appears in the Glass of Nature? So, if it were not for the Assistance of Artificial *Mediums*, false Lights, refracted Angles, Varnish, and Tinsel; there would be a mighty Level in the Felicity and Enjoyments of Mortal Men. If this were seriously considered by the World, as I have a certain Reason to suspect it hardly will; Men would no longer reckon among their high Points of Wisdom, the Art of exposing weak Sides, and publishing Infirmities; an Employment in my

[19] Of course, this does not preclude the possibility of unauthorised meanings abounding in the text. What I mean here is that in this novel, the author's intention is confidently retrievable within Hirschean parameters of validity. What Dickens might have betrayed or marginalised is another story entirely.

Opinion, neither better nor worse than that of *Unmasking*, which I think, has never been allowed fair Usage, either in the *World* or the *Play-House*.   (pp. 171–73)

The question to be asked of this passage is 'whose voice do we hear'? If we accept the terms of the traditional debate as to whether the narrator is a Hack (a sort of anti-self or reverse paragon for Swift) or a whimsically present Swift (occasionally using funny voices for rhetorical effect), which case is this passage evidence for?

Obviously it is not such an open-and-shut case as for *Bleak House*. The writing is more playful, and the divisions between stances far more fluid. Certainly, it is not possible (or, at least, not at all useful) to attempt to force the whole book into one or the other interpretation – there is something of Swift and something of other in the writing. Over the whole of *A Tale*, a rough separation might be posited between a Hack-like lunatic who writes the prefatory material and the Digressions and a Swift-like satirist who writes the allegorical tale.[20] This policy of dividing to conquer would, at least, create the conditions for interpretation in terms of Swift and anti-Swift, and remove the heavy burden of denial incumbent on proponents of one view in their attempts wholly to exclude the other. However, the acceptance of such arbitrary boundaries, if we aim to fix them as firmly as for *Bleak House*, incurs another burden of denial, another suppression of implications in the interests of systematic consistency. To mount the a priori argument that this passage comes from a digression, *therefore* it is written by the Hack is to bind reading to an inflexible preconception.

A sophistication would be to accuse both these views of exhibiting a projecting desire to subdue resonance in order to produce a crude dualism. One would then assure the reader that the text is an open-form parody, and hence that a plurality of voices, all with some more-or-less oblique relationship to Swift's plan of parodic quotation, inhabit it. One would point to the possible quotations from Thomas Tryon[21] and Erasmus[22] and the reference

---

[20] Both Starkman, *Swift's Satire on Learning*, and Harth, *Swift and Anglican Rationalism* divide the book thus between satire on religion and satire on learning. The validity of this demarcation has not been openly questioned, although its sharpness has often been considerably blurred in practice.

[21] Robert M. Philmus, 'Mechanical Operations of the Spirit and *A Tale of a Tub*', *English Studies in Canada*, 10 (1984), 391–406; quote, 397, quotes Tryon, *A Discourse of the Causes, Natures and Cure of Phrensie, Madness or Distraction* (1689), pp. 255–56: 'As the "Martial Property" attempts to take over, the "Soul" withdraws itself, and flings up the Reins of Government, and lets *Reason*, like a wilde Horse that hath cast off Bit and Bridle, and thrown his Rider, ramble confusedly whithersoever the Imagination shall hurry it.' While there is a clear similarity between this and the sentence commencing 'But when a Man's Fancy gets *astride* on his Reason', there is, as Philmus acknowledges, no positive evidence that Swift ever read Tryon's treatise.

[22] Hammond, 'In Praise of Wisdom', p. 263, remarks on the similarity between Erasmus, 'If a person were to try stripping the disguises from actors while they were playing a scene upon the stage, showing to the audience their real looks and the faces they were born with, would not such a one spoil the whole play?' and Swift's comment on '*Unmasking*, which I think, has never been allowed fair Usage, either in the *World* or the *Play-House*'. However, there is a double meaning in Swift's usage of 'allowed', entertaining opposite possibilities, which renders any debt of influence vexed, at least.

to Horatian ideology[23] in the passage under discussion as evidence of the way the Swiftian text is pieced together parodically. This proposal, conscious of the fissile capability of parody, might loosely be characterised as imagining the passage as a chorus of discordant voices, but this, in turn, raises problems. There are no markings in the printed text to divide voices authoritatively, so all attributions and their margins remain highly speculative. Also, at least in the couple of pages under analysis, there is an air of persistent utterance that belies such hermeneutic fragmentation.

Let us review, then, the metaphor of the chorus, and employ it more carefully.[24] Ideally, a chorus consists of many voices singing as one. The ideal is seldom achieved even by highly trained experts, and when more heterogeneous groups (e.g. church congregations, football teams, herds of academics, etc.) attempt communal singing, the effect can be cacophonous. The voices of Swiftian parody, being eminently unqualified for the tasks they set themselves, belong in the second category, singing in highly imperfect unison. What they do have in common, however, is the score, that is, the words on the page. It is not necessary to separate this passage into parts attributable to different voices. It can be read as the consistent, if lively, utterance of any single voice in the spectrum between Swift and anti-Swift. The voices, mutually exclusive though they be, cohabit the marks on the page persistently and irreconcilably. The source of the narrative is not determined, but claimable for any of a number of purposes. To use our chorus metaphor, then, each voice is singing the same words at the same time, but in different keys, with different emphases, and missing different notes.

Swift exploits the uncertain space between the enigmatically silent printed artefact and the sense of personal utterance it suggests. Unless it is authentically signed (and the problems and dangers of deception inherent in this seemingly simple and 'natural' act can be seen clearly in the life of Isaac Bickerstaff, Esq.;), the printed text remains anonymous and indefinite concerning its origin. Swift plays in the space provided by this anonymity by marking it with traces of narratorial integrity only to erase them.

---

[23] In the notion of happiness being 'a perpetual Possession of being well Deceived' Guthkelch and Nichol Smith (p. 171, n. 3) note, unenthusiastically, that 'Swift is thought by Sir Henry Craik to have had in mind the passage in Horace (*Ep.* II. ii. 140).' The similarity is indeed distant, the passage referred to concerning a man who, otherwise sane and good, *'qui se credebat miros audire tragoedos / in vacuo sessor plausorque theatro'* ('who used to fancy that he was listening to wonderful tragic actors while he sat happy and applauded in the empty theatre'). At great expense to his family, he was cured, whereupon he exclaimed *"'pol, me occidistis, amici, / non servastis," ait,"mi sic extorta voluptas / et demptus per vim mentis gratissimus error"'* ('Egod! you have killed me, my friends, not saved me; for thus you have robbed me of a pleasure and taken away perforce the dearest illusion of my heart.' (*Horace: Satires, Epistles and Ars Poetica*, H. Rushton Fairclough, ed. and trans. (London: Heinemann, 1926)) Again, if a debt be said to exist, it is not a simple one.

[24] One could as well undertake this analysis in terms of Bakhtinian heteroglossia or even of the more ancient idea of irony. I employ the metaphor of a chorus because it has its uses as a conceptual tool, not because I believe that it possesses any ultimate or exclusive hermeneutic validity.

Originating from (or, at least, mediated by) the mute page, these suggestions of uttering identity remain radically negotiable in a sense that relies on the silent anonymity of print. Swift may have felt that 'When I am reading a Book, whether wise or silly, it seemeth to me to be alive and talking to me',[25] but to try to imagine a dramatised reading of *A Tale*, is to be struck first by the absurdity of the task, and second by the profundity of the decisions that would need to made so that a coherent reading could be produced. Furthermore, the other readings that would be necessary to accommodate the possibilities excluded would not, like alternative readings of *Hamlet*, deepen our comprehension of the central character or widen our sense of his (still unified) potentialities. The alternative readings of *A Tale* would not offer more comprehensive knowledge of our nameless narrator, but rather propose alternative narrators, all displaying various flaws and degrees of shallowness, and all blissfully unaware of the others' existences. To illustrate this multivocality, I will outline a few of the narrators audible in the passage under discussion.

Coming as it does in the middle of the 'Digression on Madness', the role of narrator in this piece falls most naturally to the Grub Street Hack. This enthusiast for madness foolishly assumes that it is a failure in the 'Owner' of a serene brain to be happy 'to pass his Life in the common Forms, without any Thought of subduing Multitudes to his own *Power*'. We can sense his delight in the imagery of 'a Man's Fancy gets *astride* on his Reason' as the archetypal Modern projector rides off with his proselytes into the '*Happiness*' of '*being well Deceived*'. This Hack joyously asserts the 'mighty Advantages Fiction has over Truth', exalts Imagination over Reason, and sincerely believes that its products are quite as real as those of the Memory, or rather, more real because associated with the origin ('the *Womb* of Things') rather than mere vestiges ('the *Grave*'). Hence it is obvious that 'every Thing, as it appears in the Glass of Nature' should appear 'shrunk' and 'fade and insipid' without being 'convey'd in the Vehicle of *Delusion*', or (to express it in more post-modern imagery) without exhibiting 'the Assistance of Artificial *Mediums*, false Lights, refracted Angles, Varnish, and Tinsel'. It therefore follows logically enough that 'the Art of exposing weak Sides, and publishing Infirmities' is unwise, unjust, and fundamentally misguided; that unmasking ruins the show.

To read in this manner turns the narrator into a dramatised character, an un-Swift and perhaps an anti-Swift who cannot tell us the intended meaning of the author, only reflect (or perhaps distort) it in his indirections. However, the Grub Street Hack is not the only such character discernible here. The passage could be read as the utterance of a personification of folly in a more traditional, less historically specific manner, cognate with Erasmus' Folly. Here the ironies, paradoxes, and sublime ridiculousness of thought and diction would be relished and the impossible miracles of life and language finally affirmed. On the other hand, we could hear in it the moral power of the Augustinian conviction of the Fall, denouncing human nature with a bitter sarcasm; or (the moralist's subversive secret sharer), the cynical raciness of a Restoration wit, snidely ridiculing commonplace assumptions and degrading traditional canons of wisdom. This character exposes himself to censure by the irresponsible way he sports with sense and morality. However, in doing so he does much to expose the arbitrariness of received opinion and the pointlessness of all shows of morality or doctrines of pious obedience to higher wisdom. For him, all 'Objects' are 'fade[d] and insipid' and can only (and only momentarily) be made to appear otherwise by conveyance in 'the Vehicle of *Delusion*' accompanied by the ornamental *frisson* of 'the Assistance of Artificial *Mediums*, false Lights, refracted Angles, Varnish, and Tinsel'. He sneeringly asserts that the nearest thing to happiness that we are likely to experience is '*a perpetual Possession of being well Deceived*', and exults derisively in his destructive art of '*Unmasking*, which I think, has never been allowed fair Usage, either in the *World* or the *Play-House*'.

Yet if we can hear the voice of Rochester, so too we can hear that of his confessor, Bishop Burnet. One of the more discordant voices debatably present is that of a pompous Latitudinarian preacher moralising a little ineptly on the inconvenience of lunacy and the frailty of reason. Speaking more in sorrow than in anger, this figure commences with sonorous reassurance:

For, the Brain, in its natural Position and State of Serenity, disposeth its Owner to pass his Life in the common Forms, without any Thought of subduing Multitudes to his own *Power*, his *Reasons* or his *Visions*; and the more he shapes his Understanding by the Pattern of Human Learning, the less he is inclined to form Parties after his particular Notions; because that instructs him in his private Infirmities, as well as in the stubborn Ignorance of the People.

This solemn magniloquence gives way to a strangely ponderous invocation of the destructive power of too much liberty, of fancy too much indulged:

But when a Man's Fancy gets *astride* on his Reason, when Imagination is at Cuffs with the Senses, and common Understanding, as well as common Sense, is Kickt out of Doors; the first Proselyte he makes, is Himself, and when that is once compass'd, the Difficulty is not so great in bringing over others; A strong Delusion always operating from *without*, as vigorously as from *within*.

Wary of striking too paralysing a fear into his congregation, the preacher moralises the point in such a way that we cannot ignore the risk of seduction:

For, Cant and Vision are to the Ear and the Eye, the same that Tickling is to the Touch. Those Entertainments and Pleasures we most value in Life, are such as *Dupe* and play the Wag with the Senses.

He is carried away by his rhetoric so far as to attempt very stable irony on the theme of the emptiness of worldly happiness:

For, if we take an Examination of what is generally understood by Happiness, as it has Respect, either to the Understanding or the Senses, we shall find all its Properties and Adjuncts will herd under this short Definition: That, *it is a perpetual Possession of being well Deceived.*

To hammer home the point, he then expounds in methodical fashion on the false attractiveness of this miserable deception, betraying his excitement and/or his dubious competence with the rhetorical slip of writing 'first' without later going on to a second:

And first, with Relation to the Mind or Understanding; 'tis manifest, what mighty Advantages Fiction has over Truth; and the Reason is just at our Elbow; because Imagination can build nobler Scenes, and produce more wonderful Revolutions than Fortune or Nature will be at Expence to furnish.

Now, in the misconceived charity of his desire to justify (or explain away) the ways of men to God, he becomes decidedly convoluted. Like a good student of Locke, he attempts to go back to first principles of perception, reality, and the origins of things in order to find a plausible explanation (rather than an appropriate condemnation) for human frailty:

Nor is Mankind so much to blame in his Choice, thus determining him, if we consider that the Debate meerly lies between *Things past,* and *Things conceived;* and so the Question is only this; Whether Things that have Place in *the Imagination,* may not as properly be said to *Exist,* as those that are seated in the *Memory;* which may be justly held in the Affirmative, and very much to the Advantage of the former, since This is acknowledged to be the *Womb* of Things, and the other allowed to be no more than the *Grave.*

Sensing, perhaps, that he has lost his way a bit, he makes a fresh attempt to clarify the fatal attraction of fantasy, by way of rhetorical questions:

Again, if we take this Definition of Happiness, and examine it with Reference to the Senses, it will be acknowledged wonderfully adapt. How fade and insipid do all Objects accost us that are not convey'd in the Vehicle of *Delusion?* How shrunk is every Thing, as it appears in the Glass of Nature?

From this, he draws a conclusion which his argument has not really earned, with all the false finality of the journeyman rhetorician. He would like it to be a stern call to sober piety, but his duplicity on the matter of blame has led him astray to almost the opposite conclusion, praise of artificiality and disguise:

So, if it were not for the Assistance of Artificial *Mediums,* false Lights, refracted Angles, Varnish, and Tinsel; there would be a mighty Level in the Felicity and Enjoyments of Mortal Men.

Being no student of rhetorical economy, our preacher concludes again with a
further summary, collapsing into a confusion that exposes his lack of moral
rigour to hilarious ridicule and actually advocates the hypocrisy of masks and
appearances rather than resonating on the vanity of human wishes:

> If this were seriously considered by the World, as I have a certain Reason to suspect
> it hardly will; Men would no longer reckon among their high Points of Wisdom, the
> Art of exposing weak Sides, and publishing Infirmities; an Employment in my
> Opinion, neither better nor worse than that of *Unmasking*, which I think, has never
> been allowed fair Usage, either in the *World* or the *Play-House*.

With a faint glimmer of awareness that he has weak sides and infirmities on
show himself, our pompous ass declaims against any exposure (such as this
one) which he might have earned.

It may come as a surprise to find a little sermon (somewhat disfigured) in
these words, but the correct oratorical moves are all there, and we will all
remember the pulpit as one of the three rhetorical machines in 'The
Introduction'. We could also recombine the passage's elements with little difficulty to turn it into a Dissenting preacher's peroration, or into an anatomy
of imagination from some virtuoso anatomist of human nature. It can also,
as our Latitudinarian indicates at one point, be an extrapolation of Lockean
psychology. The possibilities are presumably not endless, but it is difficult to
see where they might end, even if we restrict our scope to historically available mock sources. This seems a helpful set of flood-gates to keep closed, but,
because the intertextuality of parody is constituted in an actual, undisciplined
reader, it is impossible to confine interpretation to a rigorous retrospectivity.
It is, for example, difficult to see why one should be forbidden to read the
next few lines as a premonitory parody of Derridean deconstruction and its
rejection of the logocentric mystifications of western thought:

> In the Proportion that Credulity is a more peaceful Possession of the Mind, than
> Curiosity, so far preferable is that Wisdom, which converses about the Surface, to
> that pretended Philosophy which enters into the Depth of Things, and then comes
> gravely back with the Informations and Discoveries, that in the inside they are good
> for nothing. (p. 173)

The final wisdom of a rhetoric of surfaces is here predicted and ridiculed –
though the cap be centuries older than the head it fits, it may yet be worn.
And there is also a distinctly dangerous and transgressive supplementarity,
left as a hint in the ridicule, about how Swiftian parody operates, conversing
about surfaces and identifying insides that 'are good for nothing'.

We will not pursue any further the many voices of 'other' – past, present,
and to come – which can be drawn into the vortex of this passage, for the
indeterminacy does not end at this disconcertingly plural level of 'what they
call Parodies, where the Author personates the Style and Manner of other
Writers, whom he has a mind to expose' (p. 7). These words which easily

accommodate so many disciples of error can also be claimed as the genuine and/or ironic utterance of Swift. By this I do not mean merely that we can reconstruct Swift's intention by correctly interpreting the ironic implications and judgements traced out for us by the parodies; in other words, that we are taught to understand what a true voice should sound like by controlled exposure to false voices. This would maintain a dramatic dimension where the author could be deemed to be present beneath the surface, orchestrating the conduct of his narrators for higher (or deeper, or more comprehensive, or ideologically motivated, etc.) purposes. If this were so, the narratorial vestiges I have so far traced would become merely (if complexly) instrumental, and persona scholarship would be essentially right, though in need of some sophistication. However, the text is more open than this. We can hear the 'unmediated' and 'authentic' utterance of Swift, or, to be more exact, we can hear the unmediated utterance of several authentic Swifts. The range of Swifts available is broad and inconsistent, and most of them can be heard to be the informing intelligence of this specular passage. Let us see how it works.

The passage enunciates the monstrous, sado-masochistic sarcasm of that ogre, Thackeray's Swift,[26] in its savage condemnation of our inability to be happy with peaceful serenity and in the sarcastic description of the way we culpably submit to the empty attractions of self-satisfying delusions, the 'false Lights, refracted Angles, Varnish, and Tinsel' by which we disguise the harsh realities of life. Thackeray's descendents, those who see in Swift a verbal and emotional extremist,[27] would point to the savage economy of the sarcasm which identifies all human pretense to civilisation and transcendence as empty and hypocritical self-delusion. Indeed, Leavis has famously used this very passage to demonstrate his hypothesis that in Swift's writings: 'We have...probably the most remarkable expression of negative feelings and attitudes that literature can offer – the spectacle of creative powers (the paradoxical description seems right) exhibited consistently in negation and rejection.'[28] This Swift is a dark prophet of the emptiness of the human con-

[26] See 'Swift' in *The English Humourists; Charity and Humour; The Four Georges* (London: Dent, 1854; reprint 1968).
[27] I am thinking here of writers such as Rawson, *Gulliver and the Gentle Reader;* Patrick Reilly, *Jonathan Swift: The Brave Desponder* (Manchester: Manchester University Press, 1982); David Nokes, *Jonathan Swift, A Hypocrite Reversed: A Critical Biography* (Oxford: Oxford University Press, 1985); Denis Donoghue, *Jonathan Swift: A Critical Introduction* (Cambridge: Cambridge University Press, 1969); John Traugott, '*A Tale of a Tub*', *The Character of Swift's Satire: A Revised Focus*, Claude Rawson, ed. (Newark: University of Delaware Press, 1983), pp. 83–126; and Leavis, Said, and others who stress the minimalism and Tory anarchy of Swift's work. It is interesting that this group tends to engage more directly with the words on the page rather than looking to biographical or historical detail for support (Nokes, particularly in *A Hypocrite Reversed*, is an exception to this rule). This may be seen as a limitation, but it also has the benefit of freeing the reader from the taming power of the historicist's desire to assimilate all things strange and extraordinary to perfectly natural types in the terms of the age, and the biographer's desire to justify his hero and friend (the subject) against the accusations of the world.
[28] The Irony of Swift', p. 28.

dition and the unattainability of moral and ontological security. His irony strands the reader between the minimally convincing happiness of '*a perpetual Possession of being well Deceived*', or the boring serenity of 'common forms', and the abyss of human existence unmasked. He is conducting a deeply disconcerting investigation into the mental processes of humans, where we fondly assume our essential uniqueness and majesty lie. Evacuating significance, often with a shockingly scatological focus, he shows us that human nature is erratic and unreliable at best, and an empty lie at worst.

A much less frenzied tone will be heard by more continent (and commonly more traditionally historicist) interpreters. They would acquit Swift of such savage engagement in his sad task of exposing truth and disabusing the credulous, to hear him as a pious humanist or an orthodox churchman.[29] A careful shepherd of his flock, this Swift enacts the terms of error almost sympathetically, that they may display their seductiveness with their absurdity and be seen for the self-serving delusions they are. To comprehend the orthodox values we need only to look through the enacted error with the sober eye of piety. The ironic praise of the insubstantial and dispraise of the substantial needs only to be reversed so that we learn to value the poor-but-honest over the extraordinary-but-ephemeral. Thus we should admire non-intrusive serenity, be governed by reason, and avoid the false happiness of delusion with all its blandishments. We should prefer truth to fiction, nature/experience/memory (i.e. fact) to imagination, natural images to artificial ornamentation, 'weak Sides, and...Infirmities' to masks. In humble piety before the fallen nature of earthly existence, we should forever decipher the world as Swift's stably ironic voice teaches us to decipher this text. We should learn the eternal lesson that the things of this world are no more than seductive delusion and should place our faith only in God and the authorities He has instituted.[30]

Another, and a very different, Swift is also audible here, one for whom there has been little support since the very early days when *A Tale* was first read by a scandalised audience. It is Swift as a Whiggish, cynical wit, not unlike the Restoration wit identified above, who snidely ridicules the pieties of organised culture and the comic pride of human endeavour. This mocker of all that is sacred, sincere, and significant was Swift as his contemporary enemies saw him. This renegade divine – Wotton's Swift, Queen Anne's and Archbishop Sharp's Swift – was damningly labelled (and libelled) by

---

[29] From a biographical viewpoint, it is fallacious, or very difficult at least, to conflate the humanist and the priest in Swift – see Louis A. Landa, *Swift and the Church of Ireland* (Oxford: Oxford University Press, 1954). However, in matters of rhetoric the distinction becomes very subtle.

[30] This exaggerates the tone but not, I think, the substance of Ehrenpreis' argument in 'The Doctrine of *A Tale of a Tub*'. In a formalist analysis of this passage that now seems very dated, Ricardo Quintana comes to much the same conclusions; see 'Two Paragraphs in *A Tale of a Tub*, Section IX', *MP*, 73 (1975), 15–32.

polemicists as 'the Author of *A Tale of a Tub*' whenever they had a mind to slur his character, at least until the 1720s. They did not recognise any deep strain of piety in the text, which had, after all, been dedicated to Baron Somers, the fast-living, politically cynical patron of extreme liberal thought and impious forces in politics. Certainly (and in spite of the pious but dubious ejaculations of the 'Apology'), Swift can be seen in this passage to be playing dangerously with speculations and the limits of decorous language. The slipperiness comes from the fact that, while the underlying doctrine *may* be orthodox, the tone altogether belies and deconstructs any stable piety. This Swift revels in the raciness of 'when a Man's Fancy gets *astride* on his Reason, when Imagination is at Cuffs with the Senses, and common Understanding, as well as common Sense, is Kickt out of Doors'; here sex and violence are inexplicitly suggested and language is made to combine more and more indecorous images. He relishes the carnal yet ludicrously appropriate analogy in 'For, Cant and Vision are to the Ear and the Eye, the same that Tickling is to the Touch', and takes a most unchristian pleasure in ripping the mask off our pretensions while suggesting as their source the shameful weakness of self-delusion. We are moved to bitter admiration by his brilliant display of destructive and self-promoting cleverness. Obviously Swift explicitly denied such motivations in the 'Apology' of 1710 – as an aspiring Tory propagandist nothing could be further from his desired self-image. However, it is less obvious that he must have felt the same way a few years earlier, when his contacts were with the Whigs and the only instrument available to lift him up in the world was his verbal wit. J.A. Downie has argued that Swift remained a Whig in politics throughout his career.[31] Might we not go a step further and suggest that *A Tale* provides evidence that, at this early stage of his career, Swift was toying with the idea of shaping his cultural affiliations along Whiggish lines, that he made some attempt to fit his mind and loyalties to the company he kept (or would like to have kept) in England, rather than to the bankrupt Church of Ireland to which he was tied institutionally? This passage in particular, and *A Tale* in general, are at least open to such a possibility.

Finally there are those among us who like to take innocent pleasure in comic inventiveness (or writerly *jouissance*, if one desires more fashionable terminology) and would like to claim that the passage expresses the exuberance of Swift, the comedian. These happy souls hear Swift the joker-*bricoleur* here, displaying his formidable verbal and intellectual flexibility by expanding a simple truism (appearance can appear to improve on reality, but it is

---

[31] See *Jonathan Swift: Political Writer* (London: Routledge & Kegan Paul, 1984) and 'Swift's Politics', *Proceedings of the First Münster Symposium on Jonathan Swift* Hermann J. Real and Heinz J. Vienken, eds. (München: Wilhelm Fink Verlag, 1985), pp. 47–58. Eilon, *Factions Fictions* offers a comprehensive and compelling summary of Swift's political views to follow the 'Whig in politics, Tory in Church' line.

not really real) into a hilarious extravaganza of comic images and surprising implications. This Swift is not worried about enciphering deep meanings into the shape and fabric of the argument for the careful and attentive reader to decipher. Only a pedant could miss the joke so completely. We 'Men of Wit and Tast' (p. 20) should simply laugh, enjoy, and admire the brilliance. The vividness of the imagery, the breathless syntax which combines ideas of imagination, invention, and the vertiginous joys of delusion, these defy moral and intellectual analysis. Swift is a ringmaster in a comic circus, the master of aristocratic repartee and its gnomic wisdom of recognition, and that is all we need to know.

I have still not exhausted the possibilities. There are many more Swifts available to those willing either to speculate more wildly or differentiate more subtly. Psychoanalytic readings abound, for example, and I am sure they could be shown to inform our present passage, but I leave that to the *adepti*. The point has been fully enough illustrated that the voices we can hear (or the origins we can assume) remain radically plural. Very different (indeed, logically irreconcilable) threads of parody and of 'genuine' or 'sincere' self-expression can persist simultaneously, in the same words. It is worth remarking, however, that no single voice will bear too much scrutiny. An argument for the immanence of any single voice can be mounted with considerable plausibility, but the text will always keep it a little on edge, even within its own terms, which is, perhaps, the most abiding Swiftian characteristic. The text frustrates the reader, involving her or him in the construction of meanings and their contexts while simultaneously sowing the seeds of deconstruction and promiscuously plural meaning. We are drawn into the ways of error, of language slippery and bereft of contact with true authority, and stranded in the wreckage of flawed attempts to speak authentically.

We are told in the 'Apology' that 'there generally runs an Irony through the Thread of the whole Book' (p. 8), and it is this which resists even provisional closure here. The image of 'Fancy...*astride*...Reason' (like the later image of 'a Woman *flay'd*' (p. 173)) flagrantly breaches the propriety of any reading, and the openness of implication in the notion that ''tis manifest, what mighty Advantages Fiction has over Truth' can only be closed by the reader's unilateral (and fallible) choice. Most clearly, we can see an irreducible ambiguity in the final lines, concerning '*Unmasking*, which I think, has never been allowed fair Usage, either in the *World* or the *Play-House*'. Whichever thread we are following, the slipperiness of language must defeat us here. The obvious meaning (which we can treat as conscious irony, parodic exposure, or naive expostulation) is that neither taking the masks from actors to expose their everyday appearance nor stripping off the public face people present to the world is fair or appropriate. However, if we look again at the words 'allowed fair Usage' a completely different possibility looms.

The words can mean that both forms of unmasking have not been given a fair go, have not been used enough; in other words, that there should be rather more unmasking both in playhouses and the world at large. There is nothing particularly radical or extraordinary about this meaning. Indeed, it fits well with the most sober and orthodox direction of interpretation. The problem is that such a reading subverts the other: no single interpretation can reconcile the two halves of the ambiguity, so that even the most single-minded reader must accept the frustration of his or her certainty.

The result is that we have a very strange sort of text here, where the mechanically reproduced words are cut off from authority (from authentic origins) and enact this separation by allowing the generation of many straw-narrators. This rootlessness, most apparent in the rapid multiplication of roots and sources, is like the separation wrought by the brothers between themselves and the unified, seminal power of command in the father's will and Will. Access to the one, true authority has been lost, and feral authorities (or fantasies of authority) sprout like mushrooms. Given the nature of parody and the textuality it inhabits, it might be more precise to suggest that they sprout like Modern texts, from the fertile but inorganic mechanism of the printing press. The parodic text is specular in that it mirrors the reader's preoccupations, always with a degree of distortion (it is a fairground mirror), but it is like a mirror in another sense as well. No matter how intently we look into a mirror, we cannot see what is going on behind it. Swift and his authorised meaning (if such marvellous creatures exist) have withdrawn into this space, leaving us to recombine the reflective words and discourses into some harmony, despite irreconcilable (and simultaneous) differences. Parody becomes *satura lanx*, a well-filled bowl, but not in the cornucopian sense. The bowl's contents will not mix or multiply. They exist in their own solipsistic silences, cut off from all possibility of filiation to true sources of meaning or even from affiliation among themselves. They are discourses trying to construct their own primal legitimacy and/or their objective rationality, so they cannot acknowledge kinship with anything but themselves. Ultimately they must disown different constructions of truth as error. What this passage illustrates (and Swiftian parody at large demonstrates) is that error takes many forms, but its name is legion and its (constantly denied) bonds of kinship are strong. Each voice in the chorus thinks it is singing well and alone, but what we hear is the cacophonous self-exposure of multiple selves.

8

A Tale of A Tub as Swift's own
illegitimate issue

He thinks it no fair Proceeding, that any Person should offer determinately to fix a name upon the Author of this Discourse, who hath all along concealed himself from most of his nearest Friends: Yet several have gone a farther Step, and pronounced another Book to have been the Work of the same Hand with this; which the Author directly affirms to be a thorough mistake; he having yet never so much as read that Discourse, a plain Instance how little Truth, there often is in general Surmises, or in Conjectures drawn from a Similitude of Style, or way of thinking.   (p. 6)

Fair proceeding or not, Swift concealed himself so carefully that *A Tale* was fathered on several possible authors at the time of publication, and the task of determinately fixing a name to it cannot even now be said to be complete.[1] He was always elusive about the publication of his writings, but his attitude to *A Tale* was uncommonly evasive and prickly. An anxious desire for anonymity, at odds with a sometimes adolescent pride in virtuosity, remains a deep and problematic principle throughout the book. Although the author, using the proprietorial metaphors of conception and origin, aggressively proclaims that 'He conceived it was never disputed to be an Original, whatever Faults it might have' (p. 13), he shows no eagerness to disclose the identity of this original artist. The strident note of indignation struck by the superfluous inclusion of 'determinately' in 'determinately to fix a name' is a verbal trace of uncertainty and even of a sense of recoil. Yet, as can be seen in all of Swift's contacts with *A Tale*, this ambivalence is in tension with a confidence of brilliant achievement. There is a grey area between the original text and Swift's private opinions; a space, which includes the notes (both Swift's and those appropriated from others) appended to the fifth edition, the 'Apology', letters to publishers and friends, and reported comments. This space is marked by a neatly appropriate paradox, the apparent desire simultaneously to proclaim, to vindicate, and to suppress.

At the level of literary biography, it is extremely difficult to trace connections between Swift and this most brilliant child of his literary youth.

---

[1] See ch. 6, n. 15.

Though he presents 'Truth' here as an important virtue, there is little of it in his willingness to falsify the record in the 'Apology'. In the passage quoted above, for example, he disclaims authorship of a book identified in the margin as the *Letter Concerning Enthusiasm*. It is true that he did not write this – Shaftesbury did –but it is an outright lie to claim that he had 'never so much as read that Discourse'. The 'Apology' is dated 'June 3, 1709' (p. 20), but nine months before this (14 September 1708) he wrote to Ambrose Phillips: 'Here has been an Essay of Enthusiasm lately publisht that has run mightily, and is very well writt, All my Friends will have me to be the Author, *sed ego non credulus illis*.'[2] This is not a particularly significant lie, but the overdetermination of the disavowal gives us cause to wonder whether other positive statements about *A Tale* might be similarly distorted in ways that can no longer be verified. It at least casts doubt on the candour of the 'Apology', and there are few other sources of information. Little is stated and much is left to conjecture in the recorded traces which remain in letters and legend of Swift's involvement with the book. We have looked for the origin of the text's meaning in other texts, in its own fantasies of origin, and in its constructions of narratorial identity. As we turn now to search for the grail of the book's origin in the historical Swift (his attitude to it and its place in his career), we will find another tale of subversion, evasion, and suppression of sources, ambitions, and identifications. Given the trouble I have gone to in previous chapters to kill off the author, it may come as something of a surprise for readers to discover so much interest in Swift here, at the end of the book. Yet the logic of origins within the text demands that we speculate about origins outside the text, and that we discuss 'Swift' not as the key to all mysteries but as an explanatory hypothesis which is itself open to various interpretations.[3] It is fruitful and interesting to fit what we know of Swift to what we know of *A Tale*, even if the book's original purpose remains as elusive as all the other potential sources of authentic meaning.

The evidence concerning Swift's attitude to *A Tale of A Tub*

The few traces of Swift's attitude from outside the text and its dangerous supplement, the 'Apology', will bear careful inspection because, in a lifetime of suppression, they suggest at least a furtive pride in a work of amazing if dubious virtuosity. The clearest opinion attributed to Swift is also the latest

---

[2] *Corr.*, I, p. 100.
[3] For a deconstructionist explanation of the desire to continue talking about authors, see Roland Barthes, 'From Work to Text' in *Image – Music – Text*, pp. 155–64, especially p. 161, 'the Author may..."come back" in the Text...as a "guest"'; *Bruissement*, p, 74. And for a trenchant defence of authorial intention as a necessary category in the interpretation of satire, see John Sitter, *Arguments of Augustan Wit* (Cambridge: Cambridge University Press, 1991), pp. 155–62.

(it dates from the 1730s) and most doubtful of authenticity. He is reported by Scott (who got the story from Theophilus Swift) to have muttered in his old age, 'Good God! what a genius I had when I wrote that book.'[4] What appears likely to be a more reliable recension of the same story has recently been uncovered by David Woolley in a letter from Deane Swift, transcribed for the Earl of Orrery:

> There is no doubt but that he was Author of the Tale of the Tub. He never owned it: but as he one day made his Relation Mrs Whiteway read it to him, he made use of This expression. 'Good God! what a flow of imagination had I, when I wrote this.'[5]

If the reports be true (and they offer at least very strong hearsay evidence), they would seem to suggest quite straightforwardly an old man's surprise at his youthful virility of mind; the book could, after all, do him no more harm by then, and he could hardly be said to be making a public acknowledgement of authorship in this simple, private statement. It is tempting to take this (possibly apocryphal) judgement as Swift's sincere opinion.

Less direct is the cryptic comment in the *Journal to Stella* which is generally held to refer to *A Tale*: 'They may talk of the *you know what*; but, gad, if it had not been for that, I should never have been able to get the access I have had; and if that helps me to succeed, then the *same thing* will be serviceable to the church.'[6] If we accept that the '*you know what*' is *A Tale* – and it is hard to imagine what else it might be – this admission is very interesting. Late 1710 was perhaps the most exciting and promising time of Swift's career, when he was being courted by Harley to join the Tory cause and it looked as if he would soon have the power and importance he had always craved. If there was ever a time in Swift's life when possibilities seemed endless, this was it, and the letter where we find this statement is full of excitement at the first flush of being invited into the great secrets of statecraft. Nevertheless, as an admission of authorship, this remains remarkably furtive. Certainly, little secrets abound in the *Journal* despite (or because of) its intense privacy, but this sentence seems to betray unresolved attitudes, even at the summit of Swift's self-confidence. Clearly the secret of his authorship was known by then to quite a wide circle of acquaintance among men and women of taste and influence (or how could 'the *you know what*' have opened doors for him?), but he could not bring himself to name *A Tale*, even to his most intimate correspondent. Furthermore, he seems to half-admit that the loud accusations of infidelity made against it may have a

---

[4] See Scott, *Works of Swift* (1824), I, p. 89; quoted in *A Tale*, p. xix.
[5] In a manuscript in the Houghton Library at Harvard (MS. Eng, 218.14); quoted from Woolley, 'Joint Authorship and *A Tale*', pp. 7–8.
[6] 7 October 1710; *Journal*, I, p. 47.

degree of validity when he suggests that 'the *same thing*' will now be of service to the Church by helping him to gain recognition. There can be no doubting Swift's practical loyalty to the Church, but the surprising thing is the (perhaps, not fully thought out) implication that, while *A Tale* had served the Church in bringing its author to prominence so that he might become her public defender, the book's content may have done nothing (or worse than nothing) for her. This may only have been allowing the opinions of his detractors for the sake of argument, but even if this is all, it betrays a distinct uneasiness about *A Tale*'s orthodoxy only months after the first publication of the stridently defensive 'Apology'.

A more uneasy balancing of cost and benefit occurs in another allusion which has often been held to refer to *A Tale*, the pissing on the palace scene in *Gulliver's Travels*:

It was not long before I had an Opportunity of doing his Majesty, at least, as I then thought, a most signal Service. I was alarmed at Midnight with the Cries of many Hundred People at my Door; by which being suddenly awaked, I was in some Kind of Terror. I heard the word *Burglum* repeated incessantly; several of the Emperor's Court making their Way through the Croud, intreated me to come immediately to the Palace, where her Imperial Majesty's Apartment was on fire, by the Carelessness of a Maid of Honour, who fell asleep while she was reading a Romance. I got up in an Instant; and Orders being given to clear the way before me; and it being likewise a Moonshine Night, I made a shift to get to the Palace without trampling on any of the People. I found they had already applied Ladders to the Walls of the Apartment, and were well provided with Buckets, but the Water was at some Distance. These Buckets were about the Size of a large Thimble, and the poor People supplied me with them as fast as they could; but the Flame was so violent, that they did little Good. I might easily have stifled it with my Coat, which I unfortunately left behind me for haste, and came away only in my Leathern Jerkin. The Case seemed wholly desperate and deplorable; and this magnificent Palace would have infallibly been burnt down to the Ground, if by a Presence of Mind, unusual to me, I had not suddenly thought of an Expedient. I had the Evening before drank plentifully of a most delicious Wine, called *Glimgrim*, (the *Blefuscudians* call it *Flunec*, but ours is esteemed the better Sort) which is very diuretick. By the luckiest Chance in the World, I had not discharged myself of any Part of it. The Heat I had contracted by coming very near the Flames, and by my labouring to quench them, made the Wine begin to operate by Urine; which I voided in such a Quantity, and applied so well to the proper Places, that in three Minutes the Fire was wholly extinguished; and the rest of that noble Pile, which had cost so many Ages in erecting, preserved from Destruction.

It was now Day-light, and I returned to my House, without waiting to congratulate with the Emperor; because, although I had done a very eminent Piece of Service, yet I could not tell how his Majesty might resent the Manner by which I had performed it: For, by the fundamental Laws of the Realm, it is Capital in any Person, of what Quality soever to make water within the Precincts of the Palace. But I was a little comforted by a Message from his Majesty, that he would give

Orders to the Grand Justiciary for passing my Pardon in Form; which, however, I could not obtain. And I was privately assured, that the Empress conceiving the greatest Abhorrence of what I had done, removed to the most distant Side of the Court, firmly resolved that those Buildings should never be repaired for her Use; and, in the Presence of her chief Confidents, could not forbear vowing Revenge.[7]

The allegorical correspondences are not perfect. There are significant variations in detail – the maid of honour whose negligence starts the fire is not matched by any equivalently recognisable occasion for the book, for example – and there are several complex ironies to negotiate, including the obvious problem of equating even the Gulliver of the 'Voyage to Lilliput' with Swift himself. However, there are enough analogies to carry the interpretation of this being a fictionalisation of A Tale's reportedly hostile reception by Queen Anne and Archbishop Sharp. Read this way, it makes an interesting, if speculative, commentary on Swift's attitude to his first great work and to the lasting frustration he believed that its (mis-)interpretation by Queen Anne bequeathed to his career.[8] The fantasy of the fictional scene offers cover both for wish fulfilment and a degree of brutal honesty. The wish fulfilment comes in the image of Gulliver/Swift as a potent giant among ineffectual and small-minded dwarves who have insufficient spirit to recognise the great service being done them. Gulliver/Swift saves the building (roughly equivalent to the Church of England and the state of English learning) from fire (the freethinking and Dissenting incendiaries in religion as well as the Modern perverters of language and knowledge) by discharging a great stream of urine (eloquence). Of course, this greatly exaggerates the prophylactic effect of A Tale and tends to distort its nature in the interests of fantastically dignifying its purpose – in fact, it put out no fires in the worlds of religion or letters. However, a thread of clear-sighted honesty shines through the boasting in the recognition that the eloquence, though a giant's and overpoweringly effective, remains urine. The scatological correlative is exactly appropriate, for it does not disguise the fact that the stream which halts the destruction is polluted. In this allegory of misunderstood merit, the pygmies (particularly the Queen) concentrate on the tainted medium of the salvation rather than the salvation itself, and blame the potent rescuer for doing a dirty job magnificently without recognising the obvious fact that the job needed to be done. Hence, a degree of excess and smuttiness is acknowledged in A Tale (a proposition scarcely accepted in the 'Apology'), but the essential public spirit and effectiveness of the enterprise

---

[7] PW, XI, pp. 55–56.

[8] It is not certain that this was the actual reason for Anne's determination to keep Swift from preferments in her gift. Indeed it is not even probable that she read A Tale. However, Ehrenpreis (Swift, II, pp. 622–23) is inclined to believe the story of Archbishop Sharp's lasting and effective hostility towards Swift on account of A Tale. Swift also saw Sharp as 'my mortall enemy' (Journal, 23 April 1713) and seems to have found this explanation for his frustrations convincing.

are finally asserted. The greatest problem in seeing this as a clear-sighted self-justification is that it appeared more than two decades after the fact, so deeply disguised as fiction that the point could easily be missed. The episode certainly makes a general point concerning the ingratitude of monarchs, and the argument can plausibly be made that there is no allegorical dimension; or, at least, that it was never put there by Swift. If it is Swift vindicating *A Tale*, the vindication is hardly a resounding one.

There is only one extant letter wherein Swift undisputably refers to *A Tale*, and here he could hardly have avoided it. It is a letter from Dublin to his London bookseller, Tooke, concerning the publication of the fifth edition.[9] However, even here a surprising and utterly pointless degree of evasiveness is maintained. Swift mentions the 'Apology' explicitly in the second line and later talks about 'the thing' being 'abroad', but nowhere does he name *A Tale*.[10] In this passage concerning the *Key* and Thomas Swift's claims or insinuations that he was the author, Swift refers to it twice by the completely inexplicit title of the '&c.' and once also as 'the thing':

I cannot but think that little Parson-cousin of mine is at the bottom of this; for, having lent him a copy of some part of, &c. and he shewing it, after I was gone for Ireland, and the thing abroad, he affected to talk suspiciously, as if he had some share in it. If he should happen to be in town, and you light on him, I think you ought to tell him gravely, 'That, if he be the author, he should set his name to the &c.' and railly him a little upon it: and tell him, 'if he can explain some things, you will, if he pleases, set his name to the next edition.' I should be glad to see how far the foolish impudence of a dunce could go.   (p. 349)

Swift's unwillingness to name 'the &c.' certainly does not improve the letter's grammatical flow and amounts to evasiveness. It is probably not a deliberate attempt to obscure his connection, and it is certainly not an effective one, but it does allow us to witness a psychological uneasiness: he was petulantly determined that the work should not be mis-ascribed even at the same time as he was too nervous even to write its name. The tension between pride and shame is eloquently exposed. This is the most explicit reference he is known to have made to *A Tale*, and his correspondent certainly knew him to be the author, but even here he maintains a pointless and equivocal distance. He is proud of his creation, not wanting anyone else to claim the credit for it, but he wants also to be able to avoid the blame. He is certainly not at ease with it in anything like the way he was with his other great satire, *Gulliver's Travels*, which cuts a mighty and confident swathe through his correspondence.

And that is all there is. The coyness about accepting the title of 'author of

---

[9] Printed, along with Tooke's reply, in *A Tale*, pp. 349–50.

[10] Tooke is not so cautious in his reply: 'It was very indifferent to me which I proceeded on first, the Tale, or the Miscellanies' (p. 350).

A Tale of a Tub' seems to have been maintained for emotional reasons long after there was any point in trying to keep up the pretence. During the years of his prominence as chief spokesman for the Tory government, Swift was openly referred to as 'the author of *A Tale of a Tub'* by friend and foe alike.[11] However, if we want to surmise any more about his attitude to the book, we are reduced to interpreting silences and omissions. We must presume, for example, that he arranged for the 1710 edition in the interests of establishing his credentials as a brilliant writer in much the same way that he simultaneously arranged for the publication of the 1711 *Miscellanies*. These testimonials to his abilities maximise and marmorealise the impression of his achievements in the preparation for his greater role on the public stage. The two volumes offer very different sets of credentials, however.

The *Miscellanies* was closely associated with Swift, and played the role of his (nearly) authorised collected works.[12] Old material was reprinted and new material published for the first time, all with a clear editorial view to demonstrating the author's continued political and religious orthodoxy as well as his literary virtuosity. Swift was careful to pretend that the collection had not been approved by him, and even maintained the charade to Stella:

Some bookseller has raked up everything I writ, and published it t'other day in one volume; but I know nothing of it, 'twas without my knowledge or consent: it makes a four shilling book, and is called *Miscellanies in Prose and Verse*. Took pretends he knows nothing of it, but I doubt he is at the bottom. One must have patience with these things; the best of it is, I shall be plagued no more. However, I'll bring a couple of them over with me for MD, perhaps you may desire to see them. I hear they sell mightily.[13]

We know that Swift was deeply involved in the edition, and this disavowal was not meant to fool anyone, least of all Stella. Significantly, he gives the volume its full title, and his scarcely veiled pride in the production ('it makes a four shilling book', 'One must have patience with these things', 'I'll bring a couple of them over with me', and 'I hear they sell mightily') makes the subterfuge particularly hollow. Moreover, at no time does he even pretend to dissociate himself from the original texts that go to make up the collection.

Three further details emphasise the extent to which the *Miscellanies* was being treated as the legitimate formulation of Swift's credentials as the new champion of church and Tory principles. The first is that, when such a volume was first contemplated (while Swift still considered himself a supporter

---

[11] For example, as early as 1708, 'A confidential agent of Robert Harley's…referred to Swift not by name but simply as "the author of the *Tale of a Tub*"'. Ehrenpreis, *Swift*, II, p. 330. As late as 1713 a Whiggish newspaper called *The Britain* (no. 4, 13–17 January 1713) saw fit to deflect criticism reflected on its party by association with Collins' *A Discourse of Free-Thinking* by quoting parallel passages demonstrating the likeness between it and *A Tale*, which everyone knew to be by the Tories' foremost spokesman.

[12] See Kelly, 'The Semiotics of Swift's 1711 *Miscellanies*'.

[13] 28 February 1711; *Journal*, I, p. 203.

of the Whigs) it was to be introduced by Richard Steele. As the letter to
Tooke concerning both *A Tale* and the *Miscellanies* shows, this plan was side-
stepped in 1710 ostensibly because Steele would be too busy, but actually
because his sponsorship would be a considerable embarrassment for a volume that was being engineered to demonstrate that its author had been a
true Tory all along.[14] The second is that, as Swift well knew, Tooke was 'at
the bottom' of both books, though his name appeared on the title page of
neither. John Nutt (whom Ehrenpreis considers a convenient creature of
Tooke's[15]) had been the nominal, and appropriately obscure, publisher of all
the early editions of *A Tale*; he continued on the title page of the 1710 edition. At first this may have been done primarily to protect Tooke, a publisher of some reputation, from too close an association with so dangerous
(or, at least, outrageous) a text, and it later helped to keep some distance
between Swift and his notorious creation. However, when it came to the
Miscellanies, Tooke's connection with Swift's earlier, Whiggish self as
Temple's secretary and editor becomes the salient feature.[16] Consequently,
this volume of new Tory orthodoxy appeared instead under the imprint of
John Morphew, an associate of Tooke's, but also the publisher of the stridently Tory *Examiner*. The third detail links the prehistory of the 'Apology
for the &c.' with that of the *Miscellanies*. Ehrenpreis finds it astonishing that
the 'Apology' was ever considered as part of the original scheme for the
Miscellanies,[17] but if the book had originally been intended to appear as
Swift's credentials as a *Whiggish* churchman, some official explanation for *A
Tale*'s alleged improprieties would have been necessary to balance the rigorous impression of pieces like the *Project for the Advancement of Religion*. A
Whiggish churchman might have been able to acknowledge and defend his
authorship of *A Tale*, which, for all its exuberance, can at least plausibly be
argued to have its heart in the right place. However, a defence of its essential, underlying piety could only be mounted in the context of the liberal

---

[14] 'I would not have you think of Steele for a publisher; he is too busy. I will, one of these days,
send you some hints, which I would have in a preface, and you may get some friend to dress them
up.' Swift to Tooke, 29 June 1710 (*A Tale*, p. 350). On the possibility that this excuse might have
been sincere, Ehrenpreis comments, 'Swift was employing a subterfuge which the bookseller must
have seen through very easily.' *Swift*, II, p. 423.
[15] See *Swift*, II, pp. 92, 140, 336.
[16] As Michael Treadwell ('London Trade Publishers 1675–1750', *The Library*, 6th series, 4 (1982),
99–134) demonstrates, it was quite common, for a variety of reasons ranging from convenience of
distribution to protection from prosecution, for booksellers and authors to employ 'trade publishers'
like Nutt and Morphew to provide their names for title-pages, so the significance of this subterfuge
on Swift's and Tooke's part can not be considered unusually great. The point here can only contribute to my argument that the two volumes display disparate political motives rather than clinch
it, and Treadwell in another article ('Swift's Relations with the London Book Trade to 1714',
Author/Publisher Relations during the Eighteenth and Nineteenth Centuries, Robyn Myers and Michael Harris,
eds. (Oxford: Oxford Polytechnic Press, 1983), pp. 1–36) provides a different interpretation of the
course of publication.
[17] *Swift*, II, p. 332.

matrix of ideas – which is the intellectual context of the 'Apology' – while a Tory churchman could only hope to deny the text and limit the damage. The consequence of all this is that the 'Apology' was written in the terms of an apologetic which became incompatible with its author's evolving sense of his public image. It was therefore separated from the authorised and acknowledged works, where it might have eliminated misinterpretation of a moderately Whiggish Swift, but could not vindicate a Tory. Instead, it was affixed as a means of damage-control to a new, carefully distanced edition of *A Tale* in the hope of diluting its potential heterodoxy.

Thus in 1710–11 Swift had the first edition of his collected works published in two volumes by Benjamin Tooke (though under the imprint of two others). The division of his loyalties between the two books is remarkable. He basked in the glory of the *Miscellanies*, owning it as proof of his genius and reliability. The 1710 *A Tale* was, on the other hand, the dark and formally unacknowledged side of Swift's presentation of his credentials as a literary genius. He made no attempt to suppress it – he was too proud of its brilliance for that – but he did try to control the scandal by his petulant explanation of the true meanings and intentions in the 'Apology', and to set it apart from his authorised and acknowledged canon. What is most odd, however, is the way that this separation was not merely a matter of temporary convenience governed by political expedience. The subterfuge was not confined to his politically active years, but continued until the end of his days. Never in Swift's life did *A Tale* appear collected with any other of his works, not even when Faulkner was preparing the authorised (though formally disowned) edition in the 1730s. It is inconceivable that Faulkner, who dutifully hunted out and printed obscure topical pamphlets that were then a quarter of a century old, did not wish to publish *A Tale* as well. Swift must have forbidden it, even when having it appear with his legitimate literary issue could do him no possible (further) harm.

The double psychological movement, equivocating between pleasure in the *succès de scandale* and fear of being identified with heterodoxy, poses fascinating problems for the placement of *A Tale* in Swift's canon and career. It was one of his first ventures into print, and one of the most brilliant, yet throughout his life he maintained the fiction of anonymity with a perverse energy. Despite this, he never tried to suppress the work as a whole, only trying to redefine its excesses as virtues and to obscure his direct connection with it. Ehrenpreis is also made uneasy by *A Tale*, but his response is more militant. He takes the opportunity presented by the paucity of biographical material on the book to treat it primarily as a literary text abstracted from the course of Swift's life.[18] Furthermore, his reading of the book obscures

18 Ibid., I, pp. 185–246.

the wildness so that it can fit the pattern made for Swift of dutiful son to Temple and to the Church. Ehrenpreis is confident that he understands the underlying doctrine Swift advocates:

If we root ourselves firmly in principles which Swift advocates, however, we shall have to confess that these are neither original or dazzling. Literary critics who dislike the conclusions of the supreme moralists, from St Luke to Freud, will find *A Tale of a Tub* diminished by this perspective. But there is no other way to bring order into the chaos of commentary upon what is, after all, an affirmation of accessible wisdom.[19]

It is difficult to share such reductive confidence or to be sure that the chaos is exclusively in the commentary. Even if the wisdom is accessible (a proposition only a few would accept) can it be all that finally matters in so fabulously digressive and excessive a book? Ehrenpreis gives himself away further down the same page when he makes the remarkable assertion that: 'My only postulate is that behind the book stands not a list of philosophical propositions but the idea of a good man.' To create the interpretation he requires, he has to look past the text, to the image of Temple and the determinate structure of Anglican doctrine, displacing and taming the radically flexible words on the page. Ehrenpreis never really faces the question of why a book of such accessible and orthodox wisdom should immediately have gained a reputation for dangerous heterodoxy. His is a bowdlerising reading (of which Swift might well have approved) which illustrates the pressure *A Tale* places on those who try to justify its ways to men. It is a useful token to put beside Swift's only attempt to half-face the issue, in the 'Apology for the &c.'

The 'Apology': text, commentary, or confidence trick?

But I here think fit to lay hold on that great and honourable Privilege of being the *Last Writer*; I claim an absolute Authority in Right, as the *freshest Modern*, which gives me a Despotick Power over all Authors before me.   (p. 130)

It is hard to imagine a more anxious and self-divided document than 'An Apology for the &c'. It puts one in mind of the excesses of self-shrouding and self-disclosing practised by Nabokovian narrators, yet it is not – at least in any traditional sense – a work of fiction. It sets out to be a bluff clearing up of unnecessary misunderstandings, but in practice the emphasis falls on the bluff to the almost complete exclusion of any clearing up of confusion. As Zimmerman points out, 'Even in the "Apology" Swift stages a performance that maintains, as much as it dissipates, the *Tale*'s sense of authorial

---

[19] Ibid., I, p. 189.

evasiveness.'[20] As we shall see, it blurs, obscures, and misrepresents the text which it sets out to clarify, yet readers have tended to accept it straightforwardly, presumably because of its relative innocence when compared to *A Tale* itself. Veronica Kelly, one of the few writers to analyse the 'Apology' with appropriate suspicion, suggests reasons for the naivety of the common reading:

> The 'Apology' to the fifth edition of *A Tale of a Tub* has appeared to some of its readers to be a place of comparative certainty and rest, a stretch of prose where we can hear with greater confidence the voice of the *Tale*'s author, and where we can begin to learn the rhythms of his speech and to uncover his intentions before setting off again into the verbal labyrinth of the *Tale* in search of Swift. A later addition, the 'Apology' holds before the exhausted reader of the *Tale* a vision of an outermost frame, the promise of an authorial voice that will speak through the text to still its indulgence in exuberant negation and finally turn that extravagance to a clear and positive purpose. Our expectation that any author will sacrifice the distant and sly artifice of the persona to come to the defense of his work because it is, finally, the offspring and reflection of himself makes the apologist seem categorically different from, and superior to, the mad narrator of the *Tale*: it makes him seem less like a piece of dramatic rhetoric and more like a piece of Swift.[21]

The 'Apology's' offer of sincerity is seductive, and its narrating voice is certainly 'more like a piece of Swift' speaking *in propria persona* than most of the voices of *A Tale* 'proper'. However, the likeness is deceptive, for, if this is Swift, it is a Swift torn by conflicting desires concerning the impressions he wants to give; of the points he wants to defend, and those he wants to obscure. As Kelly suggests, 'the "Apology" holds before the exhausted reader of the *Tale* a vision of an outermost frame, the promise of an authorial voice that will speak through the text', but it is not in the nature of frames to be either neutral or objective. A frame is not simply a stable marking of the borders between a work of art and the world it inhabits; it is a borderland between the two states seeking to govern the transition between them. Thus the 'Apology' is less a plain statement of helpful facts than a negotiation with the readers, by which Swift seeks to control their impressions. This supplementary text is a flexible and manipulative frame which should be analysed with the sort of suspicion its Gulliverian candour deserves.

The author of the 'Apology' does not admit to being Swift or even the author of *A Tale*, but rather projects an ambiguous status, somewhere between that of an enraged and violated author and that of a knight errant charging to the rescue. He uses 'I' a lot to affirm matters of opinion and

---

[20] *Swift's Narrative Satires*, p. 63.
[21] 'Following the Stage Itinerant', p. 239; see also Judith C. Mueller, 'Writing under Constraint: Swift's "Apology" for *A Tale of a Tub*', *ELH*, 60 (1993), 101–15.

judgement, but never allows this 'I' to speak as the author of *A Tale*, always maintaining the distance of the Caesarean third person there. By doing this, he creates the grammatical and logical convention that these authors are different people and withholds a full rhetoric of presence at the point where the impression of integrity is most essential. No obvious practical benefits are gained from the maintenance of this indeterminate gap between authors – there is certainly little sense that they really are different people. However, if we view it as the rhetorical trace of Swift's conflicting attitudes, we can see it as a sign of unease, an attempt to create a breathing-space of deniability. The 'Apology's' author is a semi-detached figure, forever availing himself of a presence he also insists on erasing. For this reason, it is not strictly accurate to talk of him as Swift (an identity denied by two veneers of anonymity) but neither would it be appropriate to construct the image of a fully independent persona, an 'other' animated by the master puppeteer, Swift. Neither merely 'the *freshest Modern*' nor determinately Swift, the authorial voice of the 'Apology' has an active but self-effacing quality analogous to a frame, and should be recognised as a slippage between the roles of author and character. To mark this duplicity and keep in mind the tension between identity and other, I will use the graphic convention of (Swift) when describing this borderline construct of authority.

In (Swift)'s text, it seems to have been the historical Swift's intention to claim *A Tale* and control its implications, yet also to maintain a distance from it. The tensions between wanting proudly to defend, piously to excuse, and humbly to disown the volatile masterpiece cannot be resolved, and Swift (or is it (Swift)?) seems half to know it. His initial and most persistent reaction is to insist petulantly on his complete innocence of any possible guilt. The author of 'the &c.' has simply been misunderstood by a vocal clique of ponderous, misguided pedants. Furthermore, 'those who approve it, are a great Majority among the Men of Tast' (p. 3). With a humility so strained that it sounds more like arrogance, youthful vigour is blamed for any excess:

Not that he would have governed his Judgment by the ill-placed Cavils of the Sour, the Envious, the Stupid, and the Tastless, which he mentions with disdain. He acknowledges there are several youthful Sallies, which from the Grave and the Wise may deserve a Rebuke. But he desires to be answerable no farther than he is guilty, and that his Faults may not be multiply'd by the ignorant, the unnatural, and uncharitable Applications of those who have neither Candor to suppose good Meanings, nor Palate to distinguish true Ones.   (pp. 4–5)

The villains of this piece are the rebukers, who are neither grave nor wise and force 'the ignorant, the unnatural, and uncharitable Applications' on the good and true (if somewhat exuberant) meanings of the witty young author. The bluster is too obvious, and exposes too starkly the attempt to divide readers into us 'Men of Tast' who understand the book and those malicious buffoons who misconstrue its genius. The concession of a small degree of youthful excess – which one assumes is supposed to appear generous – is completely swamped by the venom of the attack on the critics. These are not the assured moves of an author confident of his position, but rather the anxious over-reaction of an author trying to escape judgement for a crime he is conscious of at least half-committing. So he proceeds, as grandiloquently as possible, to declare his innocence: 'he will forfeit his Life, if any one Opinion can be fairly deduced from that Book, which is contrary to Religion or Morality' (p. 5). This is a world and a direct contradiction away from the confident embrace of a dissemination of meaning free of hermeneutic controls in 'Section X' where commentators' multiple conjectures 'will be all, without the least Distortion, manifestly deduceable from the Text' (p. 185). However, for all its sound and fury, this oath is essentially hollow – who is to judge, and who carry out any sentence? Moreover, even the oath itself is subtly qualified by the quiet inclusion of the word 'fairly', which is open to a wide range of self-protective interpretation.

(Swift) now attempts to disguise unease by turning to insinuating rationalisation. He attempts to hide behind the never very generally approved theory of ridicule and to give the impression that any spirit of excess in the book tends to expose 'the Follies of Fanaticism and Superstition...in the most ridiculous Manner' (p. 5). This is the satirist's classic statement of policy, and I suppose that one is welcome to accept it. (Swift) does not display much confidence in it here, however. He immediately twists away from this statement of principle to suggest that: (1) the book 'was not intended for the Perusal' (p. 5) of clergymen and other moral guardians; (2) 'It Celebrates the Church of *England* as the most perfect of all others in Discipline and Doctrine, it advances no Opinion they reject, nor condemns any they receive' (p. 5.); and (3) even if it does fall short of perfect and rigorous orthodoxy, there are many much more appropriate targets ('heavy, illiterate Scriblers, prostitute in their Reputations, vicious in their Lives, and ruin'd in their Fortunes' (p. 5)) for the wrath of moral guardians. He seems unaware of the fact that this Hackish accumulation of excuses does not simply prop up the original principle, but tends rather to diffuse and defuse the force of each part. The anxiety to parade every possible justification overwhelms purity of line in the argument, and undermines our confidence, both in it and in the author's sincerity and conviction.

The impression of ranting does not help either:

Had the Author's Intentions met with a more candid Interpretation from some whom out of Respect he forbears to name, he might have been encouraged to an Examination of Books written by some of those Authors above-described, whose Errors, Ignorance, Dullness and Villany, he thinks he could have detected and exposed in such a Manner, that the Persons who are most conceived to be infected by them, would soon lay them aside and be ashamed: But he has now given over those Thoughts, since the *weightiest* Men in the *weightiest* Stations are pleased to think it a more dangerous Point to laugh at those Corruptions in Religion, which they themselves must disapprove, than to endeavour pulling up those very Foundations, wherein all Christians have agreed.   (pp. 5–6)

This displays all the emotional continence of Gulliver giving up visionary schemes forever, only with an added degree of petulance. If one tries to imagine this passage spoken aloud, it is tones of spite, self-importance, and vindictiveness which suggest themselves. It is a strange and evasive sort of 'Respect' which, though it refuses to name its victims, yet accuses them of 'Errors, Ignorance, Dullness and Villany', and there is more than a hint of Parthian shot in the sarcastic proposition that he could refute his detractors easily if he had a mind to but can no longer be bothered since 'the *weightiest* Men' have so absurdly misconceived the self-evident truth as to disapprove his labours. These snarling pirouettes merely beg the question which they affect to despise: just how would (Swift) set about vindicating the orthodoxy of *A Tale*? The answer is not immediately obvious, and the question is seen to be (rather gracelessly) evaded.

If (Swift) had wanted to expose his anxiety at this point, he could not have hit upon a better expedient than his next disjunctive manœuvre, for suddenly, without warning or proper preparation, the 'Apology's' other major preoccupation intrudes. There is no logical reason (let alone any need) for (Swift) suddenly to inveigh against 'any Person [who] should offer determinately to fix a name upon the Author of this Discourse' (p. 6). Indeed, if the author is indeed blameless, it is hard to see why he should be concerned at the prospect of being identified. This local outburst – the next paragraph continues as if it did not exist – only makes sense as a sudden surge of anxiety on (Swift)'s part that he might be held publicly responsible for his book. The agony of self-disclosure is particularly apparent when compared to the later testiness brought on by Wotton's accusations of plagiarism and Thomas Swift's pretensions to be the author. (Swift) is completely opposed to the idea of having Jonathan Swift's name determinately fixed to *A Tale*, but he is possessively jealous of the book's reputation for integrity and his claim to the whole credit for its creation. He wants the reputation of an original genius desperately, while withholding his name from the risk of any blame.

He guards his undivided authorship from those who would steal or dilute it with such jealousy that he is moved to make statements which (considering the densely allusive and parodic texture of *A Tale*) are little less than absurd:

But it would be good to know what *Design* this Reflecter [Wotton] was serving, when he concludes his Pamphlet with a Caution to Readers, to beware of thinking the Authors Wit was entirely his own, surely this must have had some Allay of Personal Animosity, at least mixt with the Design of serving the Publick by so useful a

Discovery; and it indeed touches the Author in a very tender Point, who insists upon it, that through the whole Book he has not borrowed one single Hint from any Writer in the World; and he thought of all Criticisms, that would never have been one. He conceived it was never disputed to be an Original, whatever Faults it might have.   (pp. 12–13)

I know nothing more contemptible in a Writer than the Character of a Plagiary.
                                                                                                (p. 14)

Let the Answerer and his Friend produce any Book they please, he defies them to shew one single Particular, where the judicious Reader will affirm he has been obliged for the smallest Hint; giving only Allowance for the accidental encountring of a single Thought, which he knows may sometimes happen; tho' he has never yet found it in that Discourse, nor has heard it objected by any body else.   (p. 15)

Were these extreme overdeterminations of the idea of originality true and applicable to *A Tale*, any recourse to the idea of parody in general (and this book in particular) would be entirely pointless. (Swift) is driven by the fury of defending his originality to such an extent that he denies the nature of his writing. As the opening sections of my reading of *A Tale* demonstrate, the book is essentially made up of hints and quotations from previous authors, cunningly transformed. Certainly, the debts are seldom simple borrowings, but I (a sympathetic and, I hope, judicious reader) can produce (and have noted) several books through which particular hints can be traced. (Swift) contradicts himself even in the 'Apology', for earlier he points out:

There is one Thing which the judicious Reader cannot but have observed, that some of those Passages in this Discourse, which appear most liable to Objection are what they call Parodies, where the Author personates the Style and Manner of other Writers, whom he has a mind to expose. I shall produce one Instance, it is on the *51st Page. Dryden, L'Estrange*, and some others I shall not name, are here levelled at, who having spent their Lives in Faction, and Apostacies, and all manner of Vice, pretended to be Sufferers for Loyalty and Religion.   (p. 7)

Of course, there is a difference between parody and plagiarism, but (Swift) over-reacts in his anxiety to assert his own originality in a way that is rendered nonsensical by his calmer attempt to avoid the blame for 'some of those Passages in this Discourse, which appear most liable to Objection'. The contradiction between these two propositions is irreconcilable – either he asserts his originality ('he has not borrowed one single Hint from any Writer in the World') and accepts responsibility for any offense, or he concedes a degree of derivativeness so that he can hide from blame behind the argument that he is merely mimicking and exposing the true offender.

(Swift)'s insistence that 'through the whole Book he has not borrowed one single Hint from any Writer in the World' is a rash over-reaction to doubts published about the book's originality (hints) and its origin (Swift's authorship). It makes little sense logically, but psychologically it expresses definite needs and formally it reflects on important concerns in a vivid if erratic manner. These two levels interpenetrate in interesting ways. The author of the 'Apology' (Swift) and the narrator of *A Tale* (un-Swift) have this in common: they are both trying and failing to exert determinate control over the same unruly text. The Hack is forever reminding us of the brilliance, clarity, uniqueness, and revelatory power of his own writing, only to have it dissolve underneath him into disjointedness, multivalence, derivativeness, and banality, while the (Swift) of the 'Apology' wants to control this process without losing (or having to renounce) the credit for its brilliance. The conflicting demands of claiming credit and denying blame push him into paradoxes similar to the Hack's excursions into rhetorical excess, the main difference being that in the 'Apology' rhetorical skill is trying to cover the gaps rather than expose them. It is only a less flagrant attempt to usurp the liberties of readers than 'the *freshest Modern*'s' claim to 'a Despotick Power over all Authors before me' (p. 130).

A similar complication of (Swift) in Hackish enterprises comes in the complaints against the printers and the pretence that he had lost control of the manuscript long before it was piratically printed. This tissue of lies differs only in degree from the Hack's complaints against a writer's weary lot:

How the Author came to be without his Papers, is a Story not proper to be told, and of very little use, being a private Fact of which the Reader would believe as little or as much as he thought good. He had however a blotted Copy by him, which he intended to have writ over, with many Alterations, and this the Publishers were well aware of, having put it into the Booksellers Preface, that they *apprehended a surreptitious Copy, which was to be altered, &c*. This though not regarded by Readers, was a real Truth, only the surreptitious Copy was rather that which was printed, and they made all the hast they could, which indeed was needless; the Author not being at all prepared; but he has been told, the Bookseller was in much Pain, having given a good sum of Money for the Copy.   (pp. 16–17)

The history of *A Tale*'s production and transmigration into print is shrouded in mystery, and so there is a remote possibility that this is an accurate (if inexplicit) rendition of a body of 'real truth'. However, if treated as obfuscation (and Swift the historical figure seems to have exerted far more control over publication than this passage implies), the duplicity of its conventional and evasive postures is readily apparent. The story of how the author came to be without his papers is neither proper nor useful because it never happened. (Swift) attempts to double-guess our scepticism concerning the 'private Fact' which is fabricated by affecting to concede that 'the Reader would believe as little or as much [of it] as he thought good' any way, so there is little point in entering into unverifiable detail. This ruse has several benefits: it saves (Swift) from having to invent a plausible story about 'How the Author came to be without his Papers', it gives the impression that the author is a reasonable fellow who does not expect his readers to believe his assertions without independent proof, and, paradoxically, it disposes us to believe this evidence-free assertion *because* its inadmissability as positive evidence is so candidly conceded. After this duplicitous opening, the paragraph can be seen to harden into outright lying. On the extraordinarily overdetermined and 'private' affirmation that it is 'a real Truth', we are required to believe that the author possessed a corrected copy which the publisher chose wilfully to ignore; that it was not Swift but the bookseller who wrote the 'Bookseller to the Reader'; and that, like all mechanic businessmen, he was motivated entirely by greed rather than any sense of duty toward the authentic publication of literary art. There is even an element of skiting in the suggestion that the manuscript of *A Tale* would have been worth a great deal of money to an enterprising publisher. This is all possible, but it is hardly likely. It is far more probable that the 'Bookseller to the Reader' was written by Swift and that the 'surreptitious Copy' (p. 29) it mentions as about to be pirated into print was a hackneyed fiction of the aristocratic tradition of letters. The pretence that this fictional surreptitious copy was the original printer's text is simply dishonest, and the suggestion that the bookseller need not have hurried because the author was unready to beat him into print with a true copy is mere embroidery on the way to a snide suggestion that the bookseller was motivated in his textual butchery by greed. This, of course, completes the circle of aristocratic self-fashioning, blaming the printer for violating the text's manuscriptural dignity and for any blemishes it may retain, while reserving the credit for its virtues.

(Swift) continues this sort of dishonest and unedifying confusion of detail in several ways. He labours to give the impression that, through no (or little) fault of his own, *A Tale* is not quite what it might be, or even what it originally was. He gives the impression that he regrets some bits, but neglects to name them, he proclaims that he has been misunderstood by small-minded pedants, but debates only minor matters of detail with them rather than their substantive accusations. All the disclaimers are carried out with rhetorical vigour, yet remain partial. The previously discussed allegations that the original printed text was made up from a botched manuscript, is followed by the assertion that a true copy would show fewer chasms (not none) and that several corrections would be made, but only in 'Passages against which nothing hath ever been objected' (p. 17). The logical consequence of this would seem to be that the author must, therefore, be entirely happy with the passages which have caused offence, and should be prepared to be held responsible for that offence and to offer an appropriate vindication. However, no such consequence follows. Assertions are made and then undermined by supplementary counter-assertions, leaving little definitely conceded or confirmed.

This is further illustrated by the seemingly magisterial claim that men of taste would realise and appreciate the irony that pervades the book and not be concerned by the quibbling misunderstandings of pedants:

> Another Thing to be observed is, that there generally runs an Irony through the Thread of the whole Book, which the Men of Tast will observe and distinguish, and which will render some Objections that have been made, very weak and insignificant.   (p. 8)

The claim of ironical intent, as Defoe's prosecution over *The Shortest Way with the Dissenters* indicates, was not considered a valid defence for causing offence at the time, but rather a compounding of malice with evasiveness. Just such suspicions are vindicated here, for a careless reader (a man of taste, perhaps) might not notice the little word 'some' in this sentence. It is unobtrusive, leaving us with the impression that tastefully apprehended irony explains all the quibbles. It is 'honest' (in Iago's manner), in admitting (at a strictly literal level) that some of the objections are neither weak nor insignificant, though the rhetoric pushes our impressions in the opposite direction. And finally, it is both unobtrusive and honest, allowing (Swift) to deny that he had claimed that irony explains all, if challenged. The only limitation to the utility of this sort of half denial is that it becomes self-defeating because it reeks of dishonesty.

The matter of his supposed ridicule of trinitarian doctrine gives a good illustration of the way (Swift) resorts to Hackish shifts to cloud issues, rather than candidly proclaiming his 'true intentions'. As Robert Adams has remarked, much is made of the number three in *A Tale*:

> The number three, which perverse ingenuity can demonstrate in so many insignificant places, thus signifies for Swift the waste of spirit in brain maggotry. But *A Tale of a Tub* is itself written to an extraordinary degree in threes. There are, for example, three sons, three varieties of critic, three engines for achieving literary eminence, three characteristics of a critic, three volumes to the proposed treatise on zeal, three distinct anima's or winds to a man, three classes of reader – not to mention three fine ladies, the three tiers to Peter's hat, and the three recommendations as to numerology. Just as *Gulliver* plays with the quirks and oddities of number while satirising both arithmeticians and numerologists, so *A Tale of a Tub* wavers between derision and fascination.[22]

This play with three is deeply inscribed in *A Tale*, a work that was written towards the end of a decade (the 1690s) in which the Trinitarian controversy had been the most hotly contested theological issue.[23] The dangerously heterodox implications of such play would have been very apparent in context, and even a sympathetic reader would have had trouble convincing herself or himself that the nearly blasphemous ramifications were not intended. Wotton makes the accusation in his 'Observations':

---

[22] *Strains of Discord: Studies in Literary Openness* (Ithaca: Cornell University Press, 1958), pp. 163–64.
[23] See Redwood, *Reason, Ridicule and Religion*, ch. 7.

The number of these Sons born thus at one Birth, looks asquint at the TRINITY, and one of the Books in our Author's Catalogue in the Off-page over-against the Title, is a Panegyric upon the Number THREE, which Word is the only one that is put in Capitals in that whole Page.

In the pursuit of his Allegory, we are entertain'd with the Lewdness of the Three Sparks. Their Mistresses are the *Dutchess d'Argent, Madamoizelle de Grands Titres*, and the *Countess d'Orgeuil* i.e. *Covetousness, Ambition and Pride*, which were the Three great Vices that the Ancient Fathers inveighed against as the first Corrupters of Christianity.[24]

(Swift) makes no attempt to justify himself against the charges, but rather tries to side-step the issue by bringing in extraneous information of dubious relevance. He focuses on only one detail of the numerology of three (the oratorical engines) and concocts a dubious and unverifiable explanation for it:

There are three or four other Passages which prejudiced or ignorant Readers have drawn by great Force to hint at ill Meanings, as if they glanced at some Tenets in Religion; in answer to all which, the Author solemnly protests he is entirely Innocent, and never had once in his Thoughts that any thing he said would in the least be capable of such Interpretations, which he will engage to deduce full as fairly from the most innocent Book in the World. And it will be obvious to every Reader, that this was not any part of his Scheme or Design, the Abuses he notes being such as all Church of *England* Men agree in, nor was it proper for his Subject to meddle with other Points, than such as have been regularly controverted since the Reformation.

To instance only in that Passage about the three wooden Machines mentioned in the Introduction: In the Original Manuscript there was a description of a Fourth, which those who had the Papers in their Power, blotted out, as having something in it of Satyr, that I suppose they thought was too particular, and therefore they were forced to change it to the Number *Three*, from whence some have endeavour'd to squeeze out a dangerous Meaning that was never thought on. And indeed the Conceit was half spoiled by changing the Numbers; that of *Four* being much more Cabalistick, and therefore better exposing the pretended Virtue of Numbers, a Superstition there intended to be ridicul'd.   (p. 8)

Standing shrilly on his honour, 'the Author solemnly protests he is entirely Innocent', then proceeds to consider only a small part of the evidence and to fabricate a 'patently implausible'[25] story to explain it away. The story of the fourth machine is immediately recognisable as a fiction introduced to escape blame. A suspicious reader can see quite clearly that (Swift)'s language betrays a lack of ease with the fabrication, unconsciously marking the deflection from the fact of three machines to the fantasy of four at the start of the passage with the guilty slide from three to four in '[t]here are three or four other Passages'. There is even a Hackish lapse of control over meaning

---

[24] Printed in *A Tale*, pp. 317–18.
[25] Zimmerman, *Swift's Narrative Satires*, p. 63.

which makes (Swift) say the literal opposite of what he 'obviously' intends in the clause 'the Abuses he notes being such as all Church of *England* Men agree in'. Surely this was supposed to come out as 'agree to oppose' or some such locution, but if we read it as it stands, it suggests that the book notes abuses *within* the Church of England. But if we put aside such quibbles over symptoms, we are left with three (!) outright obfuscations: four is no more 'Cabalistick' than three, there is no obvious candidate for the fourth machine, and we only have the author's slippery assertion for the existence of any original manuscript.[26] Certainly, if this original text was as different from the first printed edition as we are led to believe, we are within our rights to ask why it has exerted so little influence on this new edition which the 'Apology' prefaces and authorises.[27] The fifth edition contains many additions to the earlier (allegedly unauthorised) editions, but few revisions.[28] Furthermore, even if it is by some miracle true, this convoluted story only explains one of the many instances of triadic construction, and it would be ludicrous to suggest that the whole fabric of threes is the result of misconceived editorial interference. (Swift) makes no attempt to answer this objection. He merely hopes that no one will notice.

As I have by now made tediously clear, the 'Apology' is a strange and selfdivided text that stands at a number of oblique angles to the very strange text it is trying to tame or justify. One might glibly suggest that it is just another Hackish enterprise dragged into *A Tale*'s eccentric orbit like all the other prefatory material. Certainly it is not a great and impressive apologia, but it would be biographical bowdlerisation to exonerate Swift from the blame for (Swift)'s many blurrings, lies, and indirections with the pious fiction that the Apologist is merely a ridiculed persona. In dramatising a self-justifying voice, (Swift) indicates Swift's unease over self-disclosure. Swift was

---

[26] Robert M. Adams, 'In Search of Baron Somers', makes a possible case for the existence of this original manuscript and for the fourth machine being the throne. Indeed, if his speculations are correct, the 'Apology' contains a great deal more honesty than I have credited it with. Too much of his argument remains in the realm of speculation, however, to compel our assent and I have read the extant traces differently. It is worth pointing out here that I have also read the traces differently from Ian Higgins, *Swift's Politics*, where in ch. 3 a sternly Tory and potentially Jacobite Swift is discovered behind *A Tale*. Higgins' position and mine clearly not logically compatible, but they are both 'manifestly deduceable from the Text' (p. 185).

[27] Perhaps this gap between the claims of the 'Apology', that the published version of *A Tale* was unfaithful to the original, and the fact that the 1710 edition makes few changes to the text dates back to the early plan to publish the 'Apology' in the *Miscellanies*. In that context it would have appeared less duplicitous.

[28] This obvious difficulty is meagerly covered by the assertion that 'Some Overtures have been made by a third Hand to the Bookseller for the Author's altering those Passages which he thought might require it. But it seems the Bookseller will not hear of such a Thing, being apprehensive it might spoil the Sale of the Book' (p. 18). Noting the disparity between this fiction and the recorded evidence of Swift's relationship with Tooke, Guthkelch and Smith remark trenchantly: 'Respect for the bookseller's apprehensions must be taken to be only the author's device for explaining why he did not do what he never intended to do' (p. xxii).

clearly uncomfortable with his reputation as the author of *A Tale*, but lacked the will to renounce his work entirely. We modern readers can understand easily enough why he might have been proud of such brilliant work, but we need to make an effort to understand why he was also ashamed of it. The essentially anomalous status and structure of the 'Apology' is, for the want of less ambiguous evidence, the best key we have to this.

Ultimately, the 'Apology' is not about the disclosure of meaning or self, but is rather a complex attempt to shroud both in more acceptable guises. It attempts to create space for a reappraisal of *A Tale* where Swift can be both extraordinary and orthodox at once, but has to settle in the end for propaganda and concealment. For all its self-righteous bluster, everything in the 'Apology' betrays a conviction that *A Tale* is something to be ashamed of, to be explained away. Again, it is by looking to matters of naming that we can most clearly discover the anxiety. Only once in its nineteen pages of text does the 'Apology for the &c'. actually name 'the *Tale of a Tub*'. Even here, it is in a curiously distant manner, as it relates to Wotton rather than to the author: 'this Answerer would have succeeded much better, if he had stuck wholly to his Business as a Commentator upon the *Tale of a Tub*' (p. 15). Elsewhere it appears anonymously under circumlocutions, most commonly as 'the Book' or 'the &c.' The persistence of this coyness is strange and unnecessary – we have no trouble identifying the work being apologised for (it is physically attached), and there would be no point reading the apology if we could not. This is a minor subterfuge in accord with the fundamental failures of naming that riddle *A Tale* and everything in its orbit. 'The Apology for the &c.' and *A Tale of a Tub* are no more than provisional working titles; not proper names so much as marks of the absence of proper names. The mark of authenticity is withheld in the titles and the bylines, for the originator(s) of these texts are not named. While we are entertained by the paradox of a nameless author defending the honour, integrity, orthodoxy, and, above all, the unique originality of another nameless author, formal acknowledgment of responsiblity slips away. As anonymity folds over on itself, any impression of legitimacy dissipates under the influence of a process not radically different from the 'Experiment very frequent among Modern Authors; which is, to *write upon Nothing*; When the Subject is utterly exhausted, to let the Pen still move on; by some called the Ghost of Wit, delighting to walk after the death of its body' (p. 208). *A Tale* walks on as the ghost of Swift's youthful and dangerous wit because the 'Apology' can bring itself neither to own nor repudiate it.

Conflicting ambitions: the desire for a negotiable text

As to the Author, I can give no manner of Satisfaction; However, I am credibly informed that this Publication is without his Knowledge; for he concludes the Copy is lost, having lent it to a Person, since dead, and being never in Possession of it after: So that, whether the Work received his last Hand, or, whether he intended to fill up the defective Places, is like to remain a Secret.   (p. 28)

We have used this passage previously, to describe *A Tale*'s figurative abandonment, and now we will put it to a more literal-minded use in accordance with the more literal-minded mood of this chapter. The unusual digging around in matters of biographical detail and intention has been an attempt to provide empirical support for the metaphor which has governed my interpretation in this and much of the preceding chapter, the image of the text as abandoned and illegitimate. If we treat these words (which are formally uttered by the Bookseller as if to excuse *A Tale*'s notorious textual gaps) as a displacement of Swift's own mixed feelings, we can come close to the status of parody in a mind and a culture anxious for order and control, yet capable of chaos. Swift attempts to free himself from the responsibility for the feral and carnivalesque text by creating the rhetorical form of an onlooker who alleges of the 'Author' that 'this Publication is without his Knowledge; for he concludes the Copy is lost, having lent it to a Person, since dead, and being never in Possession of it after'. This figure opens to doubt the question of 'whether the Work received his last Hand, or, whether he intended to fill up the defective Places, is like to remain a Secret'. By half-erasing the prospect of damaging inferences, the originator offers the excuse of the text being unfinished (and unexpurgated) work which he never intended to make public and might have completed and/or cleansed had he a mind to render it as his legitimate creation. However, it is the first line which reflects *A Tale*'s status most clearly: 'As to the Author, I can give no manner of Satisfaction.' Imagined as emanating from Swift in rhetorical disguise (the historical truth of its production), these words offer a trope of repudiation, a stigmatisation of the text as the original author's bastard offspring, begot in secrecy and ignored in public. This is the metaphor we shall pursue here.

An image of the bastard text's furtive conception and rank growth, offered with specific reference to hermetic writings, appears in 'Section X':

For, *Night* being the universal Mother of Things, wise Philosophers hold all Writings to be *fruitful* in the Proportion they are *dark*; And therefore, the *true illuminated* (that is to say, the *Darkest* of all) have met with such numberless Commentators, whose *Scholiastick* Midwifry hath deliver'd them of Meanings, that the Authors themselves, perhaps, never conceived, and yet may very justly be allowed the Lawful Parents of them: The Words of such Writers being like Seed, which, however scattered at random, when they light upon fruitful Ground, will multiply far beyond either the Hopes or Imagination of the Sower.   (p. 186)

The imagery of illicit procreation is intense. Darkness of night leads to a random fecundity which is aided by the perverse energy of '*Scholiastick*

Midwifry' and the line back to the legitimate origin of sense is broken by the delivery of 'Meanings, that the Authors themselves, perhaps, never conceived'. This already covert activity is further shrouded in doubt by the duplicitous 'perhaps' which never allows for the positive disclosure or denial of meaning. *A Tale's* immense capacity to generate and half deny meanings starts in this moment of orphaning from authorial authority, when words are scattered randomly on the minds of readers and commentators who credit them with meanings they themselves have fathered. The illegitimate text is dangerous because it is indeterminate, and consequently nearly anything can be inscribed on the blank space: the potential for growth is immense, but control is unrealisable because lawful parenthood of language has been subverted.

Thus illegitimacy, which is formally the *prima materia* of *A Tale* sets out to parody, leaks into the text to such an extent that the book becomes the archetype of its subject, a kind of ceaselessly unstable anti-theology of determinate meaning. The Barthesian terminology is instructive, for, though the priestly Swift keeps nervously marking the indeterminacy as 'other' (as belonging only to the disciples and manifestations of error), it becomes increasingly hard to imagine a perspective outside this fallen state of language. Given the nature of the allegory of the will and the coats, and the obsessive concentration on the status of bookishness, it would not be too fanciful to imagine the book as anti-Scripture – the insistent empty scribblings of the Modern world, cut off from the life-giving source of culture and salvation. This idea proposes an apocalyptic role for *A Tale* (a sort of Antichrist of letters), but, for a text so riddled with intimations of intellectual collapse and lying promises of inspired reformation, the cap fits. The problem for readers with 'converting Imaginations' (pp. 189–90), who wish to tie the book to an instrumental satirical scheme which uses ridicule to convert laughter into wisdom, is that the lines between the parody and the texts parodied are never stable. This instability leaks everywhere and grounds for certainty recede as this parody of Modern bookishness becomes an archetype of Modern bookishness. Diseased patterns of thought and imagery are parodied with exhilarating brilliance, but they prove resilient, and become hard to escape even at the same time as their shortcomings are being exposed. Furthermore, meaning and intention, severed as they are from authority, are seldom reliable in *A Tale*. Put simply, the same words can be read in radically different ways, and the ambiguities cannot be resolved except by appeal to the reader's individual taste. This is not true of the whole of the book – the description of Jack's later career in 'Section XI' manages generally to maintain a fairly monovalent attack on the Dissenters, much in the tradition of Butler and others. However, so much of the language remains slippery that the overwhelming impression is of textual and intellectual destabilisation.

Swift's uneasy place in the trace-work of this illegitimacy can be seen through the problems of naming and the image of 'Books, the Children of the Brain':

I confess to have been somewhat liberal in the Business of Titles, having observed the Humor of multiplying them, to bear great Vogue among certain Writers, whom I exceedingly reverence. And indeed, it seems not unreasonable, that Books, the Children of the Brain, should have the Honor to be Christned with variety of Names, as well as other infants of Quality.   (p. 71)

Without the 'variety of Names' at our disposal – a note informs us that most of these were conveniently lost when the original manuscript arrived torn at the printer – we are free to speculate on what sort of a child of Swift's brain *A Tale* might be. It is not likely to be a 'proper' name, because proper names do not need to come multiplied – one true name is enough for a legitimate identity. The distinction between the present book (which comes from nowhere and has to name itself) and 'other infants of Quality' (which come by their names honestly enough in the general order of things) is a further suggestion of dubious status. This child is clearly no infant of quality, and its displacement from any naming source sheds further suspicion on its prestige. The proliferation of prefatory material, 'primarily' or 'obviously' a satire on Modern conventions of ingratiation, also provides a mad excess of naming, which betrays a deep-seated anxiety about the proper presentation of a text to the public.

The fiction of multiple names and the fiction of multiple authors which follows from it enact the function of parody, which is to 'father' disreputable texts on others (that is, to make writers own the absurdity and illegitimacy of their actual efforts by identification with their parodic distortions). However, this fathering of bastards on victims only distracts attention from parody's transgressive nature; it does not necessarily negate the bastard-status of the parody itself. The more deeply a parody engages in the errors it affects to expose, the more it becomes the thing it mocks, and *A Tale* is a pre-eminent example of this. Inscribing and subverting so many conflicting stories of origin and authority, made up of the casually collected scraps of other ridiculous books, spawning multiple allusions, confusions, and misunderstandings, *A Tale* is the archetype of the illegitimate text. The cultural implications, discussed above, are overt, but this should not distract our attention from the covert resonance of illegitimate literary production on Swift himself. The metaphor places *A Tale* in Swift's canon as the illegitimate result of a sowing of wild literary oats, and it stayed with him throughout his career as embarrassing proof of immense but dangerous verbal virility. The book may, at some level of ridicule theory, transcend its materials and enter a higher pedagogic plain of doctrinal purity. However, Swift's actions and words suggest that he, at least, had little faith in the power of this defence to convince readers or erase the primal guilt of association. He showed no courage or persistence in defending *A Tale* and, though he saw to it that it was republished at a time when he wanted to present his credentials as a literary genius, he kept it at arm's length from his canonical works, and continued to do so even decades after such an identification had ceased to offer any potential harm.

To use a Restoration analogy, Swift stood in a similar relation to *A Tale* as Charles II did to the Duke of Monmouth. He felt indulgent and fearful at once towards the magnificent but dangerous and wayward evidence of his virility; he could not legitimate it and continually had to deny it, even at the same time as he was unwilling to allow anyone else to claim it as theirs. To fill out the analogy further, the legitimate issue it was beyond Swift's capacity to produce – the equivalent of the child Charles never had with Queen Catherine – is the abstruse theological treatise recommended to him by Archbishop King in 1711[29] as the best way of getting on in the Church. It is exactly what *A Tale* could never be, and so, despite his sincere wish to be an orthodox son of the Church, Swift's reputation was forever marked by the wildness of his literary youth.

---

[29] See King's letter of 1711, *Corr.*, I, pp. 254–55: 'Say not, that most subjects in divinity are exhausted, for, if you look into Dr. Wilkins's heads of matters...you will be surprised to find so many necessary and useful heads, that no authors have meddled with.' As Ehrenpreis points out (*Swift*, I, p. 75), 'Swift never so wildly mistook his talents as to attempt such a project.'

Conclusion: parodic disguise and the negotiability of *A Tale of A Tub*

Mean while the Danger hourly increasing, by new Levies of Wits all appointed (as there is Reason to fear) with Pen, Ink, and Paper which may at an hours Warning be drawn into Pamphlets, and other Offensive Weapons, ready for immediate Execution: It was judged of absolute necessity, that some present Expedient be thought on, till the main Design can be brought to Maturity. To this End, at a Grand Committee, some Days ago, this important Discovery was made by a certain curious and refined Observer; That Sea-men have a Custom when they meet a *Whale*, to fling him out an empty *Tub*, by way of Amusement, to divert him from laying violent Hands upon the Ship. This Parable was immediately mythologiz'd: The *Whale* was interpreted to be *Hobs's Leviathan*, which tosses and plays with all other Schemes of Religion and Government, whereof a great many are hollow, and dry, and empty, and noisy, and wooden, and given to Rotation. This is the *Leviathan* from whence the Wits of our Age are said to borrow their Weapons. The *Ship* in danger, is easily understood to be its old Antitype the *Commonwealth*. But, how to analyze the *Tub*, was a Matter of difficulty; when after long Enquiry and Debate, the literal Meaning was preserved: And it was decreed, that in order to prevent these *Leviathans* from tossing and sporting with the *Commonwealth*, (which of it self is too apt to *fluctuate*) they should be diverted from that Game by a *Tale of a Tub*. And my Genius being conceived to lye not unhappily that way, I had the honor done me to be engaged in the Performance. (pp. 39–41)

A Tale embraces its tubbian status to a quite extraordinary extent. It is self-consciously provisional (a tub thrown into the sea of dispute to distract feral discourses) and empty of intrinsic meaning (an empty tub to be filled with whatever consumers require). When we discussed this passage in chapter 2, we saw how the parody in it reflects outwards, exposing the provisionality of the culture of restoration enterprise, and deconstructing the fictions of discursive closure by which writers such as Dryden, Addison, and the rest sought to construct legitimacy. Now we will rotate the image to see how it reflects (more covertly) on Swiftian parody and Swift himself. It figures *A Tale* as a negotiable rather than as a determinate text, a parody which interacts with other texts and discourses but does not claim a unique and meaningful integrity of its own. It has function rather than meaning, and that function is a complex negotiation of mixed feelings between a playfully hidden author and a potentially hostile readership. It is process, not content; dialogue, not statement. It is launched on to the textual sea, whereon it is '*light* enough to swim...for all eternity' (p. 32), but it does not commit itself to pierce the surface of language. Parody is, after all, the enactment of the negotiability of discourses: it canvasses the multiplication of their meanings and the uncertainty of their origins. By problematising sources and goals, it uncovers the illegitimacy in a discourse's structure, to engage with it deconstructively and not always with a clear set of aims. The parodic text is an 'Expedient', a dangerously supplementary creature of process rather than a solid structure of ideological conviction, and it does not need a determinate centre. Indeed, the possibility of a genuine centre, a genuine author, is reflected and refracted into many images. None of these can claim any absolute authority, and they all show a disturbing tendency to lapse into gaps in the manuscript.

This embrace of the ironic status of language creates a space where Swift plays many games. In the first place, the indeterminacy is convenient: through it outrageous propositions can be uttered while undesirable implications can be denied or ascribed to the satirised voice of folly. Secondly, it draws the readers into the satiric complications as active agents, making them discover the absurdities of the targets parodied rather than merely hearing them denounced. However, it is the indeterminacy's third aspect which will command our attention here at the book's end: the way it betrays important authorial uncertainties. In the tubbian enterprise of Swift's early parody, where language is neither monological nor entirely controllable, the construction and disclosure of self are ceaselessly unstable. By making the reader imagine an utterer, language generates a self. However, in the reflections and multiplications of parody, informing selves can be constructed and deconstructed almost as freely as can interpretations. And this is what happens for Swift – uncertainties and contradictions of identity are entertained in the parodic language, just as a tub can be filled from time to time with different substances.

What has not been sufficiently recognised by biographers and critics determined to discover a monolithic and ideologically consistent Swift is that in the early stages of his career as an author this playing with tubs and multiplication of selves is in part exploratory as well as satirical. He is a tub-maker, a youthful intellectual in Said's sense,[1] taking the role of writer and opinion-maker as his primary duty and looking for how best to fashion himself and integrate his urgent but uncoordinated cultural affiliations. In the negotiable space provided by parody he is entertaining propositions and

---

[1] See 'Swift as Intellectual'.

taking a virtuoso's pleasure in creating a text so parodically reflective that it can be claimed for any potential self, whether it be a sober churchman, a wit, a Whig, a Tory, a satirist, or a comedian. He is, in other words, using parody playfully and experimentally to try on a variety of disguises, as well as using it instrumentally to invade the discourses of others and destroy them. Not yet ready to finalise his allegiances, he writes with a brilliant yet evasive freedom which later both impressed and embarrassed him. As (Swift) concedes in the 'Apology':

> He was then a young Gentleman much in the World, and wrote to the Tast of those who were like himself; therefore in order to allure them, he gave a liberty to his Pen, which might not suit with maturer Years, or graver Characters, and which he could have easily corrected with a very few Blots, had he been Master of his Papers for a Year or two before their Publication.   (p. 4)

Craving the gentle reader's indulgence, this disclaimer glances lightly over an assortment of hints and palliations. It suggests that the author operated with an adept audience (men of 'Tast') in mind, who would not misunderstand the higher flights of fancy. This keeping of fast and witty company (only to be found among Whigs such as Somers, Addison, and Steele when *A Tale* was being written) is passed off as forgivable exuberance, a sowing of literary wild oats. While this admits a degree of self-indulgence in the book, it places that firmly in the past. The older and wiser apologist then moves to cover his younger self's tracks further by insisting that no serious indiscretions have been committed anyway. He assures us that the excesses might be 'corrected with a *very* few Blots' (my italics), and then insists that these erasing blots would infallibly have been made had the 'Papers' been in the power of an intermediate self 'for a Year or two before their Publication'.

The most intriguing aspect of this passage, however, is the way it turns on the ideologically explosive word 'Liberty'. As we have seen so often above, particularly in the controversy over Collins' *Discourse of Free-Thinking*, 'Liberty' conceived as a virtue was a Whig property, whereas its pejorative sense was distinctly Tory. If we inspect this use of the word, it is difficult to tell which sense is operative. Where does this usage belong in the spectrum, from the extreme Whig position of 'Liberty' as an inalienable right and culturally creative agent, to the reactionary Tory understanding of it as a dangerous freedom which threatens to open the flood-gates of chaos and subversion? Certainly it has a less committed and triumphant tone than either of these extremes. It has a liminal signification which contains a stubborn ambiguity, and that ambiguity marks the border between two phases of Swift's rhetorical self-fashioning. In the semantic slippage from pride to embarrassment − liberty of the pen is not condemned, but it is apologised for − we can see Swift's slippage from a Whiggish to a Tory set of allegiances being enacted emblematically. Saying a fond farewell to the writerly liberty 'which might not suit with maturer Years, or graver Characters', he (to use St Paul's turn of thought) 'put[s] away childish things'[2] and takes on the sober responsibilities of adulthood. In this sentence, the liberty of youth and faith in the benevolent operation of the aristocracy of wit are subordinated to (and in part forsaken for) the obedience to authority suitable to 'maturer years'. And in 1710, the year this sentence was published, Jonathan Swift, an intellectual who had always found his friends (literary and political) among the Whigs, 'came out' as having been a supporter of 'Church Principles' and the Tory ministry all along. The coincidence is instructive.

The sense that this is a deliberate fashioning and *publication* of self rather than naive autobiography should not be ignored. His claim to youthfulness as a published author and partly formed intellectual should not be confused with any biographical notion of Swift as a wayward adolescent genius. *A Tale* may be his earliest major work, but it cannot be treated as juvenilia in any straightforward way. 1697, the date affixed to the 'Dedication to Prince Posterity' and the epicentre of scholarly speculations about the time of writing, was the year Swift turned thirty. He was no epigone. However, he was only beginning to have a public and published self, and he appears not to have finalised the terms of that self. Before his entry into the great world of English public life in the first decade of the eighteenth century, he had had no cause to question the compatibility of his basic ideological affinities. In Ireland, 'everyone' (which is to say, nearly all Protestants) was a Whig, proclaiming Revolution principles against the threat of a Popish restoration, and 'everyone' (which is to say, nearly all Anglicans) was a High Churchman, proclaiming the rights of the established Church and its adherents against the threat from Catholic and Dissenter. We may not admire the oligarchic neurosis underlying this affiliation of loyalties, but we cannot deny that it was a logical enough connection in the Anglo-Irish context. Similarly, in the other significant context of Swift's rather cloistered intellectual youth, the family of Sir William Temple, there was no apparent tension between strongly Whiggish politics and orthodox Anglican piety. Until he entered the great world of London, there had been no practical need for Swift to choose between his two instinctive allegiances, to be 'a Whig in politics' and 'an High-Churchman' in religion.[3] Thus his earlier publications can be read as brilliant but unresolved attempts to balance these affiliations in the English ideological context, where their connection was a paradox.

Parody offers a particularly attractive option for such a project of self-fashioning, because it allows the writer to investigate discourses and their

---

[2] 1 Corinthians, 13:11 (AV).
[3] *PW*, VIII, p. 120.

attendant ideologies without committing him- or herself to the consequences. The full voice of author-ity is withheld from the text, and extra
voices can be implicated in the carnivalesque mode of restless parodies such
as *A Tale*. Language can entertain ideological paradoxes as well as ridicule
them, and the hostile satiric deconstruction of errant discourses can also
reflect backwards to project a tentative construction of potential selves. Only
in this rather anomalous sense can we maintain Ehrenpreis' assertion that
'behind the book [i.e. *A Tale*] stands not a list of philosophical propositions
but the idea of a good man'.[4] The problem is that Swift is hoping to discover rather than to expound what it means to be a good man. There are
many possibilities: behind the specular text lie both lists of propositions and
ideas of good men. Furthermore, there are also brilliant men, vindictive
men, and irresponsible men. The polyvocal text wants to publish and be
claimable for various selves, while the youthful intellectual believes opti-
mistically in his power to gain the sympathy of readers and to reconcile
apparent differences in the alchemy of writing. Experience of the rough-
and-tumble of public discourse was to teach Swift that actual readers,
weighed down by prejudice and stupidity, would not indulge the charming
idiosyncracies of genius in good faith. As Swift's subsequent and more determinate self-fashionings suggest, one has to take sides, and there are costs.

While it would take a further book to make the case in detail, it is possible at this point to map the different publications of self essayed in Swift's
career as a public intellectual and writer of prose. While not a directly biographical analysis – it does not try to explain Swift's private writings and
motivations, or to integrate them with his public and rhetorical presences –
it has biographical implications. There are four significant phases of affiliation and rhetorical self-fashioning, and they each influence both the function and the context of the parodies. In the first and most freely parodic
period, the images of authentic utterance are least settled and least forcefully felt. The focus is on parodied form rather than ideological content so
that the cohabitation of the two extremes apparent in *A Tale* (and still
retrievable from the *Argument against Abolishing Christianity*) of the Whiggish wit
and the pious Anglican censor functions more as a raising of creative tension than as a contradiction. As Swift became a player in the politics of the
last years of Anne's reign, he needed to create a stable rhetorical self with
coherent views and unquestioned authority. Consequently, by the time of
the *Abstract* of Collins' *Discourse*, Swift has entered his second (and most self-
consciously orthodox) phase by becoming the published spokesman for the
Tory ministry. The options are fewer and the allegiances have hardened, so
the ventriloquial aspect of parody (which always allows for a degree of anarchic freedom of implication) has to be brought to heel as far as possible,

[4] *Swift*, I, p. 189.

while the text is made to serve polemical purposes. This least paradoxical of Swifts (most obvious in the *Examiner* and the *Conduct of the Allies*) seeks to smooth rather than to complicate the process of communication.

Similarly, the Hibernian patriot of the *Drapier's Letters* and the other practical Irish writings of the 1720s is a dramatic but fundamentally simple construct. With the Drapier, for example, although Swift is mimicking a voice not his own, and there are significant biographical ironies between his public patriotism and his private attitudes towards Ireland, the effect is not one of parody. The Drapier speaks an idiolect which has been imitated faithfully, forcefully, and instrumentally, without the deconstructive supplement of parody being added. Unlike the Hack, he is not divided from the authority of his own text – he appears to command language rather to be comically commanded by it. This proposition may seem an absurd statement in the context of post-structuralist literary theory, where the idea of commanding language can be no more than a metaphor obscuring authoritarian duplicity, but it marks an important difference in the relations between author, text, discourse, and audience. Unless all writing is held to be pervasively parodic and self-deconstructive, there is not much point in discussing the *Examiner* or the *Drapier's Letters* as parody. They are examples of carefully modulated persuasive prose which employ a range of rhetorical effects to enunciate 'obvious' ideologies and bring about practical political results.

The same cannot be said of *Gulliver's Travels* and *A Modest Proposal*, which disclose but do not define Swift's last and most widely recognised self-publication – the majestic misanthrope. While the Dean and the Drapier clearly have an understanding, no stable relationship exists between the narrators of these works (Gulliver and the Proposer) and the misanthropic self. Meaning and authority are disguised in parody and evade restrictive definition, leaving the reader feeling attacked rather than reassured by the irony. However, satire comes before parody in these texts and with this self. Pride and cruelty are animated parodically (i.e. deconstructed) as well as being attacked satirically (i.e. destroyed), but the priority of satire is maintained – the evasion of final judgements is not as radical as in *A Tale*. The condemnation of human folly in this last stage is fundamentally more monological in utterance as well as being more coherent and narrowly motivated towards practical political or moral goals. *Gulliver's Travels* is written by a battle-scarred veteran of a lifetime of public dispute and misinterpretation, and it is also less trusting in its belief that it will be heard and understood. An explosion of all 'visionary schemes', it centres savagely and precisely on a disillusionment which is final, rather than on more reflexive parodic processes of illusionment and disillusionment.

The negotiation between parody and authority can never be a secure one, of course, but it need not be equally unstable in all parodic texts. We cannot finally decipher *A Modest Proposal*, for example, but we can be reasonably confident that the text does not advocate cannibalism. By comparison, we cannot be sure whether a true understanding of the 'Digression concerning Madness' would hold that women are better for being flayed or not. This openness to shifting and irreducibly plural projections of authority is the most extraordinary thing about *A Tale* and Swift's other early parodies. We can propose authoritative centres to these texts, and make long and complex arguments to defend them, but we will not be able to close the issue. They play ironically on the surfaces of language, making assertions and reflecting selves, but deconstructing positions too freely to come to rest on any single ideological authority or discursive authenticity. They engage extensively with the texts which surround them and from which they are pieced together, but they do not piece the lessons of parody into the privileged understandings which occur when satire is a governing principle. Rather, they retain a paradoxical claimability for disparate affiliations and implications. Particularly in *A Tale*, authenticities multiply and escape into irony, and parody makes the language of authority into the thing which is not.

Select bibliography

This bibliography is primarily a list of references, but it also includes several items, not mentioned in the footnotes, which have exerted an influence on my work. Where acronyms occur for journals, they correspond to those used in the *MLA International Bibliography*. Where early texts have been consulted in original editions, I provide the place of publication and the date, but not the name of the publisher.

Adams, Robert M. *Strains of Discord: Studies in Literary Openness*. Ithaca: Cornell University Press, 1958.

'Jonathan Swift, Thomas Swift, and the Authorship of *A Tale of a Tub*'. *MP*, 64 (1967), 198–232.

'The Mood of the Church and *A Tale of a Tub*', *England in the Restoration and Early Eighteenth Century: Essays on Culture and Society*. H. T. Swedenberg Jr, ed. Berkeley: University of California Press, 1972, pp. 71–99 .

'In Search of Baron Somers', *Culture and Politics from Puritanism to the Enlightenment*. Perez Zagorin, ed. Berkeley: University of California Press, 1980, pp. 165–202.

Addison, Joseph and Sir Richard Steele, et al. *The Spectator*. 5 vols. Donald F. Bond, ed. Oxford: Oxford University Press, 1965.

Alkon, Paul. 'Defoe's Argument in *The Shortest Way with the Dissenters*'. *MP*, 73 (1976), 512–23.

Andreasen, N. J. C. 'Swift's Satire on the Occult in *A Tale of a Tub*'. *TSLL*, 5 (1963–64), 410–21.

Andrews, William. *Extraordinary News from the Stars: Or, An Ephemeris for the Year 1708*. London, 1708.

Anselment, Raymond A. *'Betwixt Jest and Earnest': Marprelate, Milton, Marvell, Swift and the Decorum of Religious Ridicule*. Toronto: University of Toronto Press, 1979.

Astell, Mary. *A Fair Way with the Dissenters and their Patrons*. London, 1704.

Atterbury, Francis. *Sermons on Several Occasions*. 2 vols. London, 1734.

Backscheider, Paula. *Daniel Defoe: His Life*. Baltimore and London: Johns Hopkins University Press, 1989.

Bakhtin, M. M. *The Dialogical Imagination: Four Essays*. Michael Holquist and Caryl Emerson, eds. and trans. Austin: University of Texas Press, 1981.

Barthes, Roland. *Essais Critiques IV: le Bruissement de la Langue*. Paris: Editions du Seuil, 1984.

Image-Music-Text: Essays Selected and Translated by Stephen M. Heath. London: Fontana Press, 1977.

S/Z. Richard Miller, trans. New York: Hill and Wang, 1974; 1st French edn, 1970.

Bate, W. Jackson. *The Burden of the Past and the English Poet.* London: Chatto & Windus, 1971.

Beaumont, Charles A. *Swift's Classical Rhetoric.* Athens, Ga.: University of Georgia Press, 1961.

Swift's Use of the Bible: A Documentation and a Study in Allusion. Athens, Ga.: University of Georgia Press, 1965.

Bennett, G. V. *White Kennet, 1660–1728, Bishop of Peterborough: A Study of the Political and Ecclesiastical History of the Early Eighteenth Century.* London: SPCK, 1957.

The Tory Crisis in Church and State 1688–1730: The Career of Francis Atterbury, Bishop of Rochester. Oxford: Clarendon Press, 1975.

Bentley, Richard. *Remarks Upon a Late Discourse of Free-Thinking: In a Letter to FHDD. by Philaleutherus Lipsiensis.* London, 1713.

Black, Jeremy. 'Introduction: an Age of Political Stability?', *Britain in the Age of Walpole.* Jeremy Black ed. London: Macmillan, 1984, pp. 1–22.

Bloom, Harold. *The Anxiety of Influence: A Theory of Poetry.* New York and London: Oxford University Press, 1973.

Bogel, Fredric V. 'Irony, Inference, and Critical Uncertainty'. *Yale Review,* 69 (1979), 503–19.

Booth, Wayne C. *A Rhetoric of Irony.* Chicago: University of Chicago Press, 1974.

Bosher, Robert S. *The Making of the Restoration Settlement: The Influence of the Laudians, 1649–1662.* London: Dacre Press, 1951.

Bowle, John. *Hobbes and his Critics: A Study in Seventeenth Century Constitutionalism.* London: Frank Cass, 1969; 1st edn, 1951.

Boyle, Frank T. 'Profane and Debauched Deist Swift in the Contemporary Response to *A Tale of a Tub*'. *Eighteenth-Century Ireland,* 3 (1988), 25–38.

Bramhall, John, Archbishop of Armagh. *Bishop Bramhall's Vindication of himself and the Episcopal Clergy, from the Presbyterian Charge of Popery, as it is managed by Mr Baxter in his Treatise of the Grotian Religion.* London, 1672.

Brett, R. L. *The Third Earl of Shaftesbury: A Study in Eighteenth-Century Literary Theory.* London: Hutchinson University Library, 1951.

Brown, Laura. 'Reading Race and Gender: Jonathan Swift'. *ECS,* 23 (1990), 425–43.

Burnet, Gilbert, Bishop of Salisbury. *Bishop Burnet's History of His Own Time: With Notes by the Earls of Dartmouth and Hardwicke, Speaker Onslow, and Dean Swift. To which are Added Other Annotations.* 2nd edn (enlarged), 6 vols. Oxford: Oxford University Press, 1833; 1st edn, 1724–34.

Burnham, Frederic B. 'The More-Vaughan Controversy: The Revolt against Philosophical Enthusiasm'. *JHI,* 35 (1974), 33–49.

Burton, Robert *The Anatomy of Melancholy.* Holbrook Jackson, ed. London: Dent, 1932.

Burtt, Shelley. *Virtue Transformed: Political Argument in England, 1688–1740.* Cambridge: Cambridge University Press, 1992.

Butler, Samuel. *Hudibras.* John Wilders, ed. Oxford: Clarendon Press, 1967.

Canavan, Thomas L. 'Robert Burton, Jonathan Swift, and the Tradition of Anti-Puritan Invective'. *JHI*, 34 (1973), 227–42.

Capp, Bernard. *English Almanacs, 1500–1800: Astrology and the Popular Press.* Ithaca: Cornell University Press, 1979.

Carnochan, W. B. 'Swift, Locke, and the *Tale*'. *Swift Studies*, 1 (1986), 55–56.

Casaubon, Meric. *A Treatise Concerning Enthusiasme (1655): A Facsimile Reproduction of the Second Edition of 1656 with an Introduction.* Paul J. Korshin, ed. Gainesvelle: Scholars Facsimiles & Reprints, 1970.

Castle, Terry. 'Why the Houyhnhnms Don't Write: Swift, Satire, and the Fear of the Text'. *Essays in Literature*, 7 (1980), 31–44.

Champion, J. A. I. *The Pillars of Priestcraft Shaken: The Church of England and its Enemies, 1660–1730.* Cambridge: Cambridge University Press, 1992.

Clarendon, Edward Hyde, Earl of. *The History of the Rebellion and Civil Wars in England, begun in the Year 1641.* 6 vols. W. Dunn Macray, ed. Oxford: Clarendon Press, 1888.

Clark, J. C. D. *English Society, 1688–1832: Ideology, Social Structure and Political Practice During the Ancien Régime.* Cambridge: Cambridge University Press, 1985.

Revolution and Rebellion: State and Society in England in the Seventeenth and Eighteenth Centuries. Cambridge: Cambridge University Press, 1986.

Clark, John R. *Form and Frenzy in Swift's 'Tale of a Tub'.* Ithaca: Cornell University Press, 1970.

Clifford, Gay. *The Transformations of Allegory.* London: Routledge & Kegan Paul, 1974.

Colie, Rosalie. *Paradoxia Epidemica: The Renaissance Tradition of Paradox.* Princeton: Princeton University Press, 1966.

Colley, Linda. *In Defence of Oligarchy: The Tory Party, 1714–60.* Cambridge: Cambridge University Press, 1982.

Collins, Anthony. *A Discourse of Free-Thinking Occasion'd by the Rise and Growth of a Sect call'd Free-Thinkers.* London, 1713.

A Discourse Concerning Ridicule and Irony in Writing, in a Letter to the Reverend Dr. Nathaniel Marshall. London, 1729.

Cook, Richard I. *Jonathan Swift as a Tory Pamphleteer.* Seattle: University of Washington Press, 1967.

Craven, Kenneth. *Jonathan Swift and the Millennium of Madness: The Information Age in Swift's A Tale of a Tub.* Leiden: E. J. Brill, 1992.

*A Tale of a Tub and the 1697 Dublin Controversy'. *Eighteenth-Century Ireland*, 1 (1986), 97–110.

Crocker, Robert. 'Mysticism and Enthusiasm in Henry More', Sarah Hutton, ed. *Henry More (1614–1687), Tercentenary Studies.* Dordrecht: Kluwer, 1990, pp. 137–55.

Cruickshanks, Eveline. *Political Untouchables: The Tories and the '45.* London: Duckworth, 1979.

'Religion and the Royal Succession: the Rage of Party', *Britain in the First Age of Party, 1680–1750: Essays Presented to Geoffrey Holmes.* Clyve Jones ed. London: Hambledon Press, 1987, pp. 14–45.

Dane, Joseph A. *Parody: Critical Concepts Versus Literary Practices, Aristophanes to Sterne.* Norman: University of Oklahoma Press, 1988.

Day, Robert Adams. 'Richard Bentley and John Dunton: Brothers under the Skin'. *SECC*, 16 (1986), 125–38.

Defoe, Daniel. *A Brief Explanation of a Late Pamphlet, entitled 'The Shortest Way with the Dissenters'*. London, 1702–03

   A Dialogue Between a Dissenter and the Observator, Concerning the Shortest Way with the Dissenters. London, 1703.

   The Present State of the Parties. London, 1712.

   The Shortest Way with the Dissenters and Other Pamphlets. Oxford: Basil Blackwell, 1927.

De Krey, Gary Stuart. *A Fractured Society: The Politics of London in the First Age of Party, 1688–1715*. Oxford: Clarendon Press, 1985.

De Porte, Michael V. *Nightmares and Hobbyhorses: Swift, Sterne, and Augustan Ideas of Madness*. San Marino, Calif.: The Huntington Library, 1974.

Derrida, Jacques. *Dissemination*. Barbara Johnson, trans. Chicago: University of Chicago Press, 1981; 1st French edn, 1972.

   Of Grammatology. Gayatri Chakravoty Spivack, trans. Baltimore: Johns Hopkins University Press, 1976; 1st French edn, 1967.

Dickinson, H. T. *Liberty and Property: Political Ideology in Eighteenth-Century Britain*. London: Weidenfield and Nicolson, 1977.

Docherty, Thomas. *On Modern Authority: The Theory and Condition of Writing, 1500 to the Present Day*. Brighton: Harvester, 1987.

Donoghue, Denis. *Jonathan Swift: A Critical Introduction*. Cambridge: Cambridge University Press, 1969.

Downie, J. A. *Robert Harley and the Press: Propaganda and Public Opinion in the Age of Swift and Defoe*. Cambridge: Cambridge University Press, 1979.

   Jonathan Swift: Political Writer. London: Routledge & Kegan Paul, 1984.

   'Swift's Politics', *Proceedings of the First Münster Symposium on Jonathan Swift*. Hermann J. Real and Heinz J. Vienken, eds. Munich: Wilhelm Fink Verlag, 1985, pp. 47–58.

   'Defoe's *Shortest Way with the Dissenters*: Irony, Intention and Reader-Response'. *Prose Studies*, 9 (1986), 120–39.

Drake, James. *The Memorial of the Church of England Humbly Offer'd to the Consideration of all True Lovers of our Church and Constitution*. London, 1705.

Dryden, John. *The Works of John Dryden: Poems, The Works of Virgil in English, 1697*. William Frost and Vinton A. Dearing, eds. Berkeley: University of California Press, 1987; vols V and VI of the California Dryden.

Duffy, Eamon. 'Primitive Christianity Revived: Religious Renewal in Augustan England'. *Studies in Church History*, 14 (1977), 287–300.

Eagleton, Terry. *The Function of Criticism: From the Spectator to Post-Structuralism*. London: Verso, 1984.

Eddy, William Alfred, ed. *Jonathan Swift: Satires and Personal Writings*. London: Oxford University Press, 1932.

Ehrenpreis, Irvin. *Swift: The Man, his Works, and the Age*. 3 vols. London: Methuen, 1962–83.

   'Personae', *Restoration and Eighteenth-Century Literature: Essays in Honor of Alan Dugald McKillop*. Carol Camden, ed. Chicago: University of Chicago Press, 1963, pp. 25–37.

   Literary Meaning and Augustan Values. Charlottesville: University of Virginia Press, 1974.

'The Doctrine of *A Tale of a Tub*', *Proceedings of the First Münster Symposium on Jonathan Swift*. Hermann J. Real and Heinz J. Vienken, eds. Munich: Wilhelm Fink Verlag, 1985, pp. 59–71.

Eilon, Daniel. 'Swift's Satiric Logic: Parsimony, Irony and Antinomian Fiction'. *YES*, 18 (1988), 18–40.

Factions Fictions: Ideological Closure in Swift's Satire. Newark: University of Delaware Press, 1991.

Elias, A. C., Jr. *Swift at Moor Park: Problems in Biography and Criticism*. Philadelphia: University of Pennsylvania Press, 1982.

Elkin, P. K. *The Augustan Defence of Satire*. Oxford: Clarendon Press, 1973.

Elliott, Robert C. *The Power of Satire: Magic, Ritual, Art*. Princeton: Princeton University Press, 1960.

The Literary Persona. Chicago: University of Chicago Press, 1982.

Ellis, Frank H. '*An Argument Against Abolishing Christianity* as an Argument against Abolishing the Test Act', *Reading Swift: Papers from the Second Münster Symposium on Jonathan Swift*. Richard H. Rodino and Hermann J. Real, eds. Munich: Wilhelm Fink Verlag, 1993, pp. 127–40.

'Notes on *A Tale of a Tub*'. *Swift Studies*, 1 (1986), 9–14.

Ewald, William Bragg, Jr. *The Masks of Jonathan Swift*. Cambridge, Mass.: Harvard University Press, 1954.

Fabricant, Carole. *Swift's Landscape*. Baltimore and London: Johns Hopkins University Press, 1982.

'The Battle of the Ancients and (Post)Moderns: Rethinking Swift through Contemporary Perspectives'. *ECent*, 32 (1991), 256–73.

Feather, John. *A History of British Publishing*. London: Routledge, 1988.

Fish, Stanley E. *Self-Consuming Artifacts: The Experience of Seventeenth-Century Literature*. Berkeley: University of California Press, 1972.

Foucault, Michel. *The Order of Things: An Archeology of the Human Sciences*. London: Tavistock, 1970; 1st French edn, *Les Mots at les Choses: une Archeologie des Sciences Humaines*. Paris Editions Gallimard, 1966.

'What is an Author?', *Textual Strategies: Perspectives in Post-Structuralist Criticism*. Josue Harari, ed. Ithaca: Cornell University Press, 1979, pp. 141–60.

Fox, Adam. *John Mill and Richard Bentley: A Study of the Textual Criticism of the New Testament, 1675–1729*. Oxford: Basil Blackwell, 1954.

Fox, Christopher. *Locke and the Scriblerians: Identity and Consciousness in Early Eighteenth-Century Britain*. Berkeley: University of California Press, 1988.

Frei, Hans W. *The Eclipse of Biblical Narrative: A Study in Eighteenth and Nineteenth Century Hermeneutics*. New Haven: Yale University Press, 1974.

Gascoigne, John. *Cambridge in the Age of the Enlightenment: Science, Religion and Politics from the Restoration to the French Revolution*. Cambridge: Cambridge University Press, 1989.

Goldgar, Bertrand A. *The Curse of Party: Swift's Relations with Addison and Steele*. Lincoln, NE: University of Nebraska Press, 1961.

Goldie, Mark. 'The Revolution of 1689 and the Structure of Political Argument: An Essay and An Annotated Bibliography of Pamphlets on the Allegiance Controversy'. *Bulletin of Research in the Humanities*, 83 (1980), 473–564.

Tory Political Thought 1689–1714. Cambridge University: unpublished Ph.D dissertation, 1978.

Graves, Robert. *The Greek Myths*. 2nd edn, 2 vols. Harmondsworth: Penguin, 1960.

Habermas, Jürgen. *The Structural Transformation of the Public Sphere: An Inquiry into a Category of Bourgeois Society*. Thomas Burger, trans. Cambridge, Mass.: MIT Press, 1989; 1st German edn, 1962.

Hall, Basil. 'An Inverted Hypocrite: Swift the Churchman', *The World of Jonathan Swift: Essays for the Tercentenary*. Brian Vickers, ed. Oxford: Basil Blackwell, 1968, pp. 38–68.

Hammond, Eugene R. '"In Praise of Wisdom and the Will of God": Erasmus' *Praise of Folly* and Swift's *A Tale of a Tub*'. *SP*, 80 (1983), 253–76.

Harth, Philip. *Swift and Anglican Rationalism: The Religious Background of A Tale of a Tub*. Chicago: University of Chicago Press, 1961.

'Ehrenpreis's Swift: The Biographer as Critic'. *MP*, 67 (1970), 273–78.

Heyd, Michael. 'The Reaction to Enthusiasm in the Seventeenth Century: Towards an Integrative Approach'. *Journal of Modern History*, 53 (1981), 258–80.

Higgins, Ian. *Swift's Politics: A Study in Disaffection*. Cambridge: Cambridge University Press, 1994.

Hill, B.W. *The Growth of Parliamentary Parties, 1689–1742*. London: Allen and Unwin, 1976.

Hill, Christopher. *The Century of Revolution: 1603–1714*. London: Thomas Nelson and Sons, 1961.

Hobbes, Thomas. *Leviathan*. C. B. McPherson, ed. Harmondsworth: Penguin, 1968; 1st edn, 1651.

Holly, Grant. 'Travel and Translation: Textuality in *Gulliver's Travels*'. *Criticism*, 21 (1979), 134–52.

Holmes, Geoffrey. *British Politics in the Age of Anne*. London: Macmillan, 1967.

The Trial of Doctor Sacheverell. London: Eyre Methuen, 1973.

Augustan England: Professions, State and Society. London: Allen and Unwin, 1982.

Holmes, Geoffrey, ed. *Britain after the Glorious Revolution 1689–1714*. London: Macmillan, 1969.

Horsley, L. S. 'Contemporary Reactions to Defoe's *Shortest Way with the Dissenters*'. *SEL*, 16 (1976), 407–20.

Hudson, Nicholas. *Samuel Johnson and Eighteenth Century Thought*. Oxford: Clarendon Press, 1988.

Hunter, Michael. *Science and Society in Restoration England*. Cambridge: Cambridge University Press, 1981.

Hutcheon, Linda. *A Theory of Parody: The Teachings of Twentieth-Century Art Forms*. New York & London: Methuen, 1985.

Hutton, Ronald. *The Restoration: A Political and Religious History of England and Wales, 1658–1667*. Oxford: Oxford University Press, 1985.

Johnson, Samuel. *Lives of the English Poets*. 3 vols. G. B. Hill, ed. Oxford: Clarendon Press, 1905.

Jones, J. R. *The Revolution of 1688 in England*. London: Weidenfield and Nicolson, 1972.

Jones, J. R., ed. *The Restored Monarchy, 1660–1688*. London: Macmillan, 1979.

Jose, Nicholas. *Ideas of the Restoration in English Literature, 1660–71*. Cambridge, Mass.: Harvard University Press, 1984.

Kelling, Harold D. and Cathy Lynn Preston. *A KWIC Concordance to Jonathan Swift's*

A Tale of a Tub, The Battle of the Books, and A Discourse Concerning the Mechanical Operation of the Spirit, a Fragment. New York: Garland Publishing, 1984.

Kelly, Anne Cline. 'The Semiotics of Swift's 1711 *Miscellanies*'. *Swift Studies*, 6 (1991), 59–68.

Swift and the English Language. Philadelphia: University of Pennsylvania Press, 1988.

Kelly, Veronica. 'Following the Stage-Itinerant: Perception, Doubt, and Death in Swift's *Tale of a Tub*'. *SECC*, 17 (1987), 239–58.

Kenner, Hugh. *The Counterfeiters: An Historical Comedy*. 2nd edn, Johns Hopkins University Press, 1985.

Kenyon, J. P. *Revolution Principles: The Politics of Party, 1689-1720*. Cambridge: Cambridge University Press, 1977.

Kernan, Alvin. *Printing Technology, Letters and Samuel Johnson*. Princeton: Princeton University Press, 1987.

Klein, Lawrence E. *Shaftesbury and the Culture of Politeness: Moral Discourse and Cultural Politics in early Eighteenth-Century England*. Cambridge: Cambridge University Press, 1994.

Kramnick, Isaac. *Bolingbroke and his Circle: The Politics of Nostalgia in the Age of Walpole*. Cambridge, Mass.: Harvard University Press, 1968.

Landa, Louis A. *Swift and the Church of Ireland*. Oxford: Oxford University Press,1954.

Essays in Eighteenth-Century English Literature. Princeton: Princeton University Press, 1980.

Leavis, F. R. 'The Irony of Swift'. *Scrutiny*, 2 (1934), 364–78. Reprinted in *Swift: A Collection of Critical Essays*. Ernest Tuveson, ed. Englewood Cliffs: Prentice Hall, 1964, pp. 15–29.

LeFanu, T. P. 'Dean Swift's Library', *Journal of the Royal Society of Antiquaries of Ireland*, 1896, 113–21.

LeFanu, William, ed. *A Catalogue of Books belonging to Dr Jonathan Swift Dean of St Patricks, Dublin, Aug.19.1715*. Cambridge: Cambridge University Library, 1988.

Leranbaum, Miriam. '"An *Irony Not Unusual*": Defoe's *Shortest Way with the Dissenters*'. *HLQ*, 37 (1973–74), 222–50.

Leslie, Charles. *The New Association of those Called Moderate-Church-Men, with the Modern Whigs and Fanaticks, to Under-mine and Blow-Up the Present Church and Government*. London, 1702.

The New Association. Part II, With Farther Improvements. London, 1705.

Reflections Upon a Late Scandalous and Malicious Pamphlet Entitl'd, The Shortest Way With the Dissenters; or Proposals for the Establishment of the Church. London, 1703.

A Short and Easy Method with the Deists. 9th edn, London, 1745; 1st edn, 1698.

Levine, Jay Arnold. 'The Design of *A Tale of A Tub* (With a Digression on a Mad Modern Critic)'. *ELH*, 33 (1966), 198–227.

Levine, Joseph M. *The Battle of the Books: History and Literature in the Augustan Age*. Ithaca: Cornell University Press, 1991.

Lock, F. P. *Swift's Tory Politics*. London: Duckworth, 1983.

Locke, John. *An Essay Concerning Human Understanding*. Peter H. Nidditch, ed. Oxford: Oxford University Press, 1975.

A Letter Concerning Toleration. London, 1689.

Two Treatises of Government. Peter Laslett, ed. Cambridge: Cambridge University Press 1960; 1st edn, 1690.

Love, Harold. *Scribal Publication in Seventeenth-Century England*. Oxford: Clarendon Press, 1993.

McCrea, Brian. 'Surprised by Swift: Entrapment and Escape in *A Tale of a Tub*'. *Papers on Language & Literature*, 18 (1982), 234–49.

Mandeville, Bernard. *The Fable of the Bees: or, Private Vices, Public Benefits*. Phillip Harth, ed. Harmondsworth: Penguin, 1970.

Marvell, Andrew. *The Rehearsal Transpros'd, and The Rehearsal Transpros'd, The Second Part*. D. I. B. Smith, ed. Oxford: Oxford University Press, 1971; 1st edn, 1672.

Meehan, Michael. 'Authorship and Imagination in Blackstone's *Commentaries on the Laws of England*', *Studies in the Eighteenth Century*, 16 (1992), 111–26.

Miller, John. *Popery and Politics in England, 1660–1688*. Cambridge: Cambridge University Press, 1973.

Mintz, Samuel I. *The Hunting of Leviathan: Seventeenth-Century Reactions to the Materialism and Moral Philosophy of Thomas Hobbes*. Cambridge: Cambridge University Press, 1962.

More, Henry. *Enthusiasmus Triumphatus; Or, A Brief Discourse of the Nature, Causes, Kinds, and Cure of Enthusiasm*. M. V. De Porte, intro. Los Angeles: Augustan Reprint Society, 1966; reprint of 2nd edn, 1662.

Mueller, Judith C. 'The Ethics of Reading in Swift's *Abstract* on Freethinking'. *SEL*, 31 (1991), 483–96.

'Writing under Constraint: Swift's "Apology" for *A Tale of a Tub*'. *ELH*, 60 (1993), 101–15.

Nokes. David. 'Swift and the Beggars'. *Essays in Criticism*, 26 (1976), 218–35.

'"Hack at Tom Poley's": Swift's Use of Puns', *The Art of Jonathan Swift*. Clive T. Probyn, ed. London: Vision Press, 1978, pp. 43–56.

'The Radical Conservatism of Swift's Irish Pamphlets'. *British Journal for Eighteenth-Century Studies*, 7 (1984), 169–76.

Jonathan Swift, A Hypocrite Reversed: A Critical Biography. Oxford: Oxford University Press, 1985.

Nussbaum, Felicity and Laura Brown. 'Revising Critical Practices: An Introductory Essay', *The New Eighteenth Century: Theory, Politics, Literature*. Felicity Nussbaum and Laura Brown, eds. New York and London: Methuen, 1987, pp. 1–22.

O'Higgins, James S. J. *Anthony Collins: The Man and his Works*. The Hague: Martinus Nijhoff, 1970.

Ong, Walter J. *Orality and Literacy: The Technologizing of the Word*. London: Methuen, 1982.

Palmeri, Frank A. '"To write upon Nothing": Narrative Satire and Swift's *A Tale of a Tub*'. *Genre*, 18 (1985), 151–72.

Parker, Samuel. *A Discourse of Ecclesiastical Polity: Wherein The Authority of the Civil Magistrate over the Consciences of Subjects in Matters of External Religion is Asserted*. 3rd edn, London, 1671; 1st edn, 1669.

A Reproof to the Rehearsal Transpos'd, in A Discourse to its Author. London, 1673.

Partridge, John. *Merlinus Liberatus: Being an Almanack For the Year of our Blessed Saviour's Incarnation 1709*. London, 1709.

Merlinus Redivivus: Being an Almanack For the Year of our Blessed Saviour's Incarnation 1714. London, 1714.

Paulson, Ronald. *Theme and Structure in Swift's Tale of a Tub*. New Haven: Yale University Press, 1960.

Perkin, J. Russell. 'Religion, Language, and Society: Swift's Anglican Writings'. *English Studies in Canada*, 15 (1989), 21–34.

Petr, Pavel, David Roberts, and Philip Thomson, eds. *Comic Relations: Studies in the Comic, Satire and Parody*. Frankfurt: Verlag Peter Lang, 1985.

Petty, Sir William. *The Political Anatomy of Ireland: with the Establishment for that Kingdom and Verbum Sapienti*. Shannon: Irish University Press, 1970. Facsimile of 1st edn, 1691.

Phiddian, Robert. 'The Reaction to Collins's *A Discourse of Free-Thinking* "Not Politicks"?'. *Swift Studies*, 4 (1989), 63–76.

'The English Swift / The Irish Swift', *Irish Writing: Exile and Subversion*. Paul Hyland and Neil Sammells, eds. London: Macmillan, 1991, pp. 32–44.

'A Name to Conjure With: Games of Verification and Identity in the Bickerstaff Controversy', *Reading Swift: Papers from the Second Münster Symposium on Jonathan Swift*. Richard H. Rodino and Hermann J. Real, eds. Munich: Wilhelm Fink Verlag, 1993, pp. 141–50.

Philmus, Robert M. 'Swift's "Lost" Answer to Tindal'. *TSLL*, 22 (1980), 367–93.

'Mechanical Operations of the Spirit and *A Tale of a Tub*'. *English Studies in Canada*, 10 (1984), 391–406.

Plumb, J. H. *The Growth of Political Stability in England, 1675–1725*. London: Macmillan, 1967.

Pocock, J. G. A. *The Ancient Constitution and the Feudal Law: English Historical Thought in the Seventeenth Century*. New York: Norton, 1967; 1st edn, 1957.

Probyn, Clive T. '"Haranguing upon Texts": Swift and the Idea of the Book', *Proceedings of the First Münster Symposium on Jonathan Swift*. Hermann J. Real and Heinz J. Vienken, eds. Munich: Wilhelm Fink Verlag, 1985, pp. 187–97.

'Swift and Typographic Man: Foul Papers, Modern Criticism, and Irish Dissenters', *Reading Swift: Papers from the Second Münster Symposium on Jonathan Swift*. Richard H. Rodino and Hermann J. Real, eds. Munich: Wilhelm Fink Verlag, 1993, pp. 25–43.

Probyn, Clive T., ed. *The Art of Jonathan Swift*. London: Vision Press, 1978.

Jonathan Swift: The Contemporary Background. Manchester: Manchester University Press, 1978.

Quilligan, Maureen. *The Language of Allegory: Defining the Genre*. Ithaca: Cornell University Press, 1979.

Quintana, Ricardo. *Swift: An Introduction*. Oxford: Oxford University Press, 1955.

'Two Paragraphs in *A Tale of a Tub*, Section IX'. *MP*, 73 (1975), 15–32.

Racevskis, Karlis. 'Genealogical Critique: Michel Foucault', *Contemporary Literary Theory*. G. D. Atkins and L. Morrow, eds. Amherst: University of Massachusetts Press, 1988, pp. 229–45.

Rawson, Claude J. *Gulliver and the Gentle Reader: Studies in Swift and our Time*. London and Boston: Routledge & Kegan Paul, 1973.

'The Character of Swift's Satire: Reflections on Swift, Johnson, and Human Restlessness', *The Character of Swift's Satire: A Revised Focus*. Claude Rawson, ed. Newark: University of Delaware Press, 1983, pp. 21–82.

Order from Confusion Sprung: Studies in Eighteenth-Century Literature from Swift to Cowper. London: George Allen & Unwin, 1985.

Real, Hermann J. and Heinz J. Vienken, eds. *Proceedings of the First Münster Symposium on Jonathan Swift*. Munich: Wilhelm Fink Verlag, 1985.

Redwood, John. *Reason, Ridicule and Religion: The Age of Enlightenment in England, 1660–1750*. London: Thames & Hudson, 1976.

Reed, Joel. 'Restoration and Repression: The Language Projects of the Royal Society'. *SECC*, 19 (1989), 399–412.

Reilly, Patrick. *Jonathan Swift: The Brave Desponder*. Manchester: Manchester University Press, 1982.

Reiss, Timothy J. *The Discourse of Modernism*. Ithaca: Cornell University Press, 1982.

Reventlow, Henning Graf. *The Authority of the Bible and the Rise of the Modern World*. London: SCM Press, 1984.

Richards, James O. *Party Propaganda Under Queen Anne: The General Elections of 1702–1713*. Athens, Ga.: University of Georgia Press, 1972.

Rivers, Isabel, ed. *Books and their Readers in Eighteenth-Century England*. Leicester Leicester University Press, 1982.

Robertson, Mary F. 'Swift's *Argument*: The Fact and Fiction of Fighting with Beasts'. *MP*, 74 (1976), 124–41.

Rodino, Richard H. and Hermann J. Real, eds. *Reading Swift: Papers from the Second Münster Symposium on Jonathan Swift*. Munich: Wilhelm Fink Verlag, 1993.

Rogers, Pat. 'Form in *A Tale of a Tub*'. *Essays in Criticism*, 22 (1972), 142–60.

Hacks and Dunces: Pope, Swift and Grub Street. London: Methuen, 1980.

Rose, Margaret A. *Parody // Meta-Fiction: An Analysis of Parody as a Critical Mirror to the Writing and Reception of Fiction*. London: Croom Helm, 1979.

Parody: Ancient, Modern, and Post-modern. Cambridge: Cambridge University Press, 1993.

Ross, Angus. 'The Books in the *Tale*: Swift and Reading in *A Tale of a Tub*', *Proceedings of the First Münster Symposium on Jonathan Swift*. Hermann J. Real and Heinz J. Vienken, eds. Munich: Wilhelm Fink Verlag, 1985, pp. 209–16.

Ross, Angus and David Wooley, eds. *Jonathan Swift*. Oxford: Oxford University Press, 1984.

Rupp, Gordon. *Religion in England, 1688–1791*. Oxford: Clarendon Press, 1986.

Saccamano, Neil. 'Authority and Publication: The Works of "Swift"'. *ECent*, 25 (1984), 241–62.

Sacheverell, Henry. *The Christian Triumph: or, the Duty of Praying for our Enemies*. London, 1713.

False Notions of Liberty in Religion and Government Destructive of Both. London, 1713.

The Perils of False Brethren, both in Church, and State. London, 1709.

The Political Union. A Discourse Shewing the Dependence of Government on Religion in General: And of the English Monarchy on the Church of England in Particular. Oxford, 1702.

Sachse, William L. *Lord Somers: A Political Portrait*. Manchester: Manchester University Press, 1975.

Said, Edward W. *The World, the Text, and the Critic*. London: Faber and Faber, 1984.

Sams, Henry W. 'Swift's Satire of the Second Person'. *ELH*, 26 (1959), 36–44.

Schochet, Gordon J. *The Authoritarian Family and Political Attitudes in Seventeenth Century England: Patriarchalism in Political Thought*. New Brunswick: Transaction Books, 1975.

Seaward, Paul. *The Cavalier Parliament and the Reconstruction of the Old Régime, 1661–1667*. Cambridge: Cambridge University Press, 1989.

Seidel, Michael. *Satiric Inheritance: Rabelais to Sterne*. Princeton: Princeton University Press, 1979.

Shaftesbury, Anthony Ashley Cooper, third Earl of. *Characteristics of Men, Manners, Opinions, Times, etc.* 2 vols. John M. Robertson, ed. Gloucester, Mass.: Peter Smith, 1963; reprint of 1900 edn, 1st edn, 1711.

    The Life, Unpublished Letters, and Philosophical Regimen of Anthony, Earl of Shaftesbury, Author of the Characteristics. Benjamin Rand, ed. London: Swan Sonnenschein, 1900.

Shapin, Steven and Simon Schaffer. *Leviathan and the Air-Pump: Hobbes, Boyle, and the Experimental Life*. Princeton: Princeton University Press, 1985.

Shapiro, Barbara J. *Probability and Certainty in Seventeenth-Century England: A Study of the Relationships between Natural Science, Religion, History, Law, and Literature*. Princeton: Princeton University Press, 1983.

Sisson, C. H., ed. *The English Sermon: Volume II:1650–1750 – An Anthology*. Cheadle, Cheshire: Carcanet Press, 1976.

Sitter, John. *Arguments of Augustan Wit*. Cambridge: Cambridge University Press, 1991.

Skinner, Quentin. 'The Context of Hobbes's Theory of Political Obligation', *Hobbes and Rousseau: A Collection of Critical Essays*. Maurice Cranston and Richard S. Peters, eds. New York: Doubleday, 1972.

Smith, Frederick N. *Language and Reality in Swift's A Tale of a Tub*. Columbus: Ohio State University Press, 1979.

Speck, W. A. *Tory and Whig: The Struggle in the Constituencies, 1701–1715*. London: Macmillan, 1970.

    Reluctant Revolutionaries: Englishmen and the Revolution of 1688. Oxford: Oxford University Press, 1988.

Sprat, Thomas. *The History of the Royal-Society of London, for the Improving of Natural Knowledge*. Jackson I. Cope and Howard Whitmore Jones, eds. St Louis: Washington University Press, 1959; 1st edn, 1667.

Starkman, Miriam Kosh. *Swift's Satire on Learning in A Tale of a Tub*. Princeton: Princeton University Press, 1950.

Steele, Peter. *Jonathan Swift: Preacher and Jester*. Oxford: Oxford University Press, 1978.

Steele, Sir Richard and Joseph Addison, et al. *The Tatler*. 3 vols. Donald F. Bond, ed. Oxford: Clarendon Press, 1987.

Steele, Sir Richard, et al. *The Guardian*. John Calhoun Stephens, ed. Lexington: University Press of Kentucky, 1982.

Straka, Gerald M. *Anglican Reaction to the Revolution of 1688*. Madison: The State Historical Society of Wisconsin, 1962.

Sullivan, Robert E. *John Toland and the Deist Controversy: A Study in Adaptations*. Cambridge, Mass.: Harvard University Press, 1982.

Sutherland, James. *The Restoration Newspaper and its Development*. Cambridge: Cambridge University Press, 1986.

Swift, Jonathan. *The Correspondence of Jonathan Swift*. 5 vols. Harold Williams, ed. Oxford: Clarendon Press, 1963–65.

    The Journal to Stella. 2 vols. Harold Williams, ed. Oxford: Clarendon Press, 1948.

    The Prose Works of Jonathan Swift. 14 vols. Herbert Davis, et al., eds. Oxford: Basil Blackwell, 1939–68.

A Tale of a Tub, to which is added the Battle of the Books and the Mechanical Operation of the Spirit. A. C. Guthkelch and D. Nichol Smith, eds. 2nd edn. Oxford: Clarendon Press, 1958; reprinted with corrections, 1973.

A Tale of a Tub and Other Works. Angus Ross and David Woolley, eds. Oxford: Oxford University Press, 1986.

Sykes, Norman. *From Sheldon to Secker: Aspects of English Church History, 1660–1768.* Cambridge: Cambridge University Press, 1959.

Teerink, Hermann and Arthur H. Scouten, eds. *A Bibliography of the Writings of Jonathan Swift.* 2nd edn. Philadelphia: University of Pennsylvania Press, 1963.

Temple, Sir William. *Five Miscellaneous Essays by Sir William Temple.* Samuel Holt Monk, ed. Ann Arbor University of Michigan Press, 1963.

Thackeray, W. M. *The English Humourists; Charity and Humour; The Four Georges.* London: Dent, 1854; reprinted 1968.

Tindal, Matthew. *The Rights of the Christian Church Asserted, Against the Romish and all other Priests, who claim an Independent Power over it.* 4th edn, London, 1709; 1st edn, 1706.

Toland, John. *Christianity not Mysterious: Or, A Treatise Shewing, That there is nothing in the Gospel Contrary to Reason, Nor Above it: And that no Christian Doctrine can be properly call'd a Mystery.* London, 1696.

The Memorial for the State of England. London, 1705.

Traugott, John. 'A Tale of a Tub', *The Character of Swift's Satire: A Revised Focus.* Claude Rawson, ed. Newark: University of Delaware Press, 1983, pp. 83–126.

Treadwell, Michael. 'London Trade Publishers 1675–1750'. *The Library,* 6th series, 4 (1982), 99–134.

Swift's Relations with the London Book Trade to 1714', *Author/Publisher Relations during the Eighteenth and Nineteenth Centuries.* Robyn Myers and Michael Harris, eds. Oxford: Oxford Polytechnic Press, 1983, pp. 1–36.

Vaughan, Thomas. *The Works of Thomas Vaughan.* Alan Rudrum and Jennifer Drake-Brockman, eds. Oxford: Clarendon Press, 1984.

Voitle, Robert. *The Third Earl of Shaftesbury, 1671–1713.* Baton Rouge: Louisiana State University Press, 1984.

Walsh, Marcus. 'Text, "Text", and Swift's *A Tale of a Tub'. MLR,* 85 (1990), 290–303.

Webster, Clarence M. 'Swift's *A Tale of a Tub* compared with Earlier Satires of the Puritans'. *PMLA,* 47 (1932), 171–78.

'Swift and Some Earlier Satirists of Puritan Enthusiasm'. *PMLA,* 48 (1933), 1141–53.

Weedon, Margaret. 'Bickerstaff Bit, Or, Merlinus Fallax'. *Swift Studies,* 2 (1987), 97–106.

Whiston, William. *Reflexions on an Anonymous Pamphlet, Entituled, A Discourse of Free Thinking.* London, 1713.

Williams, Harold. *Dean Swift's Library, With a Facsimile of the Original Sale Catalogue and some Account of the Two Manuscript Lists of His Books.* Cambridge: Cambridge University Press, 1932.

Wolf, Richard B. 'The Publication of Shaftesbury's *Letter Concerning Enthusiasm'. SB,* 32 (1979), 236–41.

Wood, P. B. 'Methodology and Apologetics: Thomas Sprat's *History of the Royal*

Society'. *British Journal for the History of Science*, 13 (1980), 1–26.

Woodmansee, Martha. 'The Genius and the Copyright: Economic and Legal Conditions of the Emergence of the "Author"'. *ECS*, 17 (1983–84), 425–48.

Woolley, David. 'Joint Authorship and *A Tale of a Tub:* Further Thoughts [A hard look at Tom Swift]', *Monash Swift Papers 1.* Clive T. Probyn and Bryan Coleborne, eds. Melbourne: Monash University, 1988, pp. 1–25.

Wyrick, Deborah Baker. *Jonathan Swift and the Vested Word.* Chapel Hill and London: University of North Carolina Press, 1988.

Yates, Frances A. *The Rosicrucian Enlightenment.* London: Routledge & Kegan Paul, 1972.

Zimbardo, Rose A. 'At Zero Point: Discourse, Politics, and Satire in Restoration England'. *ELH*, 59 (1992), 785–98.

Zimmerman, Everett. *Swift's Narrative Satires: Author and Authority.* Ithaca: Cornell University Press, 1983.

Zwicker, Steven N. *Politics and Language in Dryden's Poetry: The Arts of Disguise.* Princeton: Princeton University Press, 1984.

Index

218   Index

Downie, J. A., 48n., 57n., 169
Drake, James, 80–81
Dryden, John, 25, 27n., 29, 38, 41, 42, 123,
    127–32, 138, 142, 197
Duffy, Eamon, 30n., 31n.
Dunton, John, 125
Durfey, Thomas, 140

Eagleton, Terry, 24–25
Eddy, William Alfred, 99n.
Ehrenpreis, Irvin, 77n., 78n., 87., 93n., 117n.,
    168n., 176n., 179, 180–81, 196n., 201
Eilon, Daniel, 3, 169n.
Elkin, P. K., 3n., 42n.
Elliott, Robert C., 2n., 121n.
Ellis, Frank H., 77n.
Epicurus, 121, 146, 156
Erasmus, 117, 127n., 161
Establishment of the Church, 59n.
Ewald, William Bragg, Jr, 121n.

Fabricant, Carole, 3, 14n.
Faulkner, George, 8n., 99n., 180
Feather, John, 42n.
Filmer, Sir Robert, 43
Ford, Charles, 89
Foucault, Michel, 25, 26–27, 101–2, 103
Fox, Adam, 36n.
Frei, Hans W., 36n.
Frost, William, 128, 132

Gascoigne, John, 30n.
George I, King, 44
George III, King, 32, 44
Goldie, Mark, 43n., 44, 45n., 46
Graves, Robert, 149n.
Gray, Thomas, 35
Greenberg, Robert A., 99n.
Guthkelch, A. C., 110n., 111n., 116n.,
    133–34, 162n., 191n.

Habermas, Jürgen, 24, 25n.
Hammond, Eugene, R., 117n., 127n., 161n.
Hanover, House of, 26, 32
Harley, Robert, 1st Earl of Oxford, 54, 64, 174
Harth, Philip, 77n., 95, 116n., 117n., 118n.,
    152, 161n.
Henry VIII, King, 33n., 82, 154
Hercules, 149
Heyd, Michael, 118n.
Hickes, George, 32, 119
Higgins, Ian, 86n., 191n.
Hill, Christopher, 44n.
Hoadly, Bishop Benjamin, 45
Hobbes, Thomas, 29, 40, 47, 49–50, 84,
    121n.

Holmes, Geoffrey, 41, 52n., 78–79
Homer, 126
Hooker, Richard, 22–23
Horace, 162
Horsley, L. S., 61n.
Hunter, Michael, 37n., 49n.
Hunter, Robert, 89

Irenaeus, 117

James II, King, 32, 33, 45, 53, 61
Johnson, Esther (Stella), 174–75, 178
Johnson, Samuel, 24n., 142
Jose, Nicholas, 29–30
Juvenal, 1, 2, 20

Kelling, Harold D., 114n. 125n.
Kelly, Ann Cline, 12, 78n.
Kelly, Veronica, 121n., 182
Kenner, Hugh, 140
Kennett, Bishop White, 33n.
Kenyon, J. P., 43n., 45n., 54n., 81n.
Kernan, Alvin, 42n., 106n.
King, Archbishop William, 33, 196
Klein, Lawrence E., 86n.

Landa, Louis A., 168n.
Lauderdale, Richard Maitland, 4th Earl of,
    132
Leavis, F. R., 104, 120, 167
LeFanu, William, 116n. 125n.
Leranbaum, Miriam, 59n.
Leslie, Charles, 32, 54, 56, 59n., 66, 82, 119
L'Estrange, Roger, 119, 131, 135
Levine, Jay Arnold, 117n., 152n.
Levine, Joseph M., 116n.
Locke, John, 43, 44, 45, 54, 64n., 122–27,
    138, 165, 166
Louis XIV, King, 43, 61–62, 63
Love, Harold, 90n., 106n.
Lucretius, 121n.

Macclesfield, Ann, Countess of, 142
Magna Carta, 41
Marvell, Andrew, 29, 126, 127, 132–39
Mary II, Queen, 44, 53
Meehan , Michael, 41n.
Mill, John, 36
Milton, John, 27, 29, 35, 41, 144, 158
Mintz, Samuel I., 50n.
Monmouth, James Scott, Duke of, 196
More, Henry, 118, 119
More, Saint Thomas, 117
Morphew, John, 179
Mueller, Judith C., 65n., 182n.